"Palgrave Studies in Theatre and Performance History" is a series devoted to the best of theatre/performance scholarship currently available, accessible and free of jargon. It strives to include a wide range of topics, from the more traditional to those performance forms that in recent years have helped broaden the understanding of what theatre as a category might include (from variety forms as diverse as the circus and burlesque to street buskers, stage magic, and musical theatre, among many others). Although historical, critical, or analytical studies are of special interest, more theoretical projects, if not the dominant thrust of a study, but utilized as important underpinning or as a historiographical or analytical method of exploration, are also of interest. Textual studies of drama or other types of less traditional performance texts are also germane to the series if placed in their cultural, historical, social, or political and economic context. There is no geographical focus for this series and works of excellence of a diverse and international nature, including comparative studies, are sought.

The editor of the series is Don B. Wilmeth (EMERITUS, Brown University), Ph.D., University of Illinois, who brings to the series over a dozen years as editor of a book series on American theatre and drama, in addition to his own extensive experience as an editor of books and journals. He is the author of several award-winning books and has received numerous career achievement awards, including one for sustained excellence in editing from the Association for Theatre in Higher Education.

Undressed for Success

Beauty Contestants and Exotic Dancers as Merchants of Morality

Brenda Foley

UNDRESSED FOR SUCCESS
© Brenda Foley, 2005.

First published in 2005 by
PALGRAVE MACMILLAN™
175 Fifth Avenue, New York, N.Y. 10010 and
Houndmills, Basingstoke, Hampshire, England RG21 6XS
Companies and representatives throughout the world.

PALGRAVE MACMILLAN is the global academic imprint of the Palgrave Macmillan division of St. Martin's Press, LLC and of Palgrave Macmillan Ltd. Macmillan® is a registered trademark in the United States, United Kingdom and other countries. Palgrave is a registered trademark in the European Union and other countries.

ISBN 1–4039–6993–0

Library of Congress Cataloging-in-Publication Data

Foley, Brenda.
    Undressed for success : beauty contestants and exotic dancers as merchants of morality / Brenda Foley.
        p. cm.—(Palgrave studies in theatre and performance history)
    Includes bibliographical references and index.
    ISBN 1–4039–6993–0
    1. Striptease—Social aspects. 2. Beauty contests—Social aspects. I. Title.
II. Series.

PN1949.S7F66 2004
792.7—dc22   2004060113

A catalogue record for this book is available from the British Library.

Design by Newgen Imaging Systems (P) Ltd., Chennai, India.

First edition: September 2005

10 9 8 7 6 5 4 3 2 1

Printed in the United States of America.

For my father, who taught me never to give up,
and in memory of my mother,
who showed me the true meaning of the word grace.

Contents ∾

Illustrations ❧

Acknowledgments ⌒

A s with all mammoth endeavors, the list of people and organizations that gave support and succor during the research and writing of this book is too lengthy to catalog in full. Nonetheless, there are those, without whose contributions the project would never have been completed, who must be recognized.

I extend my sincere thanks to all the funny, opinionated, and smart women who granted me interviews. In particular I wish to acknowledge Susan Scotto, "Silver," Susan Mills, and the indomitable Laura Lawless. Also, at Brown University, I thank John Emigh, Rebecca Schneider, Rey Chow, William O. Beeman, Marida Hollos, and, especially, Coppélia Kahn, who encouraged my work, no matter the subject. Deserving of special thanks are Spencer Golub for his humor and boundless imagination, and Carolyn J. Dean for the astonishing generosity of spirit she expressed in numerous thoughtful comments. I would also like to thank St. Thomas University (New Brunswick, Canada) and its Department of English for their support.

Additionally, I must recognize the Andrew W. Mellon Foundation, Abby Smith, and the Council on Library and Information Resources for awarding me an invaluable fellowship. Their generosity enabled me to conduct research in repositories near and far. Brown University offered a Manning Fellowship and much needed summer research grants to continue my efforts. Also, I owe a debt of gratitude to Annette Fern, who trusted me enough to allow me to happily sort through uncatalogued materials at the Harvard Theatre Collection. I would also like to thank the Billy Rose Theatre Collection at the New York Public Library at Lincoln Center and the Harry Ransom Humanities Research Center in Austin, Texas. Portions of chapter 6 were previously published in the National Women's Studies Association Journal (Indiana University Press) and I am grateful to them as well.

It is hard to imagine how this book could have been completed without the help of Don B. Wilmeth. I thank him for his friendship, unflagging encouragement, kind and loyal mentoring, and his keen editor's eye. I also thank Brendan O'Malley, Melissa Nosal, Will Fain, and the entire production team at Palgrave Macmillan for their guidance and confidence in this project.

I want to thank my family for embracing every new adventure I undertake with characteristic aplomb—Maureen and Bill, Alex and Sara, Chris and Lisa, Bob and Peg and the whole Foley clan, and especially my father, Admiral S.R. Foley, Jr., who has ever been my strong supporter and staunch friend.

Finally, my husband, Kevin Gardner, deserves equal credit for any accomplishment of mine. I thank him for bringing me countless cups of hot coffee in bed in the morning and a like number of glasses of wine in the tub at night. He tolerated long absences, months of distraction, and my odd propensity for dealing with stressful situations by rescuing stray animals. He has my gratitude as well as my heart.

Introduction ❧

When I interviewed former burlesque performer Susan Mills, I began by explaining this book's principal argument: that the theatrical forms known as striptease and beauty contests are so deeply connected in historical, social, and performance terms that they are, in effect, variations of the same phenomenon.[1] As I started to elaborate their shared attributes as publicly enacted constructions of "femaleness," Mills gently but emphatically interrupted: "No, no, dear. They aren't the same at all. You'll have to pick one or the other."[2] Her succinct dismissal articulated a viewpoint that would reemerge in countless conversations with research librarians, pageant organizers, family members, cab drivers, manicurists, and strangers seated next to me on airplanes. The common thread in all their reactions was a widely held and deeply personal investment in maintaining the cultural disassociation of the forms, a disassociation grounded in every case on some form of moralistic ideology.

Mills was right in many ways. Stripping and beauty contests occupy differing theatrical venues, and are patronized by differing constituencies. Their public reputations, and their image-making rhetoric, promote apparently irreconcilable values; one of unfettered sexual availability and deviance and another of high-minded civic allegiance and traditional feminine virtue. One promises—and often delivers—the spectacle of full female nudity and even simulated sex acts, and the other never does. Perhaps above all, the forms are permanently committed to the promulgation of a pair of ancient and opposite female stereotypes. These types have come to be known by many names: Madonna and whore, Rebecca and Rowena, Eve and Lilith.

Given the apparently antagonistic positions beauty contests and striptease occupy in American popular consciousness, Susan Mills's reaction is perfectly understandable. Still, her own experience argues a more complex view. Her show business credentials include both the "legitimate" theatre and a stint in the cast of Ann Corio's *This Was Burlesque*, a revivalist production that played in New York and on tour during much of the 1960s and 1970s, and beyond.

She was married to the baggy pants comedian Steve Mills, also a sometime Corio performer, and worked with him as a "talking woman," a foil for his jokes in the show's comic sketches.

Through Corio, Mills's burlesque roots reach even deeper, back to the arguable heyday of the form in the Minsky shows of the 1930s. But she also appeared in other burlesque revivals, among them a yearlong engagement in a single theater. Her memory of this production is instructive. "Steve and I did a show in 1974 at the Pilgrim Theatre in Boston," she recalled, "When the show opened the girls were very nice like in real burlesque and by the time the show closed they were using coke bottles between the legs." With this one sentence, Mills identified some crucial elements of the perceived estrangement between forms of female display.

First, she distinguished late-twentieth-century revivals from what she called "real burlesque," an accurate assessment in view of the fact that by 1974 the form had long since largely retreated or been driven away from the big urban theaters where it had flourished in previous decades. The banishment of burlesque from mainstream theaters helped clear the commercial way for the rise of the strip clubs; smaller, more marginalized establishments that co-opted burlesque's calling card, the striptease, with single-minded devotion throughout the latter part of the twentieth century. But Mills's distinction was based on more than chronology: for her, the girls in "real burlesque" had been "very nice," a quality that separated them, on implicitly moral grounds, from latter-day female performers who degraded true burlesque with "coke bottles between the legs." If Susan Mills can be said to have experienced a compressed version of burlesque's decline during her Pilgrim engagement, her judgment of the show's legitimacy hinges on a critical bifurcation, the point at which the nice girls go one way and the naughty girls another. As always, the assessor's frame of reference is critical. Mills's basis for comparison, by extension if not directly, is the American popular stage of the 1920s and 1930s, a major career destination for young women with show business ambitions, especially the beauty queens who flocked in large numbers to the choruses of productions staged by the Minsky brothers, Florenz Ziegfeld, George White, and other impresarios. To her, these earlier performers were "nice"—cleaner, wittier, more wholesome, their sexuality a matter of coy suggestion rather than overt display. A closer affinity had once existed between the worlds of swim-suited bathing beauties and feather-waving burlesque chorines. This was no longer the case. Now the forms had hardened—you had to "pick one or the other."

Mills's insistence on absolute distinctions was puzzling, but also made a kind of sense—she had witnessed a profound split, in tone and content, between one type of female stage performance and another. Yet she also possessed, by virtue of her privileged position as a performer, ample understanding of the cross-pollination among the forms that had once made them far more similar to one another than they now appeared. The incompatibility of "very nice" girls with those who cavorted with coke bottles had precluded her from taking a longer view. This is the heart of the "difference." Even in the face of considerable contradictory evidence, a majority of individuals (and organizations) regard beauty contests and striptease as inhabitants of utterly segregated theatrical camps. It became increasingly clear that my research, originally intended to explore the development and overlap of both forms, would also need to address the following questions: What lies behind our investment in the cultural perpetuation of the forms as putative antagonists? Who benefits from such classifications? How did both forms respond over time to increasingly reductive categorizations? And, finally, why has a constructed morality based on a supposed "community standard" become the main criterion by which the forms (and their female participants) are rendered socially "deviant" or "normal?"

This study's initiating principle might best be understood in light of Alan Read's statement that "theatre begins from a point of coalescence, not polarity."[3] The overwhelming commonalities of stripping and beauty contests reveal numerous ways in which staged display informs, shapes, and insists on particular social definitions of "femaleness," or what Geraldine Maschio has characterized as a culturally "verifiable image of woman."[4] Since these images and definitions are transmitted principally in theatrical terms, my analysis situates them squarely in the realm of constructed live performance, aligning theoretical explorations with performance techniques, and investigating the intersection between means of representation and moral ideology in both.

To do this, I have employed the interdisciplinary methodology of the field of Performance Studies, exploring the links between beauty pageants and striptease through primary source archival research—newspaper accounts, journals, trade publications, photography collections, press releases, marketing publications—and through personal interviews with strippers and beauty contestants alike. In considering the emergence and refinement of the forms from the mid-nineteenth century to the present (as Rita Felski defines it, their "sociohistorical" development[5]), I have traced as well the continuing fluidity of their interplay. I have also drawn upon standard histories, memoirs and other non-scholarly writing, and the work of a number of performance and gender theorists. Popular entertainment scholarship in recent years has produced some excellent work on beauty contests and exotic dancing as entertainment forms in their own rights.[6] Yet little work has emerged that focuses systematic comparative analysis on their parallels in performance approach, gestural language, visual identifiers, moral hierarchies, and economic incentives, as well as on corporate and legislative controls imposed on performers and presenters of both forms. This multifaceted examination exposes the alleged differences between the forms as fictive constructs, promoted, mediated and policed by social mores.

Although *Undressed for Success* is continually concerned with matters of history, it nonetheless treats *performance* as its "organizing concept."[7] Rather than follow a straightforwardly chronological path, it freely enlists events, people, and historical contexts in explorations of particular conditions of performance in order to focus attention on patterns of cultural process in beauty contests, striptease, and related entertainments. Just as performances are constructed with multiple selective layers of image and information, this book employs frequent anachronistic examples as tools for the disruption of presumed trends too easily taken to be normative in standard historical terms. My approach does not seek historical linearity so much as the collapse of certain false distinctions. It employs history inclusively as a series of frames in which the cross-pollination and mutual influence of two seemingly disparate theatrical forms can be illuminated.

Accordingly, and critical to the task, the experiences of practitioners are as valuable as academic theories and analyses. Influential studies by respected scholars such as Robert C. Allen and Lois Banner coexist in chapters with the insider perspectives of Irving Zeidman and Ann "Bang Bang" Arbor. Maud Allen's popular theatrical presentation "Vision of Salome" (1908) is offered as an historical antecedent to the performance of novice beauty contestant Audra, who appropriated the costumed façade of exotic "harem" sexuality in 1999, yet rendered it palatable to pageant spectators with a sanitized physicalization. The promotional technique utilized by nineteenth-century producer George Lederer, who explicitly marketed his chorus girls as "wholly" feminine, is juxtaposed with the modern stripper's belief that breast augmentation is mandatory for an acceptably complete image of the desirable woman. Correspondences between contemporary exotic dancing and beauty pageants are thus matched and supported by similar correspondences, in practice and perception, across various historical periods.

The underlying unity of apparently disparate forms of female display is as demonstrable in impact as in its execution. Almost as soon as they appeared, for instance, female "shape artists"[8] became subject to cultural assessments of "authenticity"—whether in relation to their standing as "legit" actresses (evidenced by Olive Logan's insistence in 1870 that the public address the "nude woman question"[9]), or as representatives of explicit personal and social values.

Society increasingly sought to distinguish women on the stage by category, according to tacitly accepted community standards of morality. The linkage of female display in popular entertainment with manufactured value systems resulted in the compartmentalization of forms as "clean" (i.e., vaudeville, beauty contests) or "dirty" (i.e., burlesque, striptease), and these universally understood classifications operated as reminders of a woman's acceptable "place" in public. Thus, the relative moral value of a given entertainment depended on its classification, and its classification was determined almost exclusively by its context. The context in which female display of any kind is theatrically presented has been the critical measure by which forms are analyzed as separate entities.

But a "context" is never a neutral position, and the creation of contexts for female display was (is) inextricably linked to politically motivated notions of morality. Though these notions have been subject to significant revision over the past 150 years, they are grounded in an unaltered calculus with respect to the performances of women on the American popular stage. As Mary Douglas has noted, "the discourse of ordinating groups frequently falls back on the imagery of the body in an attempt to protect or redefine moral and social boundaries."[10]

As a visual nexus of seemingly discrete forms, the scantily clad female performer embraces an array of popular entertainments far broader than that occupied by the beauty pageant and the striptease show. The list of such displays begins in the mid-nineteenth century, ranging from Adah Issacs Menken and *Mazeppa* to Lydia Thompson's "British Blondes," to concert saloons, living pictures, bathing beauty contests, and Broadway revues. While Toni Bentley believes that "women's erotic territory at the beginning of the twentieth century was on the stage," it is easily demonstrable that female erotic display was firmly entrenched on American stages—indeed, on the American cultural landscape generally—by the time the twentieth century arrived.[11] Additionally, notwithstanding social suppositions that various entertainment forms were culturally segregated, individual performers routinely crossed from one "erotic" territory into another—whether as numerous so-called "Little Egypts" who made their way from the Carnival Midway to the burlesque stage, as revue chorus girls who became burlesque "parade girls," as performers like Crystal Ames, who, according to Irving Zeidman, was a "stripper recruit from George White's *Scandals*,"[12] or as bathing beauties like Miss Texas, Ann de Brow, (see figure I.1) who followed in her mother's footsteps and joined Ziegfeld's Follies. Clearly, the boundaries of what Bentley refers to as a "flesh-for-cash transaction" in theatrical entertainment proved both permeable and illusory almost from the beginning. Nevertheless, claims and

Figure I.1   Ann De Brow, former Miss Texas and Ziegfeld performer

imputations of moral value have doggedly distinguished the social visibility—
and status—of forms of female display in the public consciousness.

By the end of the nineteenth century, the word *nude*, as Lois Banner has
pointed out, was unquestionably synonymous with *woman*, and increasingly

became an etymological site of moral contestation. Social purity campaigns such as Anthony Comstock's Society for the Suppression of Vice encouraged fears about sexualized images of women as contributors to a crumbling social fiber. The dangers inherent in the public's alleged ocular vulnerability, according to the reformers, dictated a need for containment, metaphoric and actual, of female display, and led to the pathologization of both the forms and the performers. It was a short cultural leap from pathologizing women engaged in sexualized display (or, as Barbara Johnson phrases it, "woman as symptom"[13]) to the social call for quarantine of the contagious performances.

Following in Olive Logan's rhetorical wake, an additional development appeared that would carry permanent repercussions for practitioners of all kinds: female display began to acquire an assumptive public definition not as constructed, fictive performance, but as personal behavior presented on stage, individual conduct rather than acting. This assumption became enormously useful, not just as a component of various strategies for suppression of the offending performances, but also as a crucial element of commercial appeals to particular markets. A performer's exterior appearance, both visually and contextually, thus became a powerful signifier of her personal morality. The conflation worked both ways: beauty onstage could function with equal power as sinful transgression or unsullied virtue.

Long before the Miss America pageant, for instance, Florenz Ziegfeld successfully promoted a notion of "refined" female display with ambiguously inoffensive descriptives attached specifically to his "girls"—charming, demure, alluring, pulchritudinous, to name a few. Suggesting the appearance of an entirely acceptable womanly exhibition, Ziegfeld's "tasteful" bevies of identically groomed and, for the most part, silent women were intended to distinguish his "glorified American girls" from others in competing productions with (presumably) weaker commitments to rectitude. Later on, the Miss America pageant elaborated on the concept with the introduction of a "civic" agenda in its performances. Its public-spirited, altruistic competition could then be promoted as the antithesis of racier female displays that presumably threatened society's moral fiber. The civic female body onstage was more readily interpretable as a socially "useful" body, therefore a virtuous one. Meanwhile, striptease producers decided that if "morality" could be a successful promotional tool, why not employ its inverse, "immorality," as a means of developing their particular niche market? "Naughtiness," as a commodity, announced itself in everything from performer names such as "Jeanette 'Flash' O'Farrell" and "Irma the Body" to the designation of the forms themselves as "turkey shows," "behind-the-tent companies," "scratch burlesque,"[14] and others.

Relative degrees of perceived virtue and vice, of higher or lower status, took hold not just among observers and commentators, but within the industry itself.

Performers engaged in such displays enacted an institutional hierarchy of their own based on an insider code of morality that mimicked that of society at large. Burlesquers considered carnival strippers "crude" and carnival strippers thought of cooch dancers as "lowdown." Such insider classifications exist in beauty pageants too; one would seldom find a Miss America contestant participating in the Miss Budweiser contest, and the undiluted, frankly commercial sexuality of the Miss Universe Pageant is generally scorned by promoters and participants in civic and scholarship pageant systems. In fact, as recently as the summer of 2004, responding to the Miss America Organization's decision to eliminate most of the talent competition from the televised event, former Miss America Heather French tellingly remarked: "It's a tragedy [. . .] That's what separates us from the type of contestant that goes to Miss USA."[15]

The hierarchical ways in which forms of female display define themselves, and the complex transactions revealed in the histories of their marketing and their perception by audiences and commentators, have been cited, in selective and predictable ways, as evidence of the forms' disparity. Yet this superficial analysis also yields to a broader view that, as before, interprets female display fundamentally as an act of performance. This view consistently finds more correspondence than disjuncture. According to their own accounts, for instance, performers in both forms employ specific gestural and movement vocabularies to create an impression of "authenticity" in their performances. These socially agreed-upon, hence recognizable, patterns of walking, turning, posing, and gesticulating, while highly stylized in themselves, carry a series of messages meant to effect a paradoxical impression of "realness." Quite aside from their technical similarities, such theatrical conventions further compli- cate cultural assumptions of an exposed "self," revealing it instead as a con- sumer/spectator's fantasy of sexual interest or potential. This is confirmed by stripper Elisabeth Eaves, who speaks of "trolling the room systematically, as if I were on a search-and-rescue mission," to find the mark who will pay the most for her work.[16] In the moment of performance, however, each seeks to project an image of "authenticity," according to the conventions of her particular form. "For a price," says Eaves, "a stripper will pretend to be a kind of woman that doesn't exist outside the imagination."[17] Similarly, beauty contestants and pageant organizers manipulate spectator expectations and presumptions to enable sexualized display acceptable to the audience as "appropriate" female behavior.

Early in the last century, presidential candidate Warren Harding used the term "normalcy" to promulgate a political agenda (and election strategy) based on a mythically happy pre–World War I America. His slogan, "Return to Normalcy," was understood as an implicit rejection of the previous administration's policies. "Poise has been disturbed," Harding announced in a 1920 speech in Boston.[18] Similarly, pageants and stripping use a fictive presentation of the "normal feminine" to promote and sustain their own political agendas. Just as the forms share physical and gestural characteristics, they also employ and exploit culturally constructed notions of what "appropriate" feminine behavior looks like. Relying on astonishingly narrow definitions of "normal" and "deviant," these performers skillfully confirm spectator expectations whether in the role of gyrating come-hither stripper or docile feminine beauty contestant. The stripper adopts a guise of recognizable "deviance," theatrically ritualized and presented according to familiar conventions that render it acceptably "normal" within its genre. Beauty contests, of course, also traffic in images of the "normal" feminine that are, in fact, carefully constructed and ideologically based prescriptions for an alternative form of acceptable female behavior. These classifications of "deviance" or "normalcy" are equally conventional because of their shared dependence on image recognition. In striptease and beauty contests, both are presented as embodied conditions, commodified for sale by startlingly similar theatrical means. Moreover, youth as a criterion for the feminine normal is inescapable in the performance of a stripper's aroused sexuality and a pageant contestant's restrained wholesomeness. Women in both forms achieve homogeneous bodies with the use of cosmetics, costumes, hairpieces, and plastic surgery that serve to conform to and accentuate a social preoccupation with female youthfulness that has become a standard measure of the value of female bodies, and of women themselves.

Youth, appearance, and variant degrees of sexual promise are not the only signifiers of the normal. Both beauty contests and stripping also make use of immediately recognizable occupational images in ways that suggest not only the elasticity of the images themselves, but also a kind of response of one form to the other. The beauty contestant's cheerleader image is frequently appropriated by strippers, for instance, to play upon the heterosexual fantasy of the "good girl gone bad," just as the stripper's harem dance, with its pelvic thrust and shimmy, is utilized by the beauty contestant to suggest the potential for misbehavior underneath her controlled reserve. The talent segments in pageants often employ overtly sexualized images of harem dancers, famous operatic courtesans, and "sassy" jazz numbers performed to tunes extolling sexual passion such as "Fever," "I'm Just a Girl Who Can't Say No," or "All that Jazz," in which the contestants threaten to "roll their stockings down." The occupational characterizations of striptease include nurses, teachers, brides, and even housewives.

The rigid conventionalism with which images of the acceptably "feminine" are transmitted in performance has become something of an ironic skill, appropriated by scores of contests for female impersonators, in which they are judged according to how effectively they convey the standard gestural vocabulary of "femaleness." In fact, one Miss America 2002 contestant turned to her drag queen friend for pointers in perfecting her presentation. Following his expert advice, she finished in the top fifteen.

Similarities between stripping and beauty contests extend well beyond the areas of performance and perception. Exploration of (as Nancy Etcoff phrases it in *Survival of the Prettiest*) the "economics of being female" reveals a fundamental reliance in both forms on the ancient Cinderella myth that explicitly promotes beauty and desirability as the path to success in a gender economy.[19] On the American stage, successful early performers such as the Floradora Sextette helped establish a widespread cultural misapprehension of the actual economic advancement enjoyed by performing women. Media coverage stressed the attention and gifts showered on them by male admirers, and the reported fact that all the group's members married millionaires. Yet their story is far from representative. According to one source quoted by Lois Banner, sixty thousand women applied for every *one* position in a chorus line casting call as early as 1904.[20] In spite of such realities, the stage acquired a permanent reputation for offering female performers an opportunity to get ahead, and the myth enjoys robust life today, expressed in the attitude of neophyte stripper "Lolita," who hopes to gain stardom by competing in the *Miss Exotic World* competition, or beauty contestant Miss Maine 2002, who believes going into debt is "worth it" for the chance to be crowned a winner. Research shows that while monetary rewards do occur for some women, many female performers in stripping and beauty contests are actually engaged in subsistence occupations rather than careers. More than one Miss America contestant has admitted to being in debt and/or on government assistance as a direct result of her participation in the contest.

As institutions, strip clubs and beauty contests both engage in metaphoric containment of female display and actual regulation of the performers in terms of how, what, and where such display is allowed by managerial, legal, and cultural authorities. These mechanisms of regulation and containment have traditionally functioned as sources of tension that contributed significantly to the development of the forms of display themselves. Calibrating performances to circumvent the law became an essential theatrical tool in striptease, as striptease artists and promoters developed techniques such as a "flash" and costumes such as flesh-colored pasties. Legalistic and moral sanctions functioned much the same way in more "wholesome" entertainments, as beauty contests marketed the same nearly nude women yet dodged the self-appointed "morality police" with body constraining techniques such as the "suck-and-tuck" glide and political cover in the form of rhetorical platforms touting "self-improvement."

Regulation against female display is often predicated on a belief in the contagious effects of such presentment, whether symbolic or actual. The institutional forms themselves enact rules ranging from a contestant's contractual obligation to divulge her medical records to the Pageant organization, to the allowable duration of eye contact between a stripper and her customer (five seconds maximum at a particular Las Vegas club). Court cases involving beauty contestants are almost exclusively centered on an individual's complaint against a pageant organization, as in the recent Rebekah Revels case against the MAO (Miss America Organization), in which the apparent existence of photos of Revels's breasts taken by her then-boyfriend resulted in the loss of her state title. Lawsuits involving stripping tend to attract larger sanctioning bodies, from municipalities that fear overtly sexualized female display will result in "harmful secondary effects" on the community, to the U.S. Supreme Court, which has asserted, among numerous other pronouncements, that nude dancing is "widely accepted to be immoral."[21] For individuals and institutions alike, fears of moral, hence social, contagion mandate the regulation of women in beauty contests and stripping, and serve to further link the forms.

In his analysis of the burlesque dancer Nadja, who attached a small piece of fake fur in a strategic spot under her skirt in order to convince her audience it had glimpsed what it wanted to see, H.M. Alexander observed that she disclosed, "something that is not something."[22] With *Undressed for Success*, I hope to offer some insight into the ways in which "something that is not something" might be seen as a broadly applicable descriptive, equally appropriate of Miss America as of any carnival stripper. Perhaps it was a 1950s Miss America contestant who best conveyed both the imagistic and the tangible link between the two forms when, during her talent competition, she unabashedly declared: "I'm going to strip for you—in reverse."[23]

1. "Stripping the Light Fantastic":* Historical Cross-Pollination in Staged Female Exposure ✄

Clap Your Hands and I'll Take Off a Little Bit More
Early Burlesque Song, *The American Burlesque Show*[1]

"The first public striptease act ever witnessed in a theatre," according to Wolf Mankowitz, was performed by Adah Issacs Menken in the New York production of the play *Mazeppa* or *The Wild Horse of Tartary*.[2] Menken reportedly undressed onstage behind the cover of several strategically placed actors and, emerging in a flesh-colored tunic and tights, produced the titillating appearance of nudity. Posters for the production feature one of *Mazeppa*'s climactic events: the arresting sight of Ms. Menken being carried across the stage in this costume while lashed to the back of a rampaging horse. Some reviewers, apparently at a loss to describe the flamboyant suggestiveness of her performance, took to calling the actress a "shape artist."[3] "Menken is without a rival in her special line," noted one clever reporter, "but it is not a clothes line."[4] The year was 1861.

Whether or not one considers Menken's act a "striptease," her notoriety undoubtedly served as a locus for the mid-nineteenth-century's escalating public debate over female display in popular entertainment. Menken was far from alone. Such companies as Lydia Thompson and her British Blondes and Michael Leavitt's Rentz-Santley Company made women in tights a ubiquitous theatrical presence by the mid-1860s, and the act of undressing onstage soon became an inherent potential of every performance in which women were posed, arranged, featured, or displayed. As early as 1870, the actress Olive Logan felt compelled to editorialize against the trend, defining it as an urgent and unexplored category of social inquiry known as "The Nude Woman Question."[5] Theatrical tensions associated with questions as to how much might be revealed, how much concealed, became characteristic features of female performance, firmly establishing the sexualized dramatic atmosphere of which Mary Russo would later observe that "making a spectacle out of oneself seemed a specifically feminine danger."[6]

In the theatre, the female body had been a discursive site of social appropriateness in behavior since women first stepped on the stage, both in terms of expectable decorum and the more problematic issue of female infiltration of public space. "Making a spectacle," a rhetorical sister to "letting herself go," confounded established disciplinary, regulatory, and cultural notions of "proper" female display. If one accepts Gillian Rose's notion that perceptions of identity, social or otherwise, are "riddled with—and even formed through—mistakes, mis-recognitions, fantasies, forced instabilities, and contradictions," the disrobed female body provoked discussion of female identity onstage in at least two ways.[7] First, as a visual confirmation of ideology, it reinforced spectators' presumptions that actresses were uniformly vested participants in a "body showing profession."[8] Additionally, as an institutional perception among many performers, such peeling performances came to be seen as potential, or even necessary, strategies for career success. Just as actresses, prostitutes, and vagrants had been conflated in public perception for centuries, many female performers were now caught up in a kind of syllogistic synecdoche—since actresses were understood to behave categorically rather than individually, and the actress Menken took off her clothes, then the potential existed for all actresses to publicly disrobe. This perception aroused fears of social decay even as it increased revenue at the box office. As the moralist H.B. Farnie observed when Menken toured in Great Britain, "People expect the voluptuous pictures scattered about London, and the voluptuous verses printed on the playbills, to be realized by the American actress, and they go for that purpose."[9]

In *Actresses as Working Women*, Tracy Davis rightly argues that the "actresses' stigma is understood as a socially produced meaning that served the interests of particular social groups to the disadvantage of female performers themselves."[10] Still, with acknowledgment of their role as active participants in social production, a reading of actresses as both contributors to public perceptions of the "Nude Woman Question" *and* as theatrical strategists lends an additional complexity to the analysis. That Adah Issacs Menken was unaware of the possibility that spectators might be titillated by her imitation of nudity seems highly unlikely given her propensity for savvy self-promotion, just as decades later the Minskys' argument that Mae Dix initiated stripping on their stages by accident smacks of promotional disingenuousness.

Whether or not female participation in the conception and execution of these performances ultimately produced "disadvantage," their proliferating appearance on the American stage came to be viewed as more or less socially acceptable. Individual theatrical strategies, evolving cultural dictates, and the preferences of the marketplace abetted this proliferation, which diversified even as it retained essential theatrical similarities. Its particularized images of undressed (and undressing) women created a broadly familiar category of popular entertainment, from living pictures, vaudeville, burlesque, and bathing beauties to carnival "girlie" shows, the emergence of revues, Miss America, and a host of other beauty pageants.

In the mid-nineteenth century, as the increasing number and variety of female displays and public expectation of such performances became mutually reinforcing, articles began to appear entreating actresses to resist the trend, insisting they did not have to take off their clothes but could escape the stain of tawdriness by holding fast to the label of "legitimate" actress. Others warned that their entire profession was degraded by increasingly reductive standards. Olive Logan opined that "it became a question with actresses seeking a situation not whether they were good actresses, but whether they were pretty and were willing to exhibit their persons."[11] While the press and certain factions of the public revived anti-theatrical versions of Joseph Swetnum's 1615 plague metaphor for beautiful women as "bright in the hedge and black in the hand," with its stigmatic characterization of female performers as carriers of social disease, countless productions across the country ignored their protests, incorporating lovely women, wearing less and less, into their acts.[12] Nonetheless, objections to the trend began to exercise influence over its development almost immediately. "In the 1860s burlesque became something for bourgeois culture to watch," notes Robert C. Allen, "both in the literal sense of deriving pleasure from its spectacle of feminine display *and* in the sense of exercising moral oversight."[13] Allen's duality of watchfulness extended far beyond the burlesque stage to include, among other forms, beauty contests, revues, concert saloons, and even carnivals. That one can read the barely clothed or fully naked woman onstage as simultaneously transgressing traditionally accepted social mores and, conversely, fulfilling certain theatrical expectations highlights the complex, codified, and consistently fluctuating position actresses occupied (and continue to occupy) on the popular entertainment stage.

In 1897, the theatrical manager Henry C. Jarrett (of Messrs. Jarrett and Palmer) announced: "legs are staple articles, and will never go out of business while the world lasts."[14] For well over 150 years, as if by an apparent cultural compulsion, the stages of American popular entertainment have been populated by countless female performers in various stages of undress ("undress" being an historically relative designation), beginning at least as early as Charlotte Cushman's chorus of one hundred women in tights in the 1841 production of *The Naiad Queen* and continuing unabated to the recently celebrated Broadway disrobings of Kathleen Turner in *The Graduate* and Nicole Kidman in *The Blue Room.*[15] The historical preponderance of nearly nude or downright naked women in American popular entertainment would seem to validate Edward F. Albee's 1905 rhetorical point: "What are we selling?" We're selling backsides, aren't we? All right, if one backside is good, a hundred backsides are as many times better."[16]

Albee's successful line of business (in collaboration with B.F. Keith) during the early years of the twentieth century was vaudeville, not burlesque, and his assertion not only exemplifies an American tendency to link economics with female display, but also illuminates a theatrical strategy somewhat paradoxically embedded within vaudeville's "wholesome" image. During the latter half of the nineteenth century, as early burlesque presented a "raucous and bawdy style of variety performance," vaudeville sought to distance itself from just such a reputation by appealing to perceived middle-class values—and pocketbooks.[17] Soon vaudeville's "veneer of elegance" was trumpeted as the antithesis of the more ribald burlesque.[18] Notwithstanding its claim to relative cleanliness, the vaudevillian reliance on "backsides" as a theatrical draw illustrates an inescapable imagistic parallel between the forms. Edward F. Albee's promotion of Annette Kellerman's posterior points not just to stripping's shared origins in disparate theatrical forms, but also to its influence on developing ones, for the specific "backside" in question belonged to a champion swimmer, vaudeville performer, author of a well-known beauty manual, and the designer of swimsuits worn by numerous beauty contestants in the early Miss America pageants. Albee's entrepreneurial promotion of Kellerman's backside under the guise of a display of wholesome athleticism would become a significant part of the corporate rationalization not only for the Miss America Organization (MAO), but for scores of other beauty pageants all over the country.

The theatrical strategy to expose as much nudity as possible and still avoid detection by the social radar of negative public opinion was never so much in view as it was in the form alternately described as "living pictures," "poses plastique," and "tableaux vivant." "The justification for these early tableaux," according to Jack McCullough, was their contribution "to the edification, refinement, or moral uplift of the audience."[19] Theatrical producers, adroitly aligning themselves with the trend in amateur groups, began as early as 1831 to compose living copies of famous paintings in the name of art, patriotism, and moral uplift that amounted to little more than staged public displays of naked women.[20] Although producers began the tableaux vivant trend by clothing their models in nude body stockings, they soon progressed to fabric-draped bodies and ultimately to naked, gilded flesh. Efforts to evade censure through promotional assurances of "artistic" display were not always success-ful. According to George G. Foster, up to the 1850s "these exhibitions had been composed exclusively of men, and we never heard of their being immodest; but the moment the ladies made their appearance, an outcry of outraged public decency rose on all sides"[21] (see figure 1.1). As the images of nude women proliferated, spurred on by resounding financial success, pro-ducers struggled to walk the theatrical line between virtue and vice. An 1876 playbill at the Thirty-fourth Street Opera House in New York promised "College girls, Female Bathers, Can-Can." The company was summarily charged with "giving indecent performances."[22] Yet many entrepreneurs were able to negotiate their way around censorship. Even Tony Pastor, historically acclaimed for his promotion of vaudeville as wholesome family entertain-ment, "jumped on the tableau bandwagon, featuring an 'Attraction Extraordinary . . . the great FORBIDDEN PLEASURE COMBINATION with MME. CORELLI'S PARISIAN STATUE TROUPE, consisting of 50 beautifully formed young ladies, in a series of elegant LIVING PICTURES.' "[23] It is not sur-prising, then, that his partner Albee would later discover similar potential for revenue in the swim-suited Annette Kellerman. As the trend took hold, numerous touring companies presented acts featuring groups of women tum-bling together and swinging above the audience while outfitted in much the same dress (or lack of it) as the female performers of less "wholesome" enter-tainments. Zeidman's *The American Burlesque Show* points out that "Hattie Leslie's Lady Athletics" defended (and promoted) their performances as "no leg or burlesque show," but rather "a perfect legitimate lady athletic company."[24] The designation "athletic" (as noted in Don Hearn's mid-twentieth-century entertainment column "Tips on Tables," in which he referred to female enter-tainers as "bumps and grinds athletes") hardly ensured the "legitimacy" prom-ised by the producer's promotional verbiage.[25] It does, however, resonate most neatly with the contemporary insistence by the MAO that its much-criticized swimsuit competition is a display of "fitness" rather than flesh.

Negotiating an image of "wholesomeness" (while enjoying the monetary rewards available to presenters of nearly naked women) not only summarizes the effort made by the living picture producers to identify their presentations as "art," but also aptly describes an early strategy of linking female display with instruction, in much the same way that the Miss America Pageant would later use its promotion of scholarships and education as a cover for the

Figure 1.1   Lyla Kavenaugh, nineteenth-century performer

swimsuit requirement. Through a complex set of schematics, entertainments that marketed themselves as socially uplifting sought to negotiate their position between ideology and sexualized image to financial advantage; a trend acerbically remarked on by critic George Jean Nathan: "anything in a diaper with a violin off-stage is 'aesthetic dancing'."[26] Notwithstanding this and many other criticisms, producers continued to experiment with devices that were more suggestive. From Tony Pastor's "forbidden pleasure combination" of fifty women in artful poses to Florenz Ziegfeld's claim that he presented nudity "artistically," a continuing attempt to define images of naked women as more or less culturally authentic through contextual and ideological rhetoric gained momentum.

In 1894, Edward Kilyani elaborated on the tableaux form by presenting an Aphrodite whose nudity "was made more real by the dripping of water over the form."[27] The running water suggested physical action without violating the imposed legal restrictions regarding movement,[28] and the sexualized image of a "wet" woman forced to remain motionless proved salacious enough to sell plenty of tickets. In the absence of overtly suggestive activity, any potential prurience could be ascribed to the spectator alone. Kilyani's innovation served as precursor to a host of subsequent variations, including images of contemporary bathing beauties frolicking by the ocean, twentieth-century carnival water shows, Salvador Dali's "Dream of Venus Show" at the 1939 World's Fair (in which "semi-nude girls dove and swam in a large tank with glass sides"), and today's wet T-shirt contests.[29]

In 1893, at Koster and Bials's Thirty-Fourth Street Theatre, two female performers "impersonating a painting" in an act titled "An Affair of Honor," "stripped nude to the waist," an event that resulted in a "police-court brawl."[30] Whether the chief objection was to the nudity itself or the onstage action of stripping was not elaborated, but the combination of movement and female nudity increasingly became a theatrical touchstone for social debates regarding the appropriateness of female display *and* female behavior. In a 1925 court case involving the Minsky brothers, a judge asked why the plaintiff, who had witnessed productions by Flo Ziegfeld and Earl Carroll without complaint, was now targeting the Minsky performers for lewd behavior. "Could you explain," he asked, "why exposed breasts are decent north of Fourteenth Street but indecent south of it?" To which the plaintiff replied, "Well . . . yes. You see, the difference is the movement."[31]

Richard Wortley, in his *Pictorial History of Striptease*, takes passing note of the historical importance of movement to the theatrical presentation of female display, but he situates it much too late, stating that strip clubs "emerged out of the nude revues of the 1950s, with the most notable difference that the girls now moved."[32] In fact, theatrical tension between movement and stillness was already well established long before the first strip clubs appeared, and its use permeated every form of female display. While the spatial and gestural links among them will be elaborated in chapter 3, it is worth noting here that the proscriptions on movement within tableaux vivant laid the groundwork for everything from the beauty contest's obligatory "pose and pivot" physicalization to (in the wake of Kilyani's "Aphrodite" display) Rita Atlanta's famous burlesque champagne-glass bath. In the early years of the twentieth century a "typical" burlesque show on the American Wheel circuit presented a number by the "Living Picture Girls,"[33] and as late as the last quarter of the twentieth century, at the Silver Slipper in Las Vegas, Sandy O'Hara, the "Improper Bostonian," performed a "Living Picture" in which, a publicity promo assures, "a life sized portrait of the flame-haired beauty seems to come to life before your very eyes."[34]

As if in response to the unease associated with such "coming to life," elaborate theatrical elements meant to suggest discipline and containment developed along with the performances themselves. Naked female display, movement, and boundaries both conceptual and tangible began operation as a visual triumvirate, simultaneously denoting behavioral, physical, and spatial control. Movement by nude women suggested a personal agency at odds with the publicly accepted representation of "the feminine." Because women, whose bodies had historically been deemed "convoluted" with "too many openings,"[35] had long been regarded as dangerously unstable and fluctuating, their unfettered movement threatened to bring about the "ruin of [such] representation."[36] Thus, female bodies were contained on revolving plat-forms, quarantined behind glass, cordoned off by footlights, and steered in safe directions by the architectural structure of runways. Containment seemed an effective tool for warding off raids by local law enforcement and satisfying at least some objections from community-elected "morality police." Further, the *ways* in which women moved onstage would become critical measures by which entertainment forms were judged socially acceptable or unacceptably deviant. Elaborations of this system of understanding have developed in numerous arcane directions: in many clubs today, according to Katherine Liepe-Levinson in *Strip Show*, "male patrons are not allowed to place money anywhere on a female stripper's body *while she is moving*."[37]

The late-nineteenth-century fascination with Orientalia contributed to proliferating theatrical displays of undressed, and undressing, female per-formers, bringing a "foreign" and "exotic" component to the stage in what has been referred to as a "colonial harem fantasy."[38] Social response to particular sexualized female movement as "foreign" resulted in the conceptual coloniz-ing of the women who performed it, situating them within a specified context as the exotic "Other." Notwithstanding the colonialist use of such classifications as a means of devaluing both their performances and the women themselves, the concept also "depended theoretically and pragmatically on making deviance visible."[39] "Exotic" and "deviant" were thus rendered as synonymous and embodied conditions. The profitable tension between display and social control of such "deviance" was highlighted, once again, at the 1893 Chicago Columbian Exposition. The Persian Palace, on the Exposition's Midway, "engaged a troupe of Parisian dancers who performed to the accompaniment of popular songs of the day" in what was described by one reporter as "very questionable entertainment."[40] Since the performers had been hired to execute a specific performance in which their movements were already sanctioned, response to their display took the form of negative and controlling rhetoric rather than the legal regulations utilized against tableaux vivant. Labeling the entertainment "questionable" segregated it on a social/moral basis, yet also assisted in its promotion. "Exotic" dancing would quickly become performatively inseparable in the public imagination from "erotic" dancing, a conflation that is still evident in clubs nationwide. As a publicity poster for the mid-twentieth century performer "Doreen, New Zealand's Tassle Tossin' Cutie," puts it: "Press agents toss the word exotic around loosely to describe just about any dancer who tosses her anatomy around."[41]

Out of the Expo Midway and its display of exotic dancing women came the legend of Little Egypt and the "hootchy kootchy" dance. Characterized as a "debased imitation version" of the Danse du Ventre, there were as many titles for such dances as there were names of the women who performed them.[42] Dances were variously identified as the "couchee couchee" or the "hooch-ma-cooch,"[43] re-interpreted as the "Danse du Vengeance" by Millie De Leon,[44] or saddled with the titularly biblical "dance of the serpentine." Continuing the trend toward colonizing nomenclature, the dancers' stage names ranged from Little Egypt to Little Africa, ensuring that race myths and simple bigotry would assist their relegation to the category of "Other." Equating female spectacle with Eve and her unfortunate disruption of Eden, the exotic dancer was metaphorically designated simultaneously as slithering seductress, tempting sinner, and the wife/mother of all humanity. The notoriety of Little Egypt and her many imitators rests on these contradictory, cross-pollinating perceptions rather than any actual performance history, for, as Donna Carlton argues, "the truth is, there is no record of Little Egypt at the 1893 exposition or at any off-Midway sideshow."[45] On the Midway, the female performers were referred to most often simply as "the dancing girls," a perceptive conflation that embraced both dancers and cooch girls, whose act is often considered the progenitress of the breast and hip wiggling "shimmie," a name "given to one of the most popular social dances of the 1920s."[46] According to Carlton, the shimmie dancer might even be seen as "the first flapper."[47] This early public refusal to distinguish among various forms of female movement/display carried immediate and profound impact that appeared even before the Expo closed. During presentations of the (presumably) respectable "Congress of Beauty," a line of women paraded in single-file across a stage not far from their cooching sisters on the Midway.

The rejection of merely plastique "posing" by female performers and their promoters endowed a legacy of sexualized movement that would soon be appropriated by seemingly less "questionable" entertainments such as the beauty contest, in which the oft performed "harem dance" is a standby of pageant talent competitions. With floating veils and anemic pelvic thrusts drained of the provocative exoticism that rendered them scandalous at the Expo, beauty contestants regularly employ the gestural vocabulary of an antecedent entertainment—the cooch—without acknowledgment, or perhaps even awareness, of its historic deviance and "otherness." Carlton argues, "It is entirely possible that Ashea Wabe, the original notorious 'Little Egypt', helped popularize theatrical strip tease in this country."[48] Why we might recognize the historical influence of cooch on striptease but not on beauty contests indicates a distinction that is far more perceptual than presenta- tional. As Zeidman notes, the female practitioners of the "hootchie-kootchie" have been referred to as, "Oriental dancers, classic dancers, Salome dancers, control dancers, interpretive dancers, shimmy shakers, tassel dancers, exotics and still other names by the puritanical."[49] Yet, in spite of their shared physical vocabulary, cooch dancers have never been referred to as beauty contestants.

The designation of sexualized display as "foreign," hence alluringly "unnat- ural," would have long-term ramifications in the entertainment business. The fabricated binary of female deviance and virtue became commodified as a saleable product, its components segregated in theory but often operating simultaneously in application. As Kathy Peiss points out, during the early twentieth-century expansion of the "beauty culture," "Businesses that used aesthetic codes to convey social and moral messages would find 'it quite pos- sible to reach two mutually antagonistic classes of prospects,'" by advertising the same product in different packaging.[50] Ziegfeld star Anna Held might earn scandalous headlines after being photographed in one of her daily, "sticky," milk baths (an early version of the publicity campaign "Milk—does a body good"), even as countless young women of more respectable reputation were encouraged to use the same technique with the goal of "purification" of their skin.[51]

As the cooch dancers' particular movement style erupted across countless stages and in seemingly discrete forms, the extremely popular impersonations of Salome during the same period expanded its implications. The very name added personality, motivation, and appetite to the sexualized motions of the dance of the seven veils (gestural cousin to the cooch), and appeared to proclaim the identity of a particular kind of woman—the female sexual predator. Salome's provenance is summarized by Toni Bentley as "a fascinating blend of Roman gossip told in cautionary tales by Seneca, Livy, Cicero, and Plutarch, New Testament Gospel, medieval legend, and Oriental Romanticism, all based on a dash of truth."[52] Personifications of Salome passed easily across the cultural boundaries of legitimacy, appearing in 1907 on the stages of both the Metropolitan Opera and Florenz Ziegfeld's "Jardin de Paris" in New York.[53] Notably, even before she had moved "from the opera to the variety stage, critics had noted her resemblance to those 'unforgotten dancers of the [Chicago World's Columbian Exposition] Midway Plaisance.'"[54] Daisy Peterkin, who preferred the stage name La Belle Dazie, opened a dancing "School for Salomes" at Ziegfeld's rooftop theatre and, according to Susan Glenn, "by the summer of 1908, an estimated 150 newly minted Salomes from Dazie's school were descending upon the vaudeville circuit every month."[55] She adds, "Many of them found work as cooch dancers in the variety theaters along 14th street in Manhattan." Theatrical producers, managers, and performers used the image of Salome, "nothing more—or less—than a striptease,"[56] to continue to explore the limits of social tolerance for, as Peter Buckley puts it, "gradations of refinement."[57]

By 1908 even the well-respected actress Gertrude Hoffman performed a version of the legendary seductress, "first [in] a black wig and a good makeup, second a lot of jewelry and chains and there is no third."[58] Contemporary predilections for Salome in fact carried a hidden benefit for actresses by allowing them a certain scope for tactical negotiation of acceptable degrees of bodily display. Maud Allen's 1908 "Vision of Salome" was described as "part art and part cooch, the dance slyly exposing the aesthetic conventions of both."[59] Allen's interpretation of the role caused a scandal—and a much publicized court case in Great Britain—but also spawned a "Maud Allen dinner dance," held for "society ladies who were asked to appear in Salome costume."[60] The appropriation of this fictive stage persona by the upper crust indicated just how widely female display and sexualized movement had established themselves in the cultural landscape since the days of immobile tableaux vivants, in spite of Marjorie Rosen's quip that, at the end of the nineteenth century, "Female appetites of any kind (save those satisfied via the pantry) were not kindly received."[61]

But Salome didn't dance alone. Her influence was readily apparent in the new "Venus" dancers—"Zallah the Dancing Venus, Jessie Keller the Venus on Wheels, and Carmelita D'Eclidere the Animated Venus."[62] Much later incarnations, even into the 1960s and 1970s, carried the "exotic" names of

"Haran," "Zamera," "Almond Joy," "Bel-Sha-Zaar," and "Sheba the Harem Girl."[63] Even the famous vaudevillian Eva Tanguay performed a Salome dance that climaxed with the image of an uncorked bottle of champagne pouring over her head. (As noted previously, from the days of early tableaux vivant images of liquid have been a favorite tool in entertainments focusing on women's bodies, in variants that include the use of phallic shaped bottles, the ritual of the toe dipping photo op at the Miss America Pageant, or the onstage showers at clubs like Rhode Island's Foxy Lady.) Salome's classical and scriptural associations have no doubt contributed enormously to the character's extraordinary longevity and to her unmatched mobility among forms. It's worth noting, however, that other associations have tagged along for the ride. As recently as March 2004, the *New York Times* previewed Karita Mattila's rehearsal for Richard Strauss's *Salome* at The Metropolitan Opera (during which "two male dancers bit at her hips and slowly pulled off her trousers with their teeth") with the caption "Do a Striptease, Sing a Big Aria, All in a Night's Work."[64] Mattila's singing was generally praised, but the brief nudity she displayed at the end of the dance of the seven veils made Met history.

According to Carlton, "The carnival's cooch shows were the first 'gal shows,' replaced ultimately by subsequent sensations such as the Forty-niner Gold Rush camp shows, beauty shows, hula shows, swimming/swimsuit exhibitions and other displays."[65] Whether or not the umbilical relegation of "gal shows" to the narrow realm of carnival is entirely accurate, the stages of carnivals were nonetheless home to what might be seen as a fascinating social paradox. Carnivals functioned as, among other things, the locus for cooch shows, burlesque performances, variety acts, *and* beauty contests. As noted earlier, beauty contests were held at fairs and carnivals from at least the 1890s onward, and beauty contestants and carnival strippers occupied that same theatrical/social carnival space well into the 1970s. The mingling of the ordinary, or everyday, with the bizarre, foreign, or seemingly "Other," had also been a favorite entertainment strategy of early dime museums, like those of P.T. Barnum, where the "Fejee Mermaid" and temperance plays like *The Drunkard* were housed under the same roof. Charles Fish has mused that fairs and carnivals were,

> devoted to the exceptional, or to the ordinary raised to the exceptional. Here were the finest cows and horses, the most daring stunts, the most bizarre deformities, the biggest pumpkins. The strippers were not the finest women as we understood the term—"She's a fine woman, your Aunt Agatha"—but they brought into the open the very excellence about which the village was most reserved and uneasy and in which Aunt Agatha might be presumed to be deficient.[66]

In carnivals of later years, the 1893 Expo's "Streets of Cairo" were renamed, less euphemistically, "The Streets of Sin." Oddly (but not surprisingly), while Fish grants the carnival "freak shows" status as "something like theatrical performances," he does not offer the same possibility to the "girlie shows."[67] Instead he remarks that "their faces told their tale too plainly, a past and future one would rather not think about [. . .] I felt what I could not have articulated, that even when most hungry, we prefer garnish, an elegant plate, a clean cloth."[68] To him, the collections of deformed, accidental (and false) "freaks" are part of a deliberate theatrical plan, yet the strippers and cooch girls portray nothing more than their degraded selves. Beauty contests, with their configured facades presumably more congruent with Fish's longing for "an elegant plate," are never mentioned, even though these performances routinely take place in the same designated temporary space of the fair, commanding the attention of many of the same spectators whose dollars sustain both the freaks and the inelegant "girlie show." What might he have said about a parade of young, maidenly women on display along with the seven-legged calves and world-weary strippers? That it was "theatrical," like the freaks, "too plainly" revealing of truths "one would rather not think about," like the strippers, or that it promulgated an uncommon "excellence" of which ordinary mortals could only dream?

The relationship of female display with conceptions of a "contest" reveals another way in which supposed boundaries between forms proved permeable. Throughout what Jay J. Hornick identifies as a thirty-year stretch between 1870 and 1900, when the "beauty contest" as we know it began to take shape, amateur nights and chorus girl competitions became immensely popular. Marketed as "novel chorus girl contests," they consisted of "garter contests, where the girls displayed their legs by the artful use of garters," and "pick-out numbers, where each girl in the chorus was given an opportunity to display her talents, whether it be dancing, singing, shimmy shaking, or straight dramatics, and sometimes even comedy impersonations."[69] Burlesque theatres also often functioned as sponsors for bathing beauty contests, "striptease chorus girl contests," and, in an innovative twist, a "strip tease auction" which featured, as Hornick explains, "the master of ceremonies actually auctioning off wearing apparel of some chosen chorus kid."[70] Hornick's description of the "opportunity" for each contestant to "display her talents" in the burlesque contests bears remarkable similarity to the format of a contemporary beauty contest, especially its "talent" segment, in which participants perform for prize money (see figure 1.2). He concludes with a practical statement: "the present-day trend is for theatres to run 'strip-tease contests,' solely for the reason that the art of strip teasing brings better financial results."[71]

Figure 1.2   1926 anonymous burlesque performer. Library of Congress, Prints and Photographs Division

Although Hornick credits burlesque producers as the "first to introduce amateur nights," beauty contests traditionally employed an image of the "amateur" in their promotional material.[72] In 1921, the Atlantic City Pageant (as the Miss America Pageant was first known) featured three different, separately judged, categories of female competition: "Professional Beauties" (actresses, showgirls, models), "Civic Beauties" (amateurs), and "Inter-city Beauties" (entrants in the newspaper contest, who were picked by the public on the basis of a photograph).[73] These categorical distinctions soon became obsolete as sponsors of the competition offered showbiz contracts as incentives and contestants from all three divisions eagerly sought professional careers in performance. The "Civic" component of the Miss America Pageant lay dormant for many years, only to re-emerge in the 1980s in the form of individual contestant "platforms," but the label "amateur" would become an integral part of the organization's claim that each of its contestants was "every girl," thus innocent of any taint or suspicion that might attach itself to "professional" women.

In 1922, as the Miss America entered the already-bustling business of female display, the women who participated in it and other beauty contests went on to become Ziegfeld girls, chorus girls, burlesque parade girls, and vaudeville performers. Performer crossover from beauty contests to other entertainment venues was hardly anathema—in fact, the talent flowed in both directions. As early as 1888, a circus producer, Adam Forepaugh, held a beauty contest with a prize worth ten thousand dollars. Eleven thousand women sent in their photos. The winner had been a chorus girl in *The Black Crook*,[74] the formerly scandalous production that, according to a 1929 *New York Times* article, "played almost continuously" at some theatre in the country from "1866 to 1894."[75] It is rarely remembered that Gypsy Rose Lee, renowned for her striptease work, began her professional career as beauty contestant Louise Hovick. After she "won a beauty contest in her native city [Seattle],"[76] she would gain fame as a Minsky star at the Republic Theatre, later opening "in the revised Ziegfeld Follies at Broadway's Winter Garden under the protective wings of the Brothers Shubert."[77] She was also a Ziegfeld showgirl in the 1932 Broadway production "Hot Cha," under the name Rose Louise. Arrested in 1936 for her striptease as "Ada Onion from Bermuda" at the Minsky's Republic Theatre (the case was dismissed), Gypsy was also considered the first girl to bring the strip act uptown. "She was—more amazingly—the first girl to appear undressed, on the stage alone [meaning without a chorus line], in any Ziegfeld Follies. She stripped, at the end of Act I, more completely than she ever had before, appearing for one tantalizing moment in nothing but two tiny bows, held to each breast by glue, and a three-inch triangle of turquoise satin on a G-string."[78] As the Miss America Pageant, under the direction of Lenora Slaughter, increasingly sought to distance itself from other forms of show business and the women who participated in such exhibitions, performers like Gypsy Rose Lee continued to ignore the distinctions in favor of making a living. According to Zeidman, by 1932 "practically all leading women in burlesque, except for any occasional singing or 'talking' principal, bared their breasts as they cooched."[79]

Gypsy Rose Lee, perhaps one of the most versatile performers of her time, enjoyed considerable mobility among entertainment forms, from beauty contests to burlesque, striptease, revues, films, journalism, and even novels. Yet she was far from alone. As noted earlier, many actresses considered "legitimate" by the public performed versions of Salome, and countless young women, as now, hoped beauty contests would serve as starting points for careers in show business. Florenz Ziegfeld and Earl Carroll, both enormously influential musical revue directors known for presenting scantily clad—or nude—female performers, were often called upon to judge beauty contests. Ziegfeld himself publicly belittled the "show" in Atlantic City, proposing that his revue competitors were "under the impression that anyone can stage a revue, so called, by going to the Atlantic City beauty contest and hiring a mob of bathing girls. The Atlantic City beauty show is a joke. Mob selections are always a failure when one is in quest of beautiful girls."[80] Yet, according to Eddie Cantor, when the Miss America Pageant in its early years requested that Carroll adjudicate, Ziegfeld, in a tiff over the perceived snub, demanded that his press agent "go down to Atlantic City and have all the prize winners report to him—and they did."[81] Notwithstanding Ziegfeld's competitive jealousy, producers as well as contestants considered experience in beauty pageants equivalent to the necessary training for employment in a professional revue. Beauty titles were also invaluable publicity assets, so much so that Earl Carroll embroiled himself in a pageant-fixing scandal.

Kathryn Ray, a nightclub performer, was handpicked by Carroll in 1924 to star in his revue *Vanities*. Feeling the need for a publicity boost, he first entered her in one of the preliminaries for the Miss America contest. He then managed to secure a position as a judge at the Coney Island event and "with the help of some private entertaining of his fellow beauty experts, had no trouble arranging for Kathryn Ray to be the winner, making her eligible to go to Atlantic City and compete for the Miss America title."[82] Miss Ray was sponsored by the *New York Evening Graphic*, which sent a reporter to cover the event. What he ended up uncovering was Carroll's involvement, and the paper ran the headline: "Beauty Contest Exposed, Frame-Up in Atlantic City." In the end, however, Carroll actually benefited from the stunt. "Hundreds of beauty aspirants flocked to audition for Carroll's next show."[83]

At times, both Carroll and Ziegfeld seem to have regarded beauty contests as little more than amateur talent showcases for their operations. In 1938, Claire James won the title of Miss California in a Miss America preliminary, finishing the national competition as first runner-up. The outcome infuriated Earl Carroll, who, "at a well-publicized press conference in New York" took it upon himself to declare her "the people's choice," crowning her the "real Miss America."[84] A 1946 article noted that, "Behind her desk and beneath her typewriter, Miss Gladys Glad concealed the most beautiful pair of legs and ankles ever to grace the *Follies*. They might have remained hidden indefinitely, but the little stenographer won a beauty contest in the Bronx and Ziegfeld kept his eye upon beauty contests."[85] Marion O'Day, "Miss Irvington, N.J.," was said to "exemplify the fact that Earl Carroll beauties come from small towns as well as large," and Violet Arnold, "Miss New Jersey," was defined as "one of the Most-Sought Beauties of the Show-Girl Type in America."[86]

Hope Dare was yet another beauty contestant, crowned "Miss Southern California," whom Ziegfeld hired and starred.[87] Genie Fursa, "Miss Bronx" of "Beauty Pageant fame," was "selected solely for charm and beauty."[88] "Miss Texas," Ann De Brow, proudly announced in the newspaper that she was following in her mother's footsteps in joining the Ziegfeld *Follies*.[89] Dorothy Britton was "acquired by Earl Carroll immediately after she won the titles of 'Miss America' and 'Miss Universe' at the Galveston Beauty Pageant," and Beryl Wallace "attained the title of 'Miss Brooklyn' " prior to her affiliation with Carroll's *Vanities*.[90] Nor did the steady cross-pollination move only one way. Marilyn Buford, an Earl Carroll "girl," who had performed in a number of his revues, won the title of Miss America in 1946 and went on to a successful international film career. "Helen O'Hara had won a beauty contest staged by the NY Illustrators Club to find the most beautiful girl in America"— she was a Ziegfeld Follies "girl."[91] At a time when stripping and beauty contests were defining their theatrical forms and developing permanent audiences, producers and performers alike regarded them as branches of the same industry. As these few examples make clear, beauty contests functioned as part of the professional landscape in much the same way as other entertainment forms— it was simply a matter of where the talent would go. Morton Minsky, in *Minsky's Burlesque* (co-authored with Milt Machlin), confirms the link: "In those days you would advertise in theatrical publications, such as *The Billboard*, *Variety*, or *Zits Weekly*. It was a matter of chance whether a girl wound up at Minsky's or in the Ziegfeld *Follies*, because we were all drawing the same girls from the same mining towns in Pennsylvania."[92]

While individual performers utilized beauty contests as career-building tools in an industry increasingly focused on display, various forms appropriated both the title of "Beauty Contest" and the images of its bathing-suited women for promotional purposes that had little to do with actual competition. Even journalists noted the parallelism; E.S. Melcher, a *New York Journal* writer attending a 1932 Ziegfeld rehearsal observed: "here came 75 first cousins of Miss America, glorified through and through." In 1922, the same year that the Miss America Pageant was born, Ziegfeld began promoting his shows with the phrase "Glorifying the American Girl," even as his star, Gilda Gray, achieved fame for her notorious "shimmy" number, an interlude that appeared along with acts carrying titles like "The Black Crook Amazons" and "Leg Dance."[93] In the early 1920s, Burlesque producer Rube Bernstein presented two shows, one called "Bathing Beauties" and the other "Girls of the USA," starring Margie Bartel, the "shimmy sensation."[94] As Eddie Cantor remembers it,

> Girls! Girls! Girls! This amazing industry of beauty [Ziegfeld] had built had attracted others to the field. The *Follies* was no longer alone. There was the *Passing Show*, the *Greenwich Village Follies*, the *Scandals* and the *Vanities* and they all wanted girls—preferably Ziegfeld girls.[95]

Despite Cantor's hyperbolic admiration, Ziegfeld had never been "alone" in his promotion of naked and nearly naked women. Unquestionably, however, his name and reputation were in large part responsible for the per-petuation of such images as socially desirable and culturally acceptable. Ziegfeld both encouraged and capitalized on the prevailing outlook, as defined by critic George Jean Nathan:

> That one good-looking girl is enough to make almost any music show agreeable is a fact known and admitted by every man save he be bribed with a salary of several thousand dollars a year professorially to deny it before the drama classes at Columbia University.[96]

Dubbed the "leading entrepreneur of sensual desire," Ziegfeld displayed more than three thousand women in his productions from 1907 to 1931.[97] Though questions of propriety were certainly raised in some quarters with respect to these productions, it is perhaps more notable how well Ziegfeld and other promoters succeeded in achieving middle-class acceptance of the dis-play form. In a far cry from Olive Logan's severe condemnations in the 1890s, the *New York Tribune's* Percy Hammond wrote in 1923:

> It is not, I trust, an impropriety to whisper to you that in one of Mr. Ziegfeld's lovely tableaux some slim and shapely ladies appear wearing no garments whatso-ever. In other Broadway revues nude women are to be seen, but not so completely as are those in the new Follies. Yet so artistic are the disclosures and so innocent withal that they evoked from the first night spectators no outcries of shocked modesty. Lest you think that these onlookers were hardened and complaisant,

I must tell you who a few of them were. Within twenty feet of me sat eighteen respectable New York dramatic critics, including myself.[98]

That a dramatic critic might appoint himself an arbiter of "innocence" is as suspect in its way as Justice Potter Stewart's self-conferred authority to identify obscenity. Nonetheless, Hammond's description of the full nudity in Ziegfeld's production seems to support Irving Zeidman's assertion that burlesque, renowned for its striptease, actually took its cue from the glamorous revues: "In imitation of Broadway Revues, burlesque shows had, from 1925 on, presented girls, nude from the waist up, in a tableau setting, stationary and supposedly in an aura of 'art'."[99]

The "aura of art" was immeasurably helpful in the promotion of female display, and rhetorical response to display performances followed suit. As early as 1918, one critic noted that the *Follies* of that year included "Miss Pennington's masterly interpretation of the hoochie-coochie."[100] Five years before Zeidman's date of 1925, a *New York Times* review characterized one of Ziegfeld's nine o'clock revues as presenting "some of the comeliest persons extant prancing about more or less clad."[101] In a personal letter to Ziegfeld written in 1920, theatrical aspirant Betty Owen wrote, "Dear sir, It is my intention to come soon to New York City, & like thousands of other girls in the profession, I would like above everything else, to become a Ziegfeld Follie [*sic*]Girl."[102] For Betty Owen, self-definition as one "in the profession," is concise enough to require little further explanation. Notwithstanding hindsight of more than eighty years later that insists her "profession" might have been any, or all, of the forms that relied on the exposed body for success, Betty Owen regarded the *Follies*, with its glamorous reputation for "artistry," as a respectable destination for ambitious young performers like herself.

The distinction between the spectacularly produced revue shows of Flo Ziegfeld, Earl Carroll, and George White, and numerous bathing beauty contests was not the clothing—there is, after all, not much difference in the amount of material in a bathing suit of the period and, for instance, the sarong worn by the "native girl" in Carroll's *White Cargo*—but rather the clothing's contextual location within the revue performance. "Out of the vulgar leg-show," critic Nathan observed, "Ziegfeld has fashioned a thing of grace and beauty."[103] The referential "vulgar" as a distinguishing feature of the leg-show, but not a Ziegfeld show, is connected not only to an increasingly vitriolic attitude toward certain kinds of female performers on moral grounds, but also to the late 1890s emergence of a particular sort of chorus girl, the "so-called show girl, who neither sang nor danced, but was included to 'show' the latest styles of fashion and beauty."[104] The use of female performers as demonstrators of style alone supported Ziegfeld's claims to respectability on the basis of "art," but also contributed an air of commercialized artifice not entirely flattering to women. Leon Errol, star of numerous Ziegfeld productions, once observed that "beauty in a woman was not so much the gift of nature as the contrivance of man."[105] While he may have meant his remark to derogate (he believed that "beautiful girls were brainless"[106]), the business entrepreneurs who promoted their subjective notions of female beauty as a gendered norm effectively contrived a presentation of women as "natural" participants in the "showing profession."[107] This notion—that a "normal" girl is delighted to display herself, carried profound and lasting implications for future developments in American popular culture.

In 1920, Louis Reid of the *Dramatic Mirror* characterized the women in Ziegfeld's revue as "exemplars of beauty in the new generation."[108] A program from a 1924 Ziegfeld *Follies* at the New Amsterdam Theatre includes an act titled "The Beauty Contest," in which one of the characters was given the appellation "The Typical Girl of Today."[109] The presentation of normalcy through elaborately constructed theatrical, hence fictive, productions did not negate the implication that "showing" was an essential part of female behavior, in much the same way that the male emcee at Mrs. America 2003 asserted that being pretty "is what it's all about."[110] Efforts such as Ziegfeld's to distinguish the "typical" from the "exotic," the high from the low, the respectable from the transgressive, brought success in the marketplace and inspired many imitators. Still, not everyone believed the message. As late as the 1960s, the editor of a carnival trade paper summarily dismissed any distinction between forms of female display: "Revues they call them, but they're actually kootch."[111]

The supposition that women were somehow made for display was enacted on revue stages as dozens, and often hundreds, of silent women either adorned in expensive costumes or displaying only milk-bathed flesh, feathers, and beads, paraded in highly choreographed, homogenous motion. According to Allen, "the Ziegfeld *Follies* represented the acceptable face of feminine sexual spectacle in America."[112] Why such revues achieved reputations as more "acceptable" than other, similar entertainments is difficult to explain. Certainly, in part, revues normalized sexual imagery through the mythology of the rise of the chorus girl, through publicity that depicted the job as lucrative and the selection process as rigorous, but also through the visual ideology that promoted such displays as the definitive image of femininity. No matter that chorus girls became burlesque parade girls, bathing beauties, and strippers, the packaging of sexuality under the subjective term "glamour," was another attempt to compartmentalize the display in a way that would render "normal" the apparent social compunction to look at naked women onstage, a compunction complexly entwined with seemingly unending attempts to justify that behavior. As George Jean Nathan tellingly declared in an editorial about chorus girls: "Once having discovered and landed her, it is necessary theatrically to authenticate her."[113]

If, by the mid-1920s, the revues regularly featured bare-breasted and even fully naked women, burlesque added the component activity of disrobing, initially avoiding the censors by having women come onstage, dance, exit into the wings, remove one piece of clothing, and then return to the stage. The roots of these demonstrations appeared as early as 1893, when Tony Pastor's star Vesta Victoria would accomplish an entire change of costume—for each song—in less than thirty seconds, a feat for which she was widely promoted in the broadsides of the period.[114] In 1920, on the Vaudeville circuit, "Petite Jennie," the "midget dancer," changed her costumes "in full view of the audience."[115] The technique was later appropriated, implicatively, by beauty contestants under the guise of "changing costume" from evening gown to bathing suit, a modification that preserved an appearance of modesty while maintaining theatrical references to images of undress. Burlesque performers knew that the mere suggestion of disrobing was a theatrical tool nearly as powerful as the act itself: "You undo the first bit of clothing and the audience does the rest," declared the famous burlesque dancer Margie Hart.[116]

Contradicting the impression that such displays were relegated to the fringes of respectability, Irving Zeidman observes that "even in the classier shows of the 1880s and 1890s stripping was not uncommon."[117] Zeidman's use of the term "classy" points to the critical tendency, even decades later, to assign various female display-performances to hierarchical categories. The designation of some forms of female spectacle as "clean" and others as "dirty" increasingly became a common strategy, as eagerly employed by social reformers bent on enforcing a moral agenda as by theatrical producers in their efforts to stay in business. "While variety became vaudeville and aligned itself with talent," continues Zeidman, "burlesque became itself and aligned itself with dirt."[118] Assumptive cultural prejudices that institutionalize certain entertainment forms as "highbrow" or "lowbrow" often function as *de facto* instruments for keeping those who participate in activities of the latter kind perpetually peripheral to the supposed construct of an acceptable center. At the end of the nineteenth century, argues Lawrence Levine, "cultural categories which no one seemed able to define with any real precision, became fixed givens that one could be skeptical of only at the price of being accused of uncritical democratic relativism."[119] Irving Zeidman's observation of the inevitable shift toward nudity—"as it all had evolved gradually, step by step, the final denouement did not seem too startling"—might just as readily describe the ultimate segmentation of female spectacles that relied on extraordinarily similar performance strategies into socially relegated, thus separate, theatrical camps.[120]

Nancy Etcoff contends, "If Mother Teresas [*sic*] always looked like Miss Universe, the world would be just and appearance would be an easy read. But no one has figured out the visible signs of saint or sinner."[121] Yet the yoking of a value system to the female body in theatrical entertainment does just that—makes visible the cultural agenda that constructs a hierarchy rooted in the imposition of a moral code of bodily deportment. "The construction," notes Jane Flax, "and choice of one story over others is not governed by a relation to truth, but by less innocent factors. These ultimately include a will to power partially constituted by and expressing a desire not to hear certain other voices or stories."[122] Numerous stories recounted by women performers attest to the cultural echoes and shared heritage of socially segregated entertainment forms. Dorian Dennis began her career as a Broadway chorus girl and ended it as a successful stripper, but considered herself in the "strip-for-stardom" trade no matter the context.[123] Carnival stripper Lulu admitted, "Years ago I broke in via the burlesque chorus line."[124] Stripper Janette Boyd, a participant in the 1986 "Golden G-string Contest," was also a beauty queen, confessing, "any contest, I entered it. I was Miss Nuts and Bolts. And I was once Miss Firecracker."[125] Stripper Gay Dawn "once entered the University of California Sophomore Doll Beauty Contest under the pseudonym of Dolores Jones. She represented the Chi Psi fraternity house." Dawn, who won handily, had arranged to have friends inform the judges of her occupation and identity following the contest. "When the judges learned that they had chosen a professional stripper and not a co-ed, they speedily disqualified her."[126] The Miss Topless Wyoming contest not only has an evening gown segment in its competition, but, as Lily Burana confirms, "in the big contests for exotic dance titles, like Miss Nude World or Miss Nude Universe, there is great emphasis placed on 'BQI,' beauty queen image."[127] That "BQI" is readily identifiable as a visual sign of Nancy Etcoff's "saint" supports a strong perceptual link between the beauty contestant and elevated morality. That it has been easily appropriated by strippers would seem to be a more socially acceptable notion than the equal co-opting of stripping's codified gestures by pageant contestants, yet the ubiquitous harem dances and other references to burlesque and striptease that enliven beauty pageants from coast to coast prove that common theatrical languages can be used by any sort of speaker.

Cultural insistence on assigning ideologically based notions of morality, or lack thereof, to an embodied performance—whether beauty contest, burlesque, or cooch show—is not only about display and concealment, order and control, but about defining place. "Ideology," argues Bill Nichols, "uses the fabrication of images and the processes of representation to persuade us that how things are is how they ought to be, and that the place provided for us is the place we ought to have."[128] Conceptual and physical marginalization allows one form to advance to prime-time television and the other to be relegated and legislated to the periphery of culture without actually disappearing, a social reminder of where "outside" is. By the twentieth century strategies of calibration by women performers had become compulsory as female display emerged as an increasingly bifurcated and codified staging of a social value system. Moral implications had inhabited the shadow of every female performer since her first step on the stage, but by the century's end they had become contextually inseparable from the performances themselves, resulting in cultural attempts to segment forms of display into socially controllable, enforced, and decidedly reductive categories. As cultural value systems have increasingly segregated the variant forms of female theatrical display, their antagonistic ideologies have emerged more and more clearly as proactive theatrical contributors to the forms themselves. Their influence, in addition to defining the products, market, and even the audience for each variant, paradoxically seeks to obscure or deny the common origins of all of them even as it freely employs theatrical devices that repeatedly betray that commonality.

the "remedies" for addressing fears of a declining moral fiber involved the attachment of social anxiety onto the bodies of female performers. As Rebecca Schneider has remarked, "bodies are stages for social theatrics, propping hosts of cultural assumptions."[4] The result was an imposition of a "moral" self on what Erving Goffman later would argue was essentially an "amoral" form—actors being neither moral nor immoral onstage, but solely concerned with the "amoral issue of engineering a convincing performance."[5] Goffman contends that performers are "*merchants* of morality" (italics mine), participating in activities which may concern moral matters, without necessarily sharing a "moral concern with them." But fifty years prior to Goffman's observation, authorities like the Reverend Herrick Johnson had repeated the moral argument raised centuries earlier against acting as a profession: "How can they mingle together as they do and make public exhibition of themselves as they do, in such positions as they must sometimes take, affecting such sentiments and passions—how can they do this without moral contamination?"[6]

Thus Adah Issacs Menken "making a spectacle of herself," a "naked hussy on horseback," was, by virtue of her display, not only enacting a particularly female version of behavioral immorality ("hussy" being a specifically gendered term, a derivation of "housewife" for which there is no male equivalent), but also functioning as a site of social contagion for self and spectator alike.[7] Just as Joseph Roach in *The Player's Passion* notes the seventeenth-century belief that the body was the "point of intersection between natural and moral philosophy," nineteenth-century discourse offers evidence of a similar opinion, this time focusing on female performers.[8] Critical analysts of the new prevalence of female spectacle on American stages thus maintained that "thinking about a disease will produce its symptoms. Imagining great heights will make us fall"[9] (see figure 2.1). Warnings to beware of "falling" carry implicatively Biblical authority, particularly when applied to the actions of women. The nearly immediate pressure brought to bear on all forms of female display by moralists and social commentators profoundly affected their theatrical development. More critically for the purposes of this study, such pressure also assisted in the establishment of a false dichotomy; the notion that some forms of female display were inherently superior to others on moral grounds. This chapter will expand on previous arguments for the forms' essential similarity by suggesting that their perceived estrangement is neither theatrical nor substantive, but rather a result of the imposition of ideological divisions intended to express particularized visions of "morality."

The notion that an actress's performance might be capable of corrupting moral sensitivity was linked to the late nineteenth-century's medical preoccupation with overt female sexuality as pathological and/or aberrant. "The

Figure 2.1 1928 anonymous burlesque performer. Library of Congress, Prints and Photographs Division

step from selling one's body onstage, to selling it offstage," according to Robert C. Allen, "was seen as a short one by many men."[10] Of course, technically, the "saleable" commodity onstage was the *image*, not the body itself, and its reception as deviant was hardly confined to male viewers alone. While

Jon Stratton argues "in striptease the woman is literally selling the visibility of her body," the same can be said of all entertainment forms that focus on bodily display and spectacle.[11] Singling out the body in striptease as somehow more "visible" than in other displays supports the established cultural tendency to accept the systematizing of the visual into highbrow and lowbrow hierarchies of exposure. Characterizing certain female displays as an affront to "ocular decorum," while defining others, such as the *Star and Garter Revue*, as "a perfect eye tonic," does, however, highlight the role "visibility" plays in constructing such theatrical hierarchies, mainly in terms of the perceived moral rectitude of a given spectacle or performer.[12]

The distinction is also linked historically to the equation of female sexuality with visualization. Corbin's 1919 insistence on the "purity of the eye" (not unlike John Ruskin's fantasy of a return to the "innocence of the eye"[13]) rather curiously recalls the sixteenth- and seventeenth-century use of the term "eye" as a euphemism or metaphor for "vagina."[14] As Jennifer Terry and Jacqueline Urla insist in *Deviant Bodies*:

> The relentless search for signs of deviance, alongside attempts to single out and align certain individuals with morbid typologies, even in the face of contrary evidence, is part of the larger history of modern life sciences and their preoccupation with naming and classifying diverse things that make up the world.[15]

Categorization of sexual display as more or less "pure" has a particular implication when the image is itself a female sexual organ.

"Classifying" women who articulated certain codified images of sexuality on the stage into categories of behavior became the practice of everyone from critics and legislators to actresses like Olive Logan, who sought to impose a perceptual barrier between her own chosen profession and that of the women who participated in the "leg business." Logan's prolific denunciations of the "leg business" might be read, in hindsight, as precursors to Mary Douglas's insight that "ideas about separating, purifying, demarcating and punishing transgressions have as their main function to impose system on an inherently untidy experience."[16] The untidiness of the mid-nineteenth-century's variety of staged female displays, coupled with spectator assumptions about the performers' moral selves, compelled Logan to analogize such displays with the most heinous of crimes. She accomplished this by singling out "leg business" women as culturally pathological on the basis of the premeditated intention of their acts:

> The intention is everything, just as it is in killing. If you intend to kill, you are a murderer, and deserve the murderer's fate. If you kill in self-defense, and in a just

and patriotic cause—like a soldier—you are not blamable but virtuous. In like manner, the scanty drapery of the ballet, for the purpose of art, and art alone, is no offense against good taste or good manners; but if the ballet girl—not for the sake of art, but for the sake of attracting lewd attention—overdoes the scantiness, and betrays the immodesty of her mind by her motions or gestures, she commits an offense, and ought to be hissed from the stage which she disgraces.[17]

Logan's emphasis on intention denied any possibility that scantily clad female entertainers might be regarded merely as actresses, just as projections of pathological deviance on interpreters of the fictive Salome had done. "Intention" as "everything" thus became a tool for the further categorization of female performers by factions opposed to particular forms of display. The strategy of linking personal motivation with performance event bolstered the argument that an individual pathology rather than an "artistic" creation was being enacted on the stage. This, as Allen notes, amounted to a social disassociation of spectacle from narrative: "In place of that larger narrative is the self-evident rationale provided by spectacle: the stripper is what she does, and she does what she does because of who she is."[18] Arguments of this kind have enjoyed a long life: they remain popular to this day in the anti-pornography writings of those who, like Catherine Mackinnon, refuse to recognize the construction of performative artifice in entertainments like exotic dancing: "to express eroticism is to engage in eroticism, meaning to perform a sex act. To say it is to do it, and to do it is to say it."[19] Erroneous conflations of spectacle with "self" will be addressed in chapter 3, but the cultural insistence on the "authenticity" of the image presented in striptease, as well as in other forms like beauty contests, cannot be disassociated from ideological prescriptions for acceptable female behavior. Perceptions of ingenuous revelation, while crucial for success in both forms, have also contributed significantly to their fundamental misinterpretation by critics who believe that imitations of virtue or transgression are equivalent to those values in and of themselves.

Maud Allen's infamous libel case following her performance as Salome (brought about by an article in *The Vigilante*, under the headline "The Cult of the Clitoris") is an apt example of social attempts to control certain female behaviors on the stage by labeling them pathological. In testimony for the defense, Dr. Serrell Cooke, whose responsibilities included overseeing the Paddington Hospital asylum inmates, pronounced that "a person performing the part of Salome must be a Sadist," unable to "get any sexual excitement unless they bite with violence enough to draw blood, even suck it, taste it, and then they have a violent sexual orgasm."[20] Much as an earlier "scientific" theory of the "wandering uterus" had been used to connote female instability, the charge of sexual depravity became a favorite tool of critics who sought cultural quarantine of female performers on the basis of their personal deviance. Conceptions of women as hysterics had been employed to great effect by the French clinician Jean-Martin Charcot, who linked hysteria to "an enormous development of the tendency to imitation."[21] Theories of the psychology of women at the beginning of the twentieth century characterized them not only as "instinctively imitative, but, as reproducers of other bodies, they were ipso facto less capable than men of maintaining the boundaries between self and other."[22] Although not necessarily mutually constitutive, circulating theories of female behavior and the attempts to regulate female staged display might be read as contributors to the notion of performers as individuals conveying varying degrees of personal morality. In the end, Allen lost the libel case. The judgment concluded with the ambiguous statement: "Miss Allen may be a pervert, or she may not be."[23]

Schematizing tendencies with regard to staged displays of female sexuality were easily expanded from personal pathology to public contagion. Sexual disease, deviance, and sexual display were all rendered equally communicable, a practice that supports Elizabeth Grosz's definition of the body as a "series of uncoordinated potentialities which require social triggering."[24] "Woman as symptom," implicitly carries connotations both of social disease and one who is in need of "treatment," who needs to be "fixed" in the sense of contained, stabilized, in need of a cure.[25] Categorizing display might be seen as a socially viable means of "fixing" women, both in the senses of containment and repair. According to evangelist Billy Sunday in 1915, theatre audiences were literally absorbing, or "drinking in" at the "leg show" morally toxic "gutterish ideas."[26] Public resistance to the dissemination of moral decay from the stage predictably focused on female reprobacy. Notwithstanding Alexander Woollcott's dry assertion that "the chief difference between the Minsky's burlesques and the ordinary Broadway musical comedy is $2.20," the cultural segmentation of entertainment forms featuring displays of women that began in the late nineteenth century gained momentum. This theatrical fragmenting was aided and abetted by, among others, Anthony Comstock and the Society for the Suppression of Vice, feminists operating as moral reformers, and, perhaps most significantly, entertainment practitioners who saw the segmenting of forms as an opportunity for the creation of niche markets.[27]

In a discussion of the relationship between the social purity campaign and the theater, Lois Banner observes that while critical inquiry into the links has yet to be fully explored, "indications are that the new social conservatism had a substantial impact there as elsewhere."[28] She further states, "available evidence suggests that respectable audiences who came to see the British Blondes did not long frequent this kind of entertainment."[29] Not without irony, the ambiguity of the phrase "kind of entertainment" constitutes an explicit cultural location to which sexualized display is consigned as part of its annexation within the realm of an aesthetic hierarchy based on imposed morality. Notwithstanding the thundering rhetorical excesses and passionately melodramatic characterizations of American nineteenth-century theatre, the moral litmus test applied to sexualized display consisted principally of assessments of a performer's capacity for restraint. If, as Joseph Roach has noted, "the esteem in which an actor was held by his public seems to have depended on the degree to which he was perceived as capable of keeping his bodily powers in check,"[30] for actresses, according to Angela Latham, "the care with which a woman cloaked rather than displayed her sexuality was a crucial measure of her worth."[31] Where displays of mastery of the powerful body have resulted in public applause for men, restrained sexuality has been the hallmark of appropriate "womanly" behavior.[32]

In such an atmosphere, it is not surprising that female sexualized presentations would be declared legalistically illegitimate. By the 1930s, governing social bodies such as the Massachusetts Supreme Court characterized burlesque as "not an art, not acting, but among the lowest if not the lowest forms of production on the stage."[33] This occurred in part because the generalized historical significance of women on the stage had been clearly established by the early twentieth century as inseparable from particular notions of "feminine" sexuality. Such notions, and their antitheses, had been reinforced time after time in popular Victorian-era plays like *East Lynne, Margaret Fleming, The Ticket-of-Leave Man*, and the florid outpourings associated with the so-called School of Emotionalism. With the emergence of explicitly sexualized display performances, however, "making a spectacle" of oneself became not only a peculiarly female behavior, but also acquired definition as a visual "production" of the "low," rather than a reputable entertainment construct. This kind of categorization allowed critics to draw immediate parallels with far older and more broadly established social presumptions about women. In *American Beauty*, Lois Banner points to the "favorite European author of post-revolutionary Americans," Lord Byron, as "establishing the convention of splitting the female personality into two characters: Rowena and Rebecca, one dark and sensuous, the other blonde and virtuous," a convention that "would haunt the beauty culture of the modern age."[34] That bifurcation of the female persona was clearly a reconstitution of the age-old madonna/ whore binary, yet the concept carried specific ramifications when imposed on the performing female, particularly evident in the moral separation of "wholesome display" from "disreputable spectacle." In some minds, the Rebecca/Rowena dichotomy not only accounted for the existence of female sexualized display, but also reinforced the assumption that personal agency—intention—was central to the motivation of its performers.

Other nineteenth-century assumptions about women were more straight-forwardly useful to proponents and promoters of female spectacle. In stark contradiction to Lord Byron's psychological dualism, "the belief in the moral superiority of women—an ideal central to pre–World War I feminism—was closely connected to democratic beauty ideals."[35] The 1927 New Amsterdam Theatre Ziegfeld *Follies* production "Glorifying the American Girl," carried the program logo "He who glorifies beauty glorifies truth."[36] Appearance as truth, a theatrical trope employed with astonishing success in the wildly popular melodramas at the end of the nineteenth century, resulted in, as Robert C. Allen has stated, "the face and the body [as] important outward signs of the true woman's inner being: one had to be able to see the latter shining through the former."[37] Railing against burlesque, a spokesman for Catholic Charities used the argument that burlesque had "no element of truth in it [. . .] no element of goodness or beauty."[38] Yet by the 1920s, when women "no longer were seen as possessing a superior spirituality, their out-ward appearance could be viewed as more important than their inner charac-ter, and external means could become central to improving their looks."[39] In 1923, Madison Square Garden was the site of a "National Beauty Meet" sponsored by the cosmetic company "Mineralava." The president of the organization, H.K. Pokress, summed up the importance of appearance:

> Believe me, each and every one of these prize-beauties that take part in this National Beauty Meet tonight will be grabbed up by some sort of a flattering pro-posal, be it business, art or marriage, on the morning of the 29th [the day after the contest]—BUT, if there were to be a BRAINS CONTEST, and eighty-eight brains prize-winners were to compete, there would be perhaps a dozen people in the whole city who would be interested enough to attend [. . .] Beauty is what counts! It is the open sesame to everything and every place.[40]

The Ziegfeld *Follies*, characterized in 1928 by *The Austin Statesman* as comprising a "hoard of Glorified Baby Dolls," capitalized on the trend toward promoting the external as the "open sesame" to womanly success.[41] Ziegfeld (aka the "virtuoso of virgins"[42]), in popularizing the notion of appearance as truth as a specifically feminine goal, exemplified Lois Banner's contention that the idea "that every woman could be beautiful was a danger-ous concept, just as easily adapted to the ends of business as to reform."[43] Dangerous, because as beauty became equated with virtue and sincerity on the stage "on a physical level, it meant transparency and consistency."[44] "Beauty is woman's supreme gift," declared Walter Kingsley in 1920, "it is sufficient in itself—it is the genius of the body. I do not wonder at the popularity of shows wherein loveliness is pageanted and decorated and exalted. The golden girl is paramount in the theater."[45]

In a 1946 *American Weekly* article recalling the influence of Ziegfeld, Adela Rogers St. John pointed out that "It wasn't just the girls in the shows that Ziegfeld glorified. It was the American girl herself. Women began to be conscious of beauty as they never did before. They imitated *Follies* girls and they saw that it was a good idea to make the most of themselves. It'll go on and on after they've forgotten Olive Thomas and Dorothy Mackail and Virginia Bruce."[46] That few readers will recognize the names listed is a testament to the prescience of Ms. Rogers St. John. The entertainer Eddie Cantor similarly identified the profound impact of Ziegfeld's efforts to glorify a national feminine type, claiming that "the touch of beauty and artistry that [Ziegfeld] bequeathed to the American theater and American womanhood has become the common heritage of the land."[47] Cantor's pronouncement is validated to this day (perhaps ironically) in the presentational choreography—and ideology—of every beauty contest. Where facade and form are the distinguishing features of success, and "appropriate" appearance the ultimate goal, the symbolic content of what is being represented requires careful definition. For Ziegfeld and other beauty merchants, that definition equated particular forms of fashion and grace with civic, even explicitly nationalist, virtue. "It is amazing how complete is the delusion that beauty is goodness," Tolstoy had observed half-a-century before Ziegfeld.[48] Such a conflation is by no means an exclusively American phenomenon. Even Libya's first beauty contest (held in 2002) offered a superficial presentation of femaleness as a signifier of national virtue (and a counterweight to its international reputation), with the pageant slogan: "Beauty will save the world."[49] Wearing T-shirts bearing the likeness of Moammar Gadhafi, contestants were employed as promoters of tourism, object-indicators that Libya, being a place of beauty, is therefore also a desirable, even a "safe" destination.

As a reinforcing indicator of truth and/or morality, onstage behavior was merely an extension of the *look* of beauty. It, too, operated as a social marker, a component of the way one "appears" in public. Notwithstanding Ziegfeld's nomination as "the acknowledged master of skin opera" for twenty years,[50] his secretary protested in a 1924 article that "the girl who makes a suggestive gesture is taken off the lists; never has there been any complaint by the public, or public censors, of his show; never has he sanctioned by giving her a place in his company the unclad nor indecent woman."[51] That Ziegfeld promoted the "unclad" is irrefutable, yet he also vigorously sought to separate nudity in the public consciousness from the "indecent." This required a theatrical strategy that equated "feminine pulchritude" with virtue, so while Ziegfeld [falsely] credited himself as "the first producer to lead the stage toward nudity," he simultaneously expressed righteous indignation at "what he called the daring and coarseness of Broadway beauty barterers."[52]

As the theatrical forms of revues, burlesque, and beauty contests became social battlefields, marked as carriers of moral (or immoral) values, the bodies of the performers were increasingly regarded as codified messengers. In 1915, actress Ada Patterson characterized a female stage performer as "a woman intensified."[53] Distilling female performance into a cultural construct of so many "Rebeccas" and "Rowenas" fit snugly into the ongoing cultural compartmentalization of the entertainment forms themselves: Rebeccas became beauty contestants and Rowenas carnival strippers. Operating as a microcosmic reflection of the larger cultural trend toward byadic female presentation, and of a social agenda that favored controlled visibility, burlesque stages like New York's famous Irving Place Theatre actually built two completely discrete manifestations of female representation into one evening's performance: "it was standard to have two chorus lines—one for dancing, and another for stripping."[54] The theatrical attempt to circumvent moral outrage by offering one "clean" show and another "dirty" one even extended to an individual performance strategy at The Republic Theater, where promoters offered "a striptease in reverse, starting with a sparsely clad girl who gradually put on her clothes."[55] Covering the exposed body in front of the audience was a variation of a common burlesque device used to situate the spectator as voyeur. Performances of "normal" female behavior (to be explored in chapter 4) often portrayed women's "private" moments—dressing, undressing, bathing, or lounging in the boudoir. Portrayals of "normal" behavior can be seen as a theatrical strategy that allowed producers to defend themselves from charges of immorality by arguing that the performers were simply doing what every female does in daily life. "The show that most cunningly capitalizes innocence," wrote George Jean Nathan in 1918, "is the show that most prosperously serves its ends."

According to Eddie Cantor, "The beginning of the twentieth-century developed three great inventions—the telephone, the telegraph and the American Beauty."[56] It is hardly a coincidence that the term "pulchritude," so often associated with Ziegfeld, became a common noun used to reference beauty contests as well.[57] "Americans are by nature girl-watchers," remarked one journalist as late as 1965, "and this pageant down by the Jersey Shore provides them annually with one of their best opportunities to inspect the latest samples of feminine pulchritude."[58] As part of the industry of "inventing" beauty, the Miss America Pageant developed as a spectacle of "pulchritude," tacitly embracing the term as a conventional label by which it might be socially situated. This strategy proved itself extraordinarily persuasive even for skeptics. One journalist for the *New York Herald Tribune* defined the pageant (in 1963) as "a grimly fascinating morality play of the tough American business of professional beauty."[59]

Characterized elsewhere as an "edifying Preakness of Pulchritude," the Miss America Pageant began in 1921 as an attempt to extend the tourist season in Atlantic City, New Jersey.[60] After only a few years in operation, however, at the request of civic leaders and, more broadly, as a response to the social inclination toward polarization of the various competing forms of female spectacle, the contest bowed out of the public eye for a short time to re-conceptualize its role. While the pageant was busy codifying its image, its past contestants, several of whom had become burlesque and subsequently striptease performers, were being relegated to its margins. Their banishment marked an early stage in the long-term polarizing process of the forms, effected in two ways; physically, in the relocation of certain risqué establishments to the outskirts of cities and towns, and culturally, in the stigmatic identification of certain practitioners and entertainment forms as "immoral."

Perfectly aware of the cultural trend toward female display, the Miss America Pageant returned to the public stage newly positioned as the antithesis of immoral performance and a model for patriotic, virtuous young women. The Miss America Pageant, "former leg-and-more show," was now primarily touted as the public presentation of a set of role models rather than an entertainment act.[61] The transformation was not an instant one, despite the pageant's promotional attempts to settle itself in the realms of the civic and the virtuous (in other words, out of show business). In a presentational paradox that remains embedded in the pageant's foundations, the 1933 contestants were required to participate in a "seven-week vaudeville tour," sponsored by "carnivals and amusement parks," and the pageant itself became known as the "Showmen's Variety Jubilee."[62]

While employing successful techniques of the show business trade, the pageant sought to establish a preeminent position within the hierarchy of female display as "the" national image of appropriate "femininity." This required efforts to promote more than just "pulchritude." According to one 1964 journalist, "the pageant planners have been careful to bring in the right sort of gal."[63] Just as "Miss Alabama was selected by Earl Carroll as a *type*," the women who participated in Miss America were now chosen for their perceived moral potential as well as their beauty.[64] As a *Time* magazine review of

Ziegfeld's *Follies* remarked, "Not only is Rome not rebuilt in a day; not only do styles in architecture change—even showgirl architecture—but there is the always irreducible need of using good bricks and mortar."[65] The Miss America Pageant actively began recruiting a particular "sort" of girl to function as its brick and mortar foundation. But, "architecture," reminds Suzanne Langer, "is a plastic art and its first achievement is always, unconsciously and inevitably, an illusion; something purely imaginary or conceptual translated into visual impressions."[66]

Because "the Miss America pageant vehemently maintains that it is an event that showcases feminine respectability and morality,"[67] the explicit tenets of its ideology, and the corresponding details of a "moral" appearance, had to be defined and rehearsed by the organization and then accepted by a viewing public. Additionally complicating the endeavor was the fact of the openly displayed female form onstage. In 1909 an article in *Variety* succinctly asked, "Were there no women in burlesque, how many men would attend? The answer is the basic principle of the burlesque business."[68] Likewise, to remain in the beauty business, the Miss America Pageant had to retain some form of sexualized female display, while simultaneously appealing to the spectator's notion of a woman's "civic" duty and moral rectitude. In order to scrupulously mediate the display, the pageant employed a strategy of recruiting women's groups as supporters and volunteers, revising the pageant "precisely in their terms: on a moral basis."[69] Of course, such a technique was not beyond the reach of other performers, and was in fact preceded by Gypsy Rose Lee's participation in the "*Herald and Times* 14th Annual Cooking School and Better Homes Exposition in 1929," an event that by any moral measure was above reproach.[70] Years later, burlesque legend Ann Corio would lay claim to the same strategy on the *Sally Jesse Raphael Show*, stating that women were her "biggest following [. . .] because I never do anything to embarrass a woman onstage, and I always put femininity in a woman on a pedestal, which they should be [*sic*]."[71]

In 1935, new director Lenora Slaughter began a makeover of the Miss America Pageant, putting as much metaphoric distance between the pageant's history and its possible associations with other forms of female display as she could. "The pageant, insisted Slaughter, needed to be transformed from a 'leg-men's' spectacle into a respectable civic venture."[72] This required some mollifying adjustments. Early in the twentieth century, the "civic," as a category of attitudes and activities, fell under the social supervision of the upper class, which had traditionally, according to Dawn Perlmutter, considered beauty contests "unacceptable for so-called refined women. The prevalent attitude was that upper-class refined women simply did not display themselves before judges or the public."[73] To erase any resemblance to lower class entertainments, the pageant immediately costumed its contestants in more than just the ubiquitous bathing suit. Slaughter further scoured away the taint of show business, and strengthened the pageant's association with civic pride, by insisting that contestants could no longer compete under the titles of commercial organizations, but would be limited to representing cities, regions, or states.[74] Hostesses were organized to act as chaperones, talent was added as a competitive category, and the college scholarship program was initiated. In other words, every aspect of the public performance of the contestants, from the preparations for the event to the actual competition, was restructured to emphasize propriety safeguarded by constant surveillance. The conceptual split between Miss America and the revue, burlesque, or exotic dancer was thus fashioned and proclaimed as a moral imperative. The pageant's new direction provided an institutional, if inverted, illustration of the axiom: "If you get three Americans in one place, two will get together to reform the morals of the third."[75]

Miss America's calculated effort to disavow its reputation as a "girlie" show depended on the successful presentation of moral, civic-minded, and hence socially "useful" women. The preachments of pageant coaches like Anna Stanley, who declared that "a beauty queen is America's number one symbol of sweetness, femininity and wholesome good looks as well as a role model for the young women in this country," has been repeated in myriad forms for so many years that it has taken on the aspect of a costume, rhetorically draped across the bodies of contestants.[76] Taken to its extreme, the beauty contestant is assured that "maintaining your body [. . .] shows judges that you can handle responsibility."[77] An authentic and "responsible" presentation of femininity, with a "maintained" body as the guarantee, became the beauty contestant's validation as a moral being. As Erving Goffman has observed, a regular pattern of behavior, and in this case appearance, becomes a "front," intended to project a particular assurance or authenticity. This projection "exerts a moral demand on others, obliging them to value and treat him [her] in the manner that persons of his [her] kind have a right to expect."[78] "Moral" became situated as the physical obverse of "letting go" or "making a spectacle." Thus, by means of maintenance and control, the display of female bodies was rendered acceptable and nonthreatening to society.

The encouragement of civic virtue and patriotic sentiment, so much a part of the beauty contest's self-identification, is rarely associated with burlesque or striptease. Yet such appeal has nonetheless frequently appeared as iconographic gimmickry in performance, as well as in promotional rhetoric designed to forestall or circumvent social regulation and legislation. Bambi

Vawn's certainty that "striptease is as American as cowboys and Indians,"[79] addresses the direct correspondence between presentations of the female body onstage and an entertainment image of the construction of nation-ness. The Mineralava Company's backing of the "Beauty Foundation of America," an organization that claimed in the 1920s "that a nation can be really great only if it has really beautiful women," announced that it had "sprung into existence as the result of a national necessity." Asserting that "a nation produces great statesmen, great educators, great scientists, and great artists only in proportion to the amount and degree of beautiful women it possesses," the company pronounced itself "dedicated to the promulgation of feminine beauty," and encouraged the nation to swell the "ranks" of attractive females until "the fame of America's beautiful women shall reach into every nook and corner of the world!"[80]

In an editorial placed in the *Follies* program by a Mr. E.D. Price ("The Ziegfeld 'Follies' after twenty-five years is a national institution glorifying the American Girl"), patriotism was used as a rousing defense against presumably spurious allegations of "foreignness":

> The champagne of life is of precious vintage, and can never be prohibited [. . .] The 1931 edition, now a sensation at the Ziegfeld Theatre, like its predecessors, is redolent with the atmosphere of Paris when it was truly Parisian. In personnel and adornment it is all American, conceived, produced and performed by Americans for America [. . .] the Follies does not, and never did cultivate personal intimacies. The glorification of the human body is not vulgarized, but is in harmony with world acknowledged canon of true artistry. Its lovely girls are chosen from the choicest gardens of American beauty. It is all, in every aspect, bubbling, sparkling, foaming with the ardent spirit of exhilarating American youth. This defines the distinctiveness of the *Follies*.[81]

Only a few years later, the Minsky brothers would stand before a House Immigration Committee and proudly claim that American girls made the best strippers. Apparently without irony, they appropriated a Spanish dance form for their example, assuring the committee, "The shed-your-shirt Fandango was born in America right on the stage of a Minsky theater, and American it will remain."[82] In 1932, Russel Crouse and Howard Lindsay, authors and producers, warned of the impact burlesque censorship would have on the legitimate theater, going so far as to pronounce burlesque the "Czechoslovakia of the stage and the legitimate theater might soon be its Poland."[83] Continuing the linkage of burlesque's enemies with antipatriotic fascists, a letter to the editor of a New York newspaper railed: "in these days when we are making every effort to defend and preserve democratic institutions it is deplorable to see our own municipal officials adopting the methods of Hitler and Mussolini."[84] Bess Myerson, Miss America 1945, offered a less histrionic version of her nation-building role: "We couldn't have realized it, standing on the bleachers, sucking in our bellies, fixing our smiles, but we were at that moment becoming the cheesecake that followed the flag."[85]

Marrying patriotism to pulchritude with promotional logos like the Minsky's "Stars and *Strips* Forever," burlesque's stripteasers performed their own versions of national pride.[86] Take, for example, the following description of a performance event with characteristics remarkably similar to the Miss America's patriotic demonstration:

> In the midst of the gaiety and laughter the entire cast suddenly formed a patriotic ensemble depicting the birth of liberty. So who was standing in the background bearing a torch and wearing a crown, her red hair flaming defiantly against tyrants—every inch the Statue of Liberty—but Margie. The only difference between her and the lady in the harbor is that Margie was stripped to the waist, with blue touches to fit the red, white, and blue color scheme.[87]

In 1928, a Ziegfeld production (*Rosalie*) presented its chorus of "rose-pink pearl pulchritude" as "West Point Cadets" who, in the eyes of one reviewer, "strike a swashing blow at pacifism."[88] Patriotism was a tool for offstage promotion as well. Performers in Michael Todd's 1943 *Star and Garter* production were publicized for their contributions to the war effort, spending all of "their spare time in various Women's Volunteer War Work."[89] In the same program, Georgia Sothern was positioned as an exemplary paradigm of the homegrown, with her "terpsichorean interpretation of a famous American institution . . . the bumps."[90] The Miss America organization's (MAO) attempt to separate itself from the "lowbrow" on the basis of civic contributions and volunteerism would be met toe to toe by producers and performers who refused to accept their relegation to a constructed cultural fringe as second-class citizens.

Even as the language and imagery of civic pride and patriotism attached themselves to female displays of various kinds, distinctions founded on assumptive moral considerations grew sharper among forms. Scratch burlesque, nightclubs, carnival strippers, and cooch shows dropped any pretense of "cleanliness." According to Zeidman, the year 1924 was "the last in which the fetish of clean burlesque was upheld."[91] In an inverse of the beauty contest's attempts to camouflage its sexualized imagery, the overt marketing of "naughtiness" became a productive tool with which certain forms of female entertainment could be promoted, and businesses and performers capitalized on their cultural relegation to a supposed marginal social space. If "morality" had proven itself a successful marketing strategy, producers soon reasoned that "immorality" might be equally useful. The business of selling seemingly transgressive behavior with come-ons like, "This is stock burlesque, strippers and tossers, hip weavers and breast bouncers—this is stock burlesque," served to accentuate the social separation between types of performance.[92]

By the 1930s, in spite of his protestations against the "beauty barterers," Ziegfeld was openly marketing nudity on his program covers. A 1931 program cover for the Ziegfeld Theater featured a topless girl wearing a feather boa, covering (caressing) one breast with her hand while the boa barely masked the other.[93] Earl Carroll routinely used drawings of naked women to offset the photos of nearly naked performers in his souvenir programs of the 1930s, capitalizing on the short imagistic leap from one to the other. It was also in the year 1931 that two press agents for the Minskys were rumored to have "coined the phrase 'striptease.' "[94] Contrary to one beauty contestant's admonition that "you are up there to entertain, not to be suggestive," theatricals focusing on female bodies regularly employed techniques that openly relied on the entertainment value of the "suggestive."[95] The proliferation of "turkey" shows and "behind-the-tent" companies might also be read as a theatrical response to the segmentation of forms into moralistic encampments.[96] Although "scratch" shows have been characterized as the "bane" of reputable burlesque, by 1936 Joe Bigelow of *Variety* could claim that, in "reputable" burlesque, "the routine remained 99 percent strip with the other one percent just there to pad out the running time."[97] Just as decades earlier, tableau vivant was defined as a category of display because it functioned as a more "socially and morally acceptable term," and "Model artist" employed because it "connoted a more sensational, voyeuristic kind of activity,"[98] terms like "scratch burlesque," "censored," and "scholarship competition," popped up on the twentieth-century cultural landscape like so many moral roadsigns.

The balkanization of female display's variant forms along lines of moral or anti-moral probity has often been linked to the disappearance of burlesque from American stages after World War II. In 1951, however, an editorial in *Cavalcade of Burlesque* categorically declared, "Let's not be kidded, burlesque is not absent from the New York scene. It is merely dressed up and sold to the public at prices that are beyond the reach of the general public, and given a different title."[99] The common misperception is that Mayor Fiorello LaGuardia's successful effort to ban burlesque in New York City in 1942 (a process discussed in detail in chapter 6) resulted in the banishment of striptease from the cultural landscape until the appearance of strip clubs some thirty years later. In fact, nationwide, actual burlesque houses (and those merely euphemistically referred to as such) took the better part of the same thirty years to fade away for good. The marketing of female "naughtiness" as entertainment was too firmly entrenched to disappear so easily. In city after city, the landmark theaters devoted to burlesque held on as long as they could.

Boston's Old Howard, a renowned theater located in the heart of Scollay Square, was finally closed down by the Boston Vice Squad in 1953 when the act of stripper Irma-the-Body (aka Mary Goodneighbor) was caught on 16 mm film.[100] It was not until 1957, with the "arrest of twenty-one performers [. . .] and a license revocation threatened by the city," that the Empire, in Newark, New Jersey, closed its doors on Valentine's Day.[101] The Gayety Burlesque in Columbus, Ohio, which did not even open until 1946, managed to attract business for twelve years before closing.[102] The Folly Theater, in Kansas, closed its doors to stripping in 1969, as the *Kansas Star's* headline announced: "Old Grind Gets Bumped at Folly Theater here."[103] The Victoria, in San Francisco, became a "burlesque" house in the 1960s and remained so until 1976.[104] And the "longest running burlesque house in Philadelphia," the Trocadero, "closed its naughty doors on April Fool's Day in 1978."[105] By then, strip clubs nationwide were in place to assume their role in the moral hierarchy of female performance. But the reduction of burlesque's formerly varied bill of fare to its essential staple began long before that.

Susan Mills remembers a burlesque show she and her husband, baggy pants comedian Steve Mills, joined in 1974 at the Pilgrim Theatre in Boston: "When the show opened the girls were very nice like in real burlesque and by the time the show closed they were using coke bottles between the legs." The run of the show was one year. "In the beginning," Mills reasoned, "you're real successful and then, of course, you know, your box office falls off." For her, that production, with its shift from comics to coke bottles, served as a metaphor for the journey from the "tasteful" displays of Ziegfeld revues and early burlesque to contemporary lap and pole dances. "Basically that was it," she said. "That was the progression of the strippers."

The tendency at the end of the nineteenth century "to equate the notion of culture with that of hierarchy" never disappeared from the North American stage.[106] Moreover, conceptions of a hierarchy of representation extended to the performers themselves, who often perpetuated and/or allowed the ideological distinctions between the forms to thrive. Performer distinctions are made between burlesque parade girls and striptease artists, exotic dancers and strippers, strippers and coochers, just as they are among Miss America, Miss Universe, and Miss Wheatheart of the Nation (a beauty contest which began in 1947 as a way to "draw attention to the record breaking wheat crop"[107]). Susan Mills, who performed in Ann Corio's long-running revivalist production *This Was Burlesque*, argues that "stripping" and "burlesque" don't share much in the way of theatrical correspondence:

> Burlesque is a kind of comedy. Stripping is stripping. Then they added what they called parade girls to break up the scenes. Then it went from bad to worse. But at that time they were still stripteasing, they didn't take off their clothes, they pretended. Later as the economy got worse, as there was work on the road, it got raunchier and raunchier.

"Pretending" to take off clothing is situated as morally less reprehensible, less "raunchy," than actual stripping. Jenny Lee, known as a striptease artist, describes the difference between an exotic dancer and a stripper as one of layers: "The difference is an exotic dancer comes on with hardly anything off—I mean, on, and a stripper comes on fully clothed and takes it off."[108] Or, as Lee Mortimer defined the separation between forms in his openly misogynistic 1960 pulp diatribe *Women Confidential*:

> Nudity is ancient and its possibilities are limited, because a girl can't have on less than nothing. But in the 'twenties a cookie who knew something about sex appeared in a café and, instead of showing herself nude, showed herself naked. There is a distinct difference. Nude means with nothing on. Naked means with everything taken off.[109]

For Jenny Lee, the stripper is more engaged in *performance* than the exotic dancer, who in effect enters the stage space already positioned as an unclothed image. In Lee Mortimer's terms, this therefore makes the exotic dancer a nude figure, while the stripper, by virtue of the activity of disrobing, ends her performance in a state of nakedness. "Silver," the manager of Charlie's bikini club in California, argues the opposite, and defines the disparity as more conceptual than physical, more of a distinction rooted in performance methodology and approach:

> An exotic dance club is exotic dancing whether you are in a costume fully clothed or in a bikini. We do not go nude. We dance a performance just like if they were dancers in Vegas. You go to Vegas and you don't call them strippers on the big screen at the MGM, they're not considered strippers. And that's what we do. We perform; we have skills. We do a lot of pole work, climb the poles, do tricks.[110]

When asked about the moral implications of her work, Jenny Lee identified the difference as a matter of pretence, "I say I just show it, I don't do it."[111]

But "showing it," as an action of performance, is, for Silver, clearly connected to an embodied moral code:

> And it doesn't have nothing to do with sex, pornography of any kind. We don't do anything crude, rude of any sort. You want to make somebody feel special. I don't believe that I have to show anything to anybody that I'm not comfortable with because I'm a performer.

Moral designations like "crude" and "rude" are used as tools to set one performer apart from another. "Because they're just taking off their clothes, you know," states Susan Mills, "they're just taking off their clothes, so you have to negate what they're doing." Silver's description of a stripper as unskilled, a lesser performer (like Donna Carlton's reference to the "untrained imitator who fakes her way through a bellygram"[112]), sounds much like the pejorative opinions of coochers offered by their rivals in burlesque. "A cooch show," maintains Grace Swank Davis, who grew up in the wings of burlesque theatres where her mother performed, "that's generally a carnival expression. They didn't have seats, guys would come in and stand, the stage would be roped off [. . .] a cooch show is pretty lowdown."[113] Davis's use of the adjective "lowdown" expresses a widely understood concept of hierarchy within the performers' world, a hierarchy supported by explicit stigmatization of the cooch show as a lesser moral form. The further implication of "low-down" as something secret, or, as Webster's dictionary terms it, as "inside information," places the woman who performs it as simultaneously one who has something to hide, but who, for a price, will reveal it. As Silver states:

> Everyone has their own opinions. You have a lot of critics who believe that no matter what if you work in a club you're a "stripper." And that's a very harsh word. Strippers need to take off everything, to show pink, to prove what they have. Exotic dancers don't need to do that. They show that they can perform. Exotic dancing is not about sexual contact, it's about tasteful fantasy.

"Showing pink," or exposing female genitalia in performance, to "prove what they have," is a compelling, and disturbing, example of the deeply embedded social assumption of an "authentic" female self that can only be bodily revealed. For Silver, the designation "stripper" is "harsh" not only because of its immediate relegation to a lesser category of performance, but also because of its associations with the morally inferior, the "less tasteful."

Distinguishing acceptable kinds of performance from others deemed "less tasteful," or hierarchically "lowdown," is precisely what beauty contests strive to do as well. Their approach, according to pageant coach Anna Stanley, also "forces" contestants "to prove that they are genuine."[114] Just as "showing pink" is used as a tool for marking a particular (im)moral authenticity in strippers, bodily proof of the "genuine" is intrinsically linked in beauty contests to a presentation of morality; morality based on visually recognizable codifiers of acceptable "femininity." The construct of hierarchy that separates sexualized spectacle in strip clubs from that displayed on pageant stages is directly connected to the presumption that some demonstrations of sexuality are more "lowdown" than others. The distinction was described by one Miss Rhode Island contestant, who positioned the "erotic" as morally on a par with the primitive, even the animalistic:

> I don't know, to me, erotic just seems to evoke all these more, um, I don't know . . . when I think of erotic I think of like, ah, books like Fanny Hill or something, you know? That have a lot more negative, I guess, more, more, um, the animal-like thoughts.[115]

The pageant's willingness to utilize sexualized images to market its program while simultaneously discouraging its contestants from similar promotion in their individual performances creates a unique double bind for contestants. So, while commercial advertising for the Miss America Scholarship Pageant 2002 offered a final image of an "artificial shot of a big pair of puffy swollen lips" that appeared "like a porn video more than anything else," contestants struggled to negotiate an image of wholesomeness while displaying themselves in a swimsuit and high heels.[116] Reacting to the disparity between the pageant's published imagery and her own efforts to project the required "wholesomeness," Miss Arizona 2002 asked, "Is that all I am? Is a pair of lips and a pair of hips?"[117] Contestants participating in the 2004 competition were faced with a similar performance conundrum. As they valiantly attempted to project health and "fitness," contestants were posed in string bikinis, draped across the steps of a pool, and surrounded by hundreds of lit candles creating an image, as one viewer phrased it, of "trying to make a cheap porno [film]."[118]

Notwithstanding its habitual use of such recognizably erotic "lips and hips" images, the pageant sticks to its ideological performance of morality, insisting that each contestant accept a clause in her contract that assures she will not do anything that would tarnish the Miss America image. Such management techniques function as devices to safeguard the separation Miss America seeks from other beauty contests that may have similar formats but lack its "moral" emphasis. (The organization may have some justification for this in view of the proliferation of parallel pageant events: In 1976, the Miss International Nude Pageant, characterized as an "imitation of the bigger one going on down the boards in convention hall," was held in Atlantic City one week prior to the Miss America pageant. One of the patrons at the event, apparently unable to distinguish which pageant he was attending, shouted out, "Hey, where's Bert Parks?"[119])

Contestants who fail to embody the tenets or imagery of the beauty contestant's moralistic code are summarily dismissed from the MAO. Jack Bushong, one-time executive director of the Miss Michigan Scholarship pageant, "remembers ordering one Miss Michigan dethroned just two days before Atlantic City because she had shacked up with her boyfriend in a motel just a few blocks from her house."[120] Vanessa Williams, who actually won the crown, was, famously, "deemed unfit for cornflakes," when posed images of her that the Organization considered "less tasteful" were later discovered to have been published.[121] Even an implication of turpitude is enough to activate Miss America's moral immune system. By the time Miss Florida 1982, Deanna Pitman, arrived in Atlantic City, she felt like a "whipped dog." Two months prior to the pageant, "this Girl Next Door had been arrested for drunk driving, and though the charges were dropped and the pageant let her compete, she knew she didn't have a chance in hell."[122] At the 2002 competition, another scandal erupted when Miss North Carolina stepped down due to the content of an e-mail sent to pageant officials by the contestant's ex-boyfriend, which allegedly contained a photograph of her bare breasts, exposed as she was dressing. Just as Susan Mills insisted that the stripper who is "just taking off her clothes" should be "negated," the MAO apparently relegated Miss North Carolina to the realm of the "lowdown," hence unacceptable. After all, as Don B. Magness, Chairman of the Miss Texas pageant in 1983, phrased it, "You can't win the Kentucky Derby with a jackass. We want to send a thoroughbred to Atlantic City [. . .] All we care about is the finished product."[123]

In spite of these and other strenuous attempts to distance themselves from what one journalist characterized as more of a promotional "emphasis on busts and gams than on education or character," pageants have never been able to entirely transcend association with other, less savory forms of female spectacle.[124] "Somehow . . . the contests just couldn't get deodorized of the carnival aroma."[125] The lingering scent of the sawdust in pageant displays may well be due, ironically, to the continuing enthusiasm with which pageants and their contestants interchangeably utilize theatrical techniques recognizable as social signifiers of both "moral" *and* erotically suggestive female behavior. One of the best-known former Miss Americas,

Mary Ann Mobley (1959), won with a talent number in which she began with a "highbrow" operatic aria, then abruptly stripped off her skirt and belted out a torch song, referred to by one reviewer of the show as "a stripped-down version of a tune much lower on the social scale."[126] Appropriations such as Mobley's reveal a continuing cross-pollination that argues a far more complex relationship among allegedly segregated theatrical forms, despite the pageant's insistence on its absolute independence from the seamier side of female spectacle.

This insistence requires pageant supporters to defend their format in occasionally elliptical ways. The beauty contest's ubiquitous display of women in swimsuits was justified by one veteran producer of preliminary pageants in Wisconsin as a kind of moral litmus test, a measure of a good girl's capacity for endurance rather than mere sexualized spectacle:

> I look on bathing suits this way; the girl is put in a difficult position. She goes out there, and she's half naked. To me, I look and see if she can take it. Does she have the poise to stand the embarrassment? Sure, you're gonna look at her shape. I am. You are. But she doesn't have to be a raving beauty to win.[127]

Fortitude, the ability to "take it," is how the contestants supposedly distance themselves from sexualization, holding fast to moral ground without tumbling down to, as Susan Mills phrased it, the realm of the "lowly."

Brendan Gill has written that, "of all topics, sex is the one that exposes in its purist form the ineradicable hypocrisy of the American people."[128] Moreover, he states, "we have been behaving in this ridiculous fashion for upwards of 300 years now. Notoriously, we are a people obsessed with sex; no less notoriously, we go on pretending the contrary, piously proclaiming that spiritual concerns are far more important to us than erotic ones."[129] So, as one pageant contestant, an "exotic belly dancer from Ohio,"[130] performs her sanitized talent segment, and another swimsuited contestant parades across the stage, "carefully programmed for the exact moment when every man in the audience is presumed to be saying to himself: 'I wonder what she looks like without her clothes on' "[131] beauty pageants continue to claim a social position as promoters of role models. This position atop the hierarchy of the female spectacle industry is dependent on an elaborate marketing device: the selling of moralistic superiority as a mask for the pageant's commonality with similar, but less sanctified, forms of entertainment. Suzette Charles, the woman who succeeded Vanessa Williams as Miss America 1984, stated in an interview that "women who wear bathing suits on the Atlantic City pageant's stage should not be compared to those seen in the meat market."[132]

Figure 2.2 "Miss Modesty," 1926 burlesque performer. Library of Congress, Prints and Photographs Division

Williams's unfortunate appearance in that market was, of course, the reason for Ms. Charles's elevation.

In spite of the evidence that beauty contests and strip shows both deal in manufactured ideologies of femininity which they package for sale in remarkably similar ways, there exists a continuing perception that the forms "should not be compared." In the artificial distinction between a beauty contestant's performance of a chaste, "moral" self and an exotic dancer's display of willing and "immoral" sexuality, morality itself becomes a malleable, ultimately fraudulent conception (see figure 2.2). Still, in disassociating the female body from its accumulated moral significance, we find a cultural catachresis, what Gayatri Spivak refers to (albeit in a different context) as "a concept-metaphor without an adequate referent."[133] Perhaps therein lies at least one of the reasons for the insistent allegiance to the illusion of moral distinction inscribed across the bodies of female performers in popular entertainment. Such a distinction allows for continuous verification of Jay Hornick's claim that such forms will never die as long as the "female leg keeps its modern curves and the patron's leg can move to the box office."[134]

That the body plays a role in the production of knowledge has been extensively analyzed, particularly in feminist theory, since the 1980s.[135] In light, however, of Elizabeth Grosz's observation that "knowledge is an activity; it is a *practice* and not a contemplative reflection," this idea seems particularly relevant to discussions of the socially composed fragmentation of forms of female display.[136] The exposed female body on American stages literally *performs* a social function, intrinsically connected to perceptions and impositions of a socialized moral center. Social knowledge of the potency of staged female spectacle as a disruptor of "ocular decorum" and moral stability has resulted in social action toward sanction and containment of such events, reducing the forms to what Guy Debord has termed, "the omnipresent celebration of a choice already made."[137] In the end, however, attempts to situate one performer as more, or less, moral than another are complicated, even contradicted, by the testimony of performing women in all the variants of female spectacle that focus on their approach to presentations as purely fictive constructs. Social investment in moral hierarchies is, ultimately, of dubious interest to the women who participate. As Ann "Bang Bang" Arbor succinctly stated when asked whether or not she was an exhibitionist: "You can call us what you like, but don't call us late on payday."[138]

3. Artifice and Authenticity: Parallels in Performance Approach ❧

They told us to be false, and that's all I'm doing.

"Some Girls," Soho Weakly News[1]

Impersonal:
Though you be endowed with grace,
Though you be passing fair,
I cannot recall your face,
I was looking otherwhere.

Jeannette, in her "Songs for the G-String"[2]

The careful construction of context is indispensable to the success of beauty contests and striptease alike, since both rely on the skillful theatrical employment of numerous visual cues to ensure the coherence of the performance event and to manipulate, and conform to, spectator perceptions and expectations. When the images presented by both forms are removed from their structured contextual positions, however, analysis of their discrete condition exposes the artifice in their constructions, irreparably damaging the illusion of the moment and often standing in blunt contradiction to the performances' announced or implied aims. This point that was not lost on Miss Arizona 2002, who noted, "we would not have 40 million dollars in scholarship to give out if we didn't have women in bikinis." Similarly, the late comedian Foster Brooks, a Miss America judge in 1982, announced to the press, "If it's not a beauty contest, then they should put bags over their heads."[3] Without a carefully constructed context (and in the absence of one or two categories of achievement), Lily Burana's account of her experience in the Miss Topless Wyoming Contest might just as easily be taken for the final staged moments of the Miss America Pageant: "We're all standing in a row, clapping for each other as winners are announced in the categories of Best Interview, Best Face, Best Breasts, Best Legs, Best Buns, and Best Pole Work."[4] This chapter will examine some of the means by which context and artifice are manipulated to produce performances that strike viewers as genuine, as authentically female in one or another of a small number of acceptable, predictable ways.

Performance approaches in stripping, beauty contests, and other forms of female display are identical in the sense that they share a common, coded language of "female" presentation familiar to all audiences. "We always project a corporeal state conforming to our own," proposes Heinrich Wolfflin, "we interpret the whole outside world according to the expressive system with which we have become familiar from our own bodies."[5] But expressive systems are also social structures, constructed and recognizable codifications. "Constant smiling," reminds Katherine Liepe-Levinson, "and a show of friendly interest or a show of attempting to please others above all else, have long been the hallmarks of 'femininity' in the West."[6] Because the smile is specifically codified in women as an indicator of, among other things, availability, passivity, interest, approval, and a nonthreatening or submissive attitude, it is readily accessible to beauty contestants and striptease artists as a theatrical tool, one of the means whereby they successfully maintain the attention of the audience.

Even William Cameron in his history of the 1893 Columbian Exposition (published that same year) remarked that for the "dancing girls," "the smile really seems to be indispensable."[7] In the Miss Topless Wyoming Contest, Lily Burana relied on the socially accepted codification of the female smile to project the all-important BQI (beauty queen image):

> For the swimsuit segment, an escort walks us to the stage one by one, then helps us up the stage stairs so we can do a brief pageant walk-and-wave before we join the other girls in a line along the back wall. When I walk across the stage wearing a black mirrored bikini Randy bought me, I beam extra wattage into my smile—as girly tradition dictates. Toothsome and irresistible, I am every babe hawking product at a trade show. I am Miss America.[8]

The fact that there is such a codified visual language that is instantly recognizable as "BQI," illustrates a western tradition of particular "feminine" behavior. The BQI smile is a gestural equivalent to the Queen of England's wave; everyone recognizes that her discreet, rotating, side-to-side hand movement represents control, decorum, and dignity befitting her station. For Burana, the forced smile assisted her winning bid for the title "Best of Show" (one must assume, although Burana confessed to trying to put it out of her mind, that the canine imagery conjured up by such a title was intentional on the part of event's organizers).

The smile, utilized as an expressive tool rather than an involuntary reflex, requires practice, according to one Miss America chaperone: "We have to coach some of them in smiling. You would be surprised how much gum some of the girls show. It looks horrible. I get them to practice in front of a mirror every day."[9] Because it disassociates context from action, smiling independently of any felt emotion enables control of the expressive gesture so it can be deployed on cue. Miss America 1949 "suggests practicing your smile on someone or something that won't smile back—like lampposts and mailboxes."[10] This fictive presentation of the genuine, like most other learned performance skills, apparently requires rehearsal uninterrupted by any external response. In the less than proficient performer, such a technique is responsible for a certain vacuousness, often noted when the level of skill hasn't developed to the point of conveying "authenticity." (On the other hand, perhaps vapidity carries its own attraction. It was Diderot who asserted that, "beauty in a woman is a vacant face," a face "innocent, naïve, still without expression."[11])

For the stripper, a practiced smile can serve as the means of reassuring the spectator that he has her full attention. Susan Scotto, an exotic dancer for more than thirty years and a Senior Lecturer of Russian Literature at Mount Holyoke College, uses the smile to define herself as "one of the helping profession, like a social worker or bartender"[12] (not unlike beauty contestants who promote themselves upon winning the crown as participating in a "year of service"). Perhaps most important to the success of the stripper and beauty contestant, the smile indicates willingness, or, as one pageant reviewer from the *New York Press* rather defensively noted, "they were all bright and pretty and they didn't look like they were being exploited, either."[13] As if to remind contestants that they wanted to be there, the director of one 1970s preliminary pageant in Wisconsin strategically positioned a sign with the "Biblical commandment," "Smile . . . Smile . . . Smile." directly under the judges' table, where it was visible only from the stage.[14] Though perhaps not precisely what the late Bert States had in mind when he noted that, "the inclination of the sign is to become more efficient," the BQI smile efficiently situates the contestant, or the stripper, within the expressive world deemed appropriate for "feminine" presentation.[15]

Disassociating the constructed context from actual presentation in beauty contests and striptease results in countless parallel images. Mae Dix, while performing in Chicago stock at the State-Congress Theatre in 1920, presented an act that featured a costume of "paper-mache [*sic*] cherries between her legs. She plucked the cherries one by one, tossing them with appropriate vocal and cooch accompaniment to an appreciative audience."[16] Dix's symbolic distribution of her virginity to the spectators is theatrically employed (in somewhat more fastidious and reassuringly paternalistic fashion) by the Miss America Pageant, which often features its contestants, in white gowns, being handed off to the audience by fathers and brothers, as though in a kind of marriage. In a 1990 "Stripper of the Year" contest in Las Vegas, a competitor used a wedding gown as her costume. Entering to the well-known wedding march, then slowly unzipping and stripping off the gown to reveal first her red G-string, then nothing, she energetically simulated an orgasmic sex act, thus rather imaginatively re-interpreting the lyrics "Here Comes the Bride."[17] Images of wedding gowns proliferate across the stages of beauty contests as well, particularly in opening numbers when contestants announce themselves, imagistically at least, as virginal potential brides.

When Adah Issacs Menken toured Nevada in the 1800s, "a line quickly formed, and men came onto the stage one by one to make their offerings to the Goddess," giving her money and gifts in an early version of dollars in the G-string.[18] Crowning the beauty queen functions in a similar manner as a pretense of worship, with an offering of money, flowers and, occasionally still, the phallic symbol of authority, a scepter. Props such as batons and canes, utilized in both forms as visual signifiers of sexuality and phallic imagery, are accepted in beauty contest talent segments as an accompaniment to "jazz" numbers and considered, as one former Miss Nebraska phrased it, "sassy," not "sexual." Likewise feather boas, a stereotype of the stripper costume, are common on the beauty pageant stage, even escaping the confines of the talent competition. One of the Miss America contestants in the 2002 competition wore a huge white boa with her very first appearance in the opening parade, over a costume that appeared almost a replica of the one worn by stripteaser Dixie Evans in her early Marilyn Monroe act. Stuffed animals abound in the "up-close and personal" video segments of beauty pageants and are routinely used in "baby doll" acts at strip clubs to convey innocence (that is, virginity) as a sexual turn-on.

For burlesque performers and strippers, the walk (which H.M. Alexander insisted should "fix character") is designed to convey open and willing sexuality, whereas the physicality of the beauty contestant is contrived and rehearsed to denote self-control and discipline.[19] Backstage pageant coaches vehemently whisper from the wings, "Flex the knees! Straighten the legs! Tummy in! Fanny under!"[20] "Girls postural training," reminds Nancy Henley, "emphasizes propriety—keeping the legs properly closed when sitting, not leaning over so as to reveal breasts."[21] The Miss America "Suck-and-Tuck glide," a particularly level step that calls for the stomach to be sucked in and the buttocks to be tucked slightly together and under the body, ensures that nothing will bounce, wiggle, or protrude too much when the contestant is in motion.[22] "At the racetrack, comments are frequently made on the beautiful gait of a thoroughbred horse," states former Miss America Donna Axum, "A woman can develop that same sort of gait."[23] Why a woman might wish to emulate the "gait" of a horse is not an indication of interest in animal husbandry, but a continuation of the social theme of "reining in" display. Still, the approaches of strippers and beauty contestants to physical presentation are far more similar than one might suppose, largely because the performers' aims are similar. As former beauty pageant winner Christy Cole explains, "Whirling around quickly doesn't give the judges a good look at what you really have under your hood!"[24]

The "Suck-and-Tuck" glide is itself a variation of earlier female stage movement, the "Ziegfeld walk," utilized successfully by revue performers. According to one newspaper article, it was Ziegfeld employee "Kathleen Mary Rose, aka Dolores, who taught the girls how to walk—'the real secret was in holding your body absolutely still and erect from the knees up.' "[25] *Variety* claimed the "Ziegfeld walk" to be "a combination of Irene Castle's flair for accenting the pelvis in her stance, the lifted shoulder—plus the slow concentrated gait."[26] The "accenting" of the pelvis in the controlled gait allowed for the implication of sexuality, but emphasized that it was held in check. Such signification of restraint ironically frees beauty contestants to adopt the physical language of burlesque and stripping without fear of misinterpretation. When a Miss New Hampshire contestant performed her "harem" dance in the 1999 competition, her limp pelvic thrusts were, perhaps more accurately than intended, accepted by the audience as "traditional" gestures.

Striptease artists and exotic dancers have traditionally employed a similar "parade" walk as they enter the stage space, progressing, usually, to a routine of choreographed abandon. Such a physical "narrative" was often standard in the days of burlesque as well:

> The "parade" which starts the stripper's act, is a modified version of the fashion model's gliding walk. The "bump" which winds it up can be described as a "fast pelvic propulsion." In between, the moulting performer may indulge in an occasional shimmy or kick. Both footlights and spotlights are progressively dimmed during the performance, until, during the last moments, severe cases of eyestrain may result.[27]

"Moulting" performers, often just before the stage lights went completely dark, used the technique known as a "flash," removing the last bit of clothing in the final seconds, or at least appearing as if they were, which accounted for the potential spectator "eyestrain." The stripper "Nadja," mentioned earlier as a performer who attached strategically placed fake fur under her costume, used the technique to give the audience what it wanted—the impression that she had exposed herself to them. Beauty contestants, well aware that the audience wants the opportunity to admire (and criticize) their bodies, employ the swimsuit segment in a similar way. By stripping down to the fabric equivalent of bra and panties, they offer themselves as "exposed." In spite of the fact that they now realize, according to Miss South Dakota 2002, "no one can take you seriously in high heels and a bathing suit,"[28] contestants appreciate that the juxtaposition of the sexualized image against the rhetoric of wholesomeness operates as their "flash," the draw that keeps the audience looking. (The Miss America Organization's continuing efforts to justify its swimsuit competition in the face of longstanding public criticism and its own tortured rhetoric of "fitness" and "wholesomeness" have included audience surveys that invariably endorse the segment by overwhelming margins.)

Mary Ann Mobley's gesture—stripping off her skirt and throwing it to the ground—during her winning performance in 1959, functioned in the same way as "Nadja's" pretend revelation. As she belted out the lyrics "there'll be a change in me," while stripping, Mobley rather boldly intimated the erotic potential beneath the beauty contestant's traditional air of control and reserve. Miss America 2003, who sang the courtesan's song from *Carmen* while dressed in red velvet, slowly pulled the rose from her hair and flung it to the ground, symbolically tossing away her sexuality like so many of Mae Dix's "paper mache" [*sic*] cherries. Even more overtly, according to *Variety*, one Miss America contestant "did a recitation of her schizo aspects," and combined in one talent piece "*Carmen* and "I'm Just a Girl Who Can't Say No."[29] Such acts are simply a reinterpretation of traditional theatrics performed years earlier, from a time when "musicians played 'refined' selections, such as 'Kiss Me Again,' or 'Beautiful Lady,' " while dozens of "showgirls paraded up and down the runway, and from one side to the other, clad only in a G-string."[30] As one performer phrased it, "in a beauty pageant you wear clothes to signify yourself."[31] Signification, rather than revelation, would seem to be the operative activity, and the "self" as fluid as the costumed moment.

Just as Ann Corio and Hinda Wassau saw the potential in abandoning "the riotous cooching of the shimmy shakers for the 'sophisticated' squirming to the strains of sweet, languorous music, all the while unfastening hooks and buttons," pageant performers capitalize on the entertainment value in what is known as "playing the opposite."[32] Even the stereotype of the pageant baton twirler has been appropriated by strippers. On stages in Las Vegas and elsewhere, exotic dancers can be found flinging flaming batons and rolling them around their well-oiled, G-string clad bodies. While Miss Virginia performs a can-can number wearing black panties, black stockings, and a garter belt, her skirt raised above her waist as she kicks,[33] contestants at the Miss Topless Wyoming contest are costumed as angel, schoolgirl, and, of course, a favorite fantasy image, the ubiquitously sexualized cheerleader.[34]

In particular, the talent segment of beauty pageant competition allows for a more open physical behavior and a sexually codified gestural vocabulary than would be deemed acceptable in other aspects of the contest. The Miss New York City 1980 pageant "started with the obligatory non-dancer production number, performed in fishnet tights and red garters [. . .] with endless hip swivels and arched-throat poses."[35] In the Miss New Hampshire 2000 pageant, a contestant performed a jazz number, complete with breast shimmy, long black evening gloves and fishnet stockings, to the sexually suggestive song "Fever." If, as pageant coach Anna Stanley argues, "the goal of this preparation is to be ready to 'sell' yourself to the judges," what is being sold at beauty contests is not only the image of innocence and wholesomeness, but a sexual display that is fully permissible within certain institutionally composed categories, legitimized by the watchful body of judges.[36]

Kathy Peiss has discussed the ways in which, in the early twentieth century, "photographers embraced specific styles of posing, camera placement, and lighting that regularized images of beauty, including those intended to be sexually arousing."[37] The regularization enabled a gestural codification that could be transmitted from performer to spectator without overt acknowledgment. In such a codification, no matter how tightly controlled the beauty contestant's swimsuit "suck-and-tuck" glide, the visual referent of accompanying high heels (which Bentley states "elongate[s] the female leg to its erotic pinnacle"[38]) is immediately, imagistically, associated with the exotic dancer, whose standard costume always includes a set of heels. "I think people recognize," allows Miss Illinois 2002, "if you're going to the beach, you're not going to be wearing the heels."[39]

At the Miss Capital Area Scholarship Program in Concord, New Hampshire, in January of 2002, the contestants all wore shoes with heels so disproportionately high that they unintentionally accentuated the visual parallel with an exotic dancer. Unused to such footwear, the contestants moved awkwardly, breasts and hips thrust out at odd angles, conveying precisely Roland Barthes' impression of novice strippers and their "clumsiness," a restoration of "erotic power."[40] The artifice didn't show in the work of the novices, not because of the skill level at which they operated, but for the opposite reason: Because they weren't yet adept at the pretense (they were most concerned with not falling down), they conveyed the impression of children trying on sexuality for size, as one would a Halloween costume, visually reiterating a Miss Rhode Island contestant's notion of showing the audience "who I *could* be." Beauty contestants are fundamentally required to calibrate their performances to suggest potential sexuality without expressing sexual knowledge, a contradictory stance for at least one young contestant who, when asked to define herself in one word, said "indecisive."[41] She didn't win the crown.

Although some of the contestants may have been unaware of the impact of their presentation, such costuming is central to the intentionally doubled image behind the event—the sexualization of youthful innocence. This is perhaps nowhere more evident than in the pageant's swimsuit segment. The swimsuit is itself an elastic metaphor, whether of healthy activity and innocent "fitness" to some viewers, or of nudity, wetness, and sexual fantasy to others. It is also remarkably similar to what was known in the burlesque trade as a "semi"; a wardrobe designator that differed from a "strip" in that the dancer "adds to or subtracts nothing from it during the number."[42] The performer in a "semi," a contemporary bikini club dancer, or the swim-suited beauty contestant are only distinguishable from one another by context, not fabric amount. "Some of the swimsuits that we're wearing," admits Miss Illinois 2002, "are more costumey [*sic*], they're not something that we would swim in. If you noticed last night, mine is velvet. I probably would never wear velvet to the beach, and so it's really a tool." The "tool's" purpose remains unarticulated by most pageant contestants, but Miss Arizona 2002, Laura Lawless, has no compunctions about admitting that sex is being marketed in the beauty pageant swimsuit segment:

> It is a very sexual image. And it's, it's a little bit disconcerting to me that in an age group that targets 17 to 24 year old women that the images that we're using to advertise the program are the sexualized images. But then again, if we don't have the ratings and we don't have the network then we don't have the pageant, and we don't have 40 million dollars in scholarship. So it's always a balancing act.

The "balancing act" of sexualized images and social acceptance extends beyond the individual performance approaches and accouterments to the performance spaces within which the displays occur. Bud Abbott and Lou Costello observed (in their introduction to the first issue of *Cavalcade of Burlesque*) that by disallowing the term "burlesque" in New York, "the authorities merely caused promoters to take burlesque out of the burlesque theatres and put it into the nightclubs."[43] Moving the venue off Broadway didn't necessarily indicate a change in the performance itself, but rather a contextual re-situating. As Rudolph Arnheim has pointed out, "[. . .] when we talk about spaces, about outer space and inner space, we are not referring primarily to physical facts. What we are dealing with is the psychological experience of our senses."[44] The construction of context in striptease and beauty contests is carefully pieced together to manipulate the "psychological experience" of the spectator. Locating strip clubs on the margins of public space, zoning them as on the "fringe," is the exact inverse of the beauty pageant choice to stage its event in a high-school auditorium, town hall, or civic center, spaces that signify order, approbation, rectitude, and mainstream centrality.

While the strip club's fantasy context might seem more apparent than that of the beauty pageant, Murray Davis points out, "Ordinary settings designated for utilitarian activities [. . .] discourage their users from actually going into erotic reality but permit them to fantasize going there."[45] Thus the beauty contest's high-school auditorium or community theater is transformed into a space where society's illusion of ideal femininity is framed, adorned, and paraded—often escorted by uniformed military guards against a backdrop of the American flag. The civic space holds a paying public invited to watch their daughters and sisters enact, under the "protection" of judges and institutional ideology, theatrical traditions of sexualized display. The beauty contest's protected, centralized location immeasurably strengthens its claim on moral acceptability.

In broadly strategic terms, strip shows and beauty contests both exist to provide formalized opportunities for gazing at women's bodies, and for making subjective assumptions about their potential. Outlined by footlights (a simultaneous illumination and barrier), the beauty contest stage allows judges to sit at eye level to the platform, a position that duplicates that of the audience at the strip club railing. So traditional is this configuration that it appears even in hybridized parodies—Lily Burana describes precisely the same arrangement at the Miss Topless Wyoming contest: "the judges, local men hand-picked [. . .], sit at the first row of tables in front of the stage, marking down our scores. No spectators are allowed to sit at the tipping rail to afford the judges an unobstructed view."[46] Tactical management of the spectators' gaze in each form depends partly on the governing subtext of its invitation to admire and to judge, and partly on the commercial realities of its respective milieu. Given their fundamental similarity as performative spectacles centered on the act of staring at women's bodies, however, it is not surprising that, although variant configurations do occur, stages for strip shows and beauty contests share certain essential features as laboratories for the creation of fantasy identities.

As nightclub disc jockey "Nightshade," notes, "Each person on the staff, whether they be management or bartender or security, and the customers as well, have all stepped into a realm of fantasy."[47] Nightshade's particular vantage point on the world of the strip club is perhaps unique in its insider/outsider status, including responsibility for an important component of the club's technical atmospherics, yet divested of personal interest in its ongoing artifice. Yet the value of elements of unreality provided by technical support are plain even to direct participants. Stripper "Candy" explains the theatrical components as essential aspects of her performance:

> I was naive and a very inhibited person. Extremely inhibited. But with the combination of lights, audience, and music, I was like a different person. It hits you before and after you come off the stage. I was scared to death of men, and the stage was a buffer between me and them. I never considered what I did "sexy," though I portrayed an animalistic sexuality that was not a basic part of my nature. In a relationship I would never be that uninhibited. Never.[48]

The created performance spaces in strip clubs or at beauty pageants are conceived as settings for an elective communal illusion that is rendered tenuous when a particular theatrical coherence is missing. As "Rita Rhinestone" discovered:

> One of the things I found out about performing in Western Canada is that there's no setting. Like, there's often no type of stage, so the times I've felt naked in the sense that it didn't seem appropriate, that rather than feeling nude or feeling like I was making a presentation of physical beauty, but just felt I didn't have my clothes on, was vulnerable in that way [. . .] Those moments when it's no longer a performance, it's just being caught not properly dressed.[49]

"Caught not properly dressed" is the end result of a poorly constructed context. "During erotic time," notes Murray Davis, "one's experience of the spatial expanse of the everyday world shrinks drastically."[50] From the phallic imagery of the strip club runway, to the dim and colored lights and the low ceilings, the spectator is encouraged to experience the event as a spatial journey inward. The space for stripping is constructed as "sexual" in the same way the beauty contest space is premeditatively positioned as "civic"—both are intentionally created contexts for the purpose of a successful theatrical presentation.

The use, or suggestion, of a runway (known in burlesque as "varicose alley"[51]), for instance, is common to both forms, and an important element of display, simultaneously offering up and cordoning off the female performers. "The concept has always been," states David Scott, "to bring the men in the audience as close as possible to what is forbidden to them."[52] Toni Bentley agrees that "the fact that these scenarios employ a theatrical device where the woman is physically separated from her audience is of central importance to these fantasies."[53] But the runway "concept" might just as easily be read, rather than a tool for separation, as a more theatrically effective means of display, literally thrusting out the female form to be viewed from all sides and angles. Characterized as "a tour de force, a swing of the pendulum that brought the visual event scandalously—and dangerously—close to the tactile," the runway also functions as a conduit between stage and audience, through which a particular theatrical, socially sanctioned, publicly ritualized affirmation of a sex-based ideology passes in both beauty contests and strip clubs.[54] The use of a runway, with its spatial insistence on controlling focus, contributes to the success of the performance and recalls Murray Davis's insistence that "those who dominate others sexually possess the greatest social power there is: the power to control another person's focus of attention."[55]

Spatial management of perspective is not confined to the use of runways, or the "bridge of thighs," as one *New York World Telegram* journalist phrased it.[56] The 1999 Miss New Hampshire Pageant's swimsuit competition featured a revolving circular dais that the contestants mounted to display themselves. This remotely operated, wedding-cake-sized pedestal evoked images of slave auctions, livestock shows, rotisseries and delicatessen pastry turntables, requiring the contestants to freeze in position as it rotated, in essence paralyzing them under the audience's gaze even as it elevated them beyond its reach. Undoubtedly borrowing from the theatrical tradition of living pictures, when turntables were used to present one pose while another was arranged on the half stage out of audience view, the use of rotating pedestals has historically been a popular tool for simultaneous presentations of female display and confinement. This approach to visualization has a long pictographic history: Rudolph Arnheim has written that, in the fifteenth century, when painters "began to define realistic space their construction of 'confined shape' served to facilitate orientation."[57] Confining displays of women to specific visual spaces with recognizable boundaries—runways, rotating pedestals, go-go cages—can only be read as a calculated attempt to "facilitate" spectator/ societal "orientation" toward the female body. As one newspaper article noted, revealingly: "Ever get that caged in feeling? The girls at the French Quarters do. They're pussy cats (14 of them) dancing in cages on the piano, and just about everywhere."[58]

Many performers consider such spatial barriers a welcome aspect of their jobs. According to *Cavalcade of Burlesque*, Ann "Bang Bang" Arbor "prefers to work in theatres rather than night clubs, since in the latter she comes into too close a proximity with her audiences."[59] Gypsy Rose Lee remarked that one of the advantages of burlesque was that "the dears who reveal their peeled forms at Minsky's are never within reach of the audience as they are in popular Broadway floor shows, where the drunks can paw them—and do."[60] Using spatial proximity as a tool, contemporary performers have developed techniques to negotiate their way through difficult encounters with spectators. "Nicki," at Charlie's bikini club in California, uses her time onstage to "train" her sometimes unruly audience. If a spectator reaches out to touch her or speaks in a disrespectful manner, "Nicki" counters upstage, distancing herself from the spectator until he "settles down," then she slowly returns to the stage edge. She repeats the process until an understanding is reached.[61] Just as Judith Lynne Hanna has referred to clothing as that which "affects the fantasy of intimacy; along with distance, it is armament that conveys unavailability and/or unapproachability,"[62] the stage setting in clubs and beauty pageants operates as a theatrical tool for management and performer alike, ensuring that the "communal illusion" remains within prescribed boundaries.

Commonalities of stage presentation, however, are overwhelmed and rendered barely noticeable by the insistence on segregating the forms in "moral" terms. According to David Scott, "The beauty queen and the fashion magazine cover girl reside at one extreme and the stripper (where she can perform in the nude) and the porn queen at the other."[63] Situating female performers at cultural "extremes" denies the shared theatrical traditions and individual performance approaches inherent in entertainment forms that use female display as their "flash." In Aubrey Beardsley's 1893 copy of *Salome*, Oscar Wilde wrote that the dance of the seven veils was an "invisible dance."[64] Eighty years later, a San Francisco club, the *Black Orchid Bar*, offered a poster promoting "Abstract a Go-Go."[65] Yet if one analyzes and accepts the numerous accounts by strippers and beauty contestants of their performance approaches as valid indicators of particular methodologies employed for successful presentations of particular "feminine types," "invisible" and "abstract" would seem more readily applicable terms than the cultural designators "moral" or "immoral," with their heavily freighted, nontheatrical prejudice. Just as in Ben Jonson's *Bartholomew Fair*, when the raised skirt of the puppet in Act V reveals that it has no sex, the underpinnings of female display in stripping and beauty contests reveal nothing more than a construction carefully calibrated for theatrical success.[66] If one reads the *performances* of beauty contestant and strippers, without their culturally imposed labels, one must consider that the women whom Scott positions at "extremes" are much more likely to be, like Jeanette "Flash" O'Farrell, "just . . . working girl[s] trying to get ahead."[67] In fact, presuppositions of moral content in forms of female display, in addition to obscuring their fundamental similarities, aggravate another common—but very ancient—misperception of theatrical performers in general.

In addition to a tendency to "grant characters in a play a peripheral life they do not have,"[68] the spectator has an even greater tendency to equate display with revelation, even going so far as George Jean Nathan, who asserted that "an actress is charming on the stage in the degree that her audience imagines she is charming off the stage."[69] Neither innately synonymous nor necessarily symbiotic, "display" and "revelation" have historically been subject to a conflation that perpetuates the reductive axiom "you are what you do." Given the regularity with which such conflation occurs, "it is hardly surprising," notes Elizabeth Grosz, "that feminists have tended to remain wary of any attempts to link women's subjectivities and social positions to the specificities of their bodies."[70] It is precisely *because* of the cultural tendency to link women's bodies to specific subjectivities that an interrogation of the forms in which such linkage operates is necessary. Teresa de Lauretis has stated that "woman is unrepresentable except as representation,"[71] that there is no "authentic" category of "woman." Nonetheless, female bodies continue to function on the radar of social perception as a kind of "hinge, or threshold"[72] through which an interior might be viewed.

Assumptions of authenticity hidden behind the presented surface in beauty contests and exotic dancing are directly tied to historically prejudicial comments such as Olive Logan's reference to Adah Issacs Menken: "Such women were never actresses in the true sense."[73] In addition to referring to the authentic, "true" carries here the sense of "agreeing with reality" and "conforming,"[74] in other words consonant with a highly conservative, text-based, performatively narrow definition of the profession of acting as it was traditionally understood in the nineteenth century. Logan's well-publicized denunciation of the "leg business" in 1870 articulated a social perception of female performers in popular entertainments that remains common: "The nude woman of today represents nothing but herself. She runs upon the stage giggling; trots down to the footlights, winks at the audience, rattles off from her tongue some stupid attempts at wit, . . . and is always peculiarly and emphatically herself."[75] Logan's opinion was supported by popular newspaper editorials. One *New World* writer banished the "nude woman" performer from the category of "legitimate" actress by refusing to accept the construction behind the display: "But the real profession of acting, the portrayal of character, and the holding up of the mirror, not to factitious calves, but to nature, is very remote from this, and deserves to be classed as a distinct profession."[76] *The New York Tribune* concurred: "the bare-legged women who tramp over the boards in burlesque, and kick up their heels in the can-can, have—with here and there an exception—no more title to be regarded as members of the dramatic profession than they have to be regarded as members of the French Academy."[77] Such a refusal to consider the point of view that, as Anthony Kubiak has noted, "performance is more a showing than a becoming,"[78] ensured that the women who danced, posed, paraded, or stripped, were rendered inauthentic as skilled practitioners of a creative craft, their performances regarded as behavioral conduct rather than constructed events. Further characterization as "a sort of fungus upon the stage," that was quickly becoming "excessive and intolerable,"[79] legitimated attempts to quarantine certain female performers and their respective forms, a reaction with profound effects that continue to this day.

Nonetheless, the dismissals of Logan and others notwithstanding, actresses who use their bodies as theatrical tools are following the same traditions as their more "legitimate" associates. Accessing aspects of one's "self" for use onstage has, arguably, been the cornerstone of Western "legitimate" actor training for at least the past one hundred years. Processes variously referred to as "methods," and exercises such as "dropping in," aimed at personalizing scripted lines, all operate to give the appearance, however oxymoronically, of "truthful" performance. Richard Gilman has argued that the actor offers the audience "possible selves," or more accurately the *idea* of possible selves"[80] [emphasis his]. Such a description of the actor's construction of performance echoes the approach employed by many strippers and beauty contestants.

These performers, contrary to presumptions of *self-revelation*, participate in the creative fraud of *self-repetition* with every performance.[81] Essentially, they repeat a rehearsed projection of a codified image, imagined and calibrated to represent a particular evocation of femaleness. The borrowed elements of such an evocation, whether from oneself or from real or imagined others, are employed as tools for a specific dramatic purpose. This fact is not lost on performers, who repeatedly draw clear distinctions between their staged and actual "selves." Debbie, a carnival stripper of the 1960s, argued bluntly that such falsehood is a critical requirement for a successful portrayal of "authenticity":

> When I'm workin', I'm there for one reason—I take my clothes off. I would never take my clothes off anyplace else. When I'm a dancer, the guys have to think I'm tempting—it's like acting, you have to be glamorous, you have to be sexy, you have to move your hips. You gotta wear a lot of lipstick, *you have to be fake.*[82]

On the beauty contest side, Bess Myerson, Miss America 1945, perhaps somewhat more euphemistically than Debbie, likewise characterized her performance as a form of disguise: "already I was in a masquerade."[83]

The manipulable nature of authenticity as a theatrical value can hardly be overstated. In an enlightening illustration, the March 1950 magazine *Night and Day: America's Picture Magazine of Entertainment,* included an article in which an audience was asked to judge whether a female performer was more authentically "herself" singing in a traditional evening gown or in a "nylon net and sequin production costume" with flowers strategically placed. The audience decided that "while the song quality remained the same, Miss Lombard put over Miss Lombard much better in nylon and sequins."[84] Because she was singing a torch song, it made more sense to the audience that she appeared nearly naked; that the image fit the act. What is more illustrative, is the audience's belief that she was more or less authentically "herself" according to her image. The article concludes: "All this goes to show you that things are as they seem." "Seeming" as a kind of truth or authenticity ensured that the torch song appeared incongruous when performed in an evening gown.

Perceptual conflations of self with performance cut both ways. Just as the torch singer is more believable as "herself" when wearing sequins, "when the stripper leaves the stage and becomes a person again, she finds that no one will allow her to leave her role behind. Everywhere she goes people see her as a gypsy from the erotic zones."[85] As Gypsy Rose Lee recounted to Louella Parsons, her act began as a calculated response to what she perceived to be the narrow range of performance possibilities in the genre, rather than any revelation of identity:

> My strip tease act all started because I thought some of the acts at Minsky's were so ridiculous, [. . .] There are three types of strip teasers, the loud and brazen girl, who comes out on the stage and shrieks; then there is the demure kind, who acts scared to death; and finally the voluptuous gal, who acts that way to cover her embarrassment.[86]

Yet when Gypsy insisted on a modicum of privacy backstage the columnist Walter Winchell mocked her choice as pretension, assuming that because she performed the act of disrobing as a theatrical event, she would display an equally liberal attitude toward nakedness in her offstage moments:

> Gypsy Rose Lee who deserted the Minsky Girleg [sic] operas for a principal assignment in "The Ziegfeld Follies" at the Winter Garden. Gypsy, our country cousins might not recall, specializes in peeling herself as she would a banana— right before your very eyes no less! She is perfectly willing to live up to her contract with the Shubert Freres and disrobe on the stage so that the audience may

feast—but she won't agree to people back stage peeking at her, by golly. And so two stage hands are assigned to her act. They stand in the wings, one on each side, holding curtains so that the other entertainers and workers cannot enjoy Gypsy's nekkid [sic] shoulders, etcetera. And don't start envying the stagehands either, while holding the curtains they must stand with their backs to Gypsy.[87]

Winchell's patronizing attitude toward Gypsy's request for privacy is illustrative not only of the lack of respect accorded entertainers of the "lowbrow" variety, but also of the social resistance to the acceptance of the onstage event as separate from the offstage person.

As a woman who grew up in the wings of burlesque theatres with the job of holding her mother's robe offstage (a task often given as well to the "catcher," the person standing in the wings responsible for, literally, catching costumes as the performer cast them off), it is Grace Swank Davis's contention that:

You would never see a girl go half-naked around the dressing room, around the stage; you'd always wear your robe. The other people wouldn't appreciate it, the stage hands wouldn't appreciate it and they thought very badly of you if you did that. You were thought of as low class. You had no respect if you were doing that backstage. You were trash, and they didn't have respect for you. Whatever you did onstage was your job, your act, but offstage you were a lady and you were treated as such.

Davis not only corroborates the existence of the performer hierarchy discussed in chapter 2 with her designators of "lowly" and "trash," but also confirms the testimony of other performers who insist that personal ethical or moral allegiances are not necessarily articulated in the entertainment event, the "act." Nor is the spectator, privileged in the moment of performance, necessarily privy to knowledge of how the actress conducts herself when away from the theatrical space. "I see it as a game," explains Susan Scotto, "and a performance, and an interaction."

Intentionally manipulating signifiers to *suggest* personal intimacy and communication of a self, female performers have consistently exploited the persistent cultural belief that they "are what they do" in the composition of their performances. In this way, according to Erving Goffman, the female performer might be seen to "set the stage for a kind of information game—a potentially infinite cycle of concealment, discovery, false revelation, and rediscovery."[88] Even more succinctly articulating the fictive moment in the construction of the performance process is "Carmen's" statement: "This is a fantasy, not a relationship."[89] In female spectacles that rely on the convention of disrobing, "calculated unintentionality"[90] is utilized by the performer so that multiple meanings emerge as each layer of clothing is removed, drawing the spectator into the *illusion* of an understanding of the intimate, and sexual, self of the performer. In that way, the physical act of undress is not unlike what might seem to be its inversion, masquerade. Both forms operate by "masking the absence of the very identity [they] appear to mask."[91]

Exemplifying the social propensity for conflating a performance with a "self" is the following exchange between a cab driver and performer Susan Scotto:

> I was in Los Angeles after a taping of "What's My Line," and my cab driver, hearing why I was there, announced, "last night I went to this stripper for the first time, some friends of mine took me and, well, I got this private dance from this dancer and it was really great. Well, do you think she liked me? She was really nice to me. Do you think she liked me?," and I answered, "well, I don't know her. I can't speak for her. Did she look to you as if she was having a good time?" and he said, "well yeah," and I said, "well then, either she was really having a good time or she's really good at her job, but in either case, she did a good job because she made you feel great."

"You could tell," remarked Professor Scotto, "that he was sort of devastated by the thought that maybe she'd been acting," that she might have been, borrowing from Roland Barthes, an "unoccupied occupant of the subject position."[92] The cab driver considered Scotto's reasoning, and then rejected it, preferring to believe, "Well, I got something extra," as though the acceptance of the performance as a construct rather than an expression of the stripper's "real" interest held the dangerous potential to render the entire experience inauthentic. "My job," according to Lily Burana, "is not to be who I am, but what the average strip club customer wants, and those things are, I am resigned to admit, quite different."[93]

Occupational awareness such as that expressed by "Kyra" is rarely considered by spectators in clubs: "It is all an act up there. When you're looking at some guy real sexy, you're not thinking, 'Oh. Gee. Wouldn't I like to screw you.' No. You're thinking, 'God! I can't stand what that guy has on his T-shirt.'"[94] Most performers remain acutely aware of what is required to "play the room." As the online advice column *Stripper Power*, written "For Strippers. By Strippers," advises: "When sparring with the customers, use the path of least resistance. Make money as easy as possible. When you first enter the main floor, look around. Make eye contact with all the suits. While you are scanning the room, look for the guy making eye contact with you."[95]

"Nicki," a performer at Charlie's bikini club, refrains from picking the music for her sequence until she sees what kind of crowd is at the edge of the stage. Because the club is located near a military base, she looks for the tell-tale buzz-cut and selects her music accordingly, employing patriotism as her tool for that set. If there are cowboy hats in the crowd, she opts for "good ole boy" tunes.

Nicki's choices are made for maximum effect, as are those of the beauty contestant who, in the wake of patriotic fervor following the tragedy of 9/11, sang "God Bless America" at her talent competition. In both instances, the performers utilize theatrical strategies to create a successful performance. As stripper Crystal Rose articulates:

> What's going through your head as a performer—you know, you have a routine down to that music and you have to do certain things at certain times and your facial expressions, your hand movements, your body movements, what you're taking off, what you're doing, is all running around in your head at the same time . . . And your facial expressions have to hide all that.[96]

Characterizing the work as a "contract," Scotto explained why the "reality" needs to remain hidden by the "authentic" performance of attraction to the customer: "It doesn't work so well if you look over at the clock, or if you look to see how many other dollars are there, because you're sort of betraying that contract between yourself and the guy who puts up the dollar." Or, as another stripper stated: "It's a good policy, really, to do something that conveys, 'I see you,' before taking a guy's money."[97] Scotto's "contract" recalls Goffman's contention that "perception" is a "form of contract,"[98] as in the example of Scotto's cab driver. Moreover, according to Goffman, "the more closely the imposter's performance approximates the real thing, the more intensely we may be threatened," so performers must "take care to enliven their performances with appropriate expressions, exclude from their performances expressions that might discredit the impression being fostered."[99]

"I know they like Luscious Lona," remarks one stripper, "They don't know Lona. They don't know that part of me and I don't want them to know that part." Moreover, "Lona" believes "*They* don't want to know that part. They just want to know the fantasy that's up on stage, that's sexy and looks like she wants everyone in the crowd."[100] Susan Scotto concurs, stating that "guys don't come in here to hear about your problems at home or how your kid threw up on you at 2:00 in the morning, they want you to pay attention to them." Once again, authenticity is a relative term in performance. An "authentic" stripper is apparently not one who has vomiting children. "Up there," according to one stripper, "when you take off your clothes, you're an actress. You're actually two different people."[101]

Stripper Power contains an article addressing the construction of a performance approach: "Stripper Kung-Fu." The artifice required for success is presented clearly from the outset: "Before you start learning Stripper Kung Fu, you have to first know yourself. Secondly, you have to be someone else. We all have to be actors. Create a persona for your work. When you are at work, don't be yourself [. . .] I call this stripper mode."[102] Yet, in spite of such emphatic illustrations of the methodology utilized in building a performance approach, misapprehensions of the means whereby a fictive stage event is constructed blend with erroneous social assumptions of performer's personal lifestyles even to the point where, as one stripper explains, "the audience often takes for granted that the rigors of the job manifesting as bruises are sexually related."[103] As Katherine Liepe-Levinson points out, "Seemingly raw or involuntary responses of the body that occur within the frames of theatre create a particular dilemma and added thrill for the viewers. For such acts lure spectators into the game of actively guessing whether the performer's pleasures or pains are real or pretend."[104] The inference of the stripper's offstage promiscuity based on her onstage body is much like the social perception of the beauty contestant as an authentic, moral person based on *her* onstage performance. In both forms the body is perceived to be the indicator of authenticity, whether visible bruises on the stripper or the tightly controlled physical movement of the beauty contestant, the external is assumptively positioned as the marker of the internal.

In spite of their confessions that onstage they "are giving the audience who they *could* be,"[105] many beauty contestants feel compelled to present a façade of authentic "wholesomeness" in public at all times. The beauty contestant projects a particular "authentic" persona created for the express purpose of convincing an audience that she is the most genuine, most beautiful, most moral, most deserving contestant in the pageant, all the while not so discreetly appearing onstage wearing increasingly less clothing. The convention of having beauty contestants appear onstage in a variety of outfits carries with it traces of the early burlesque strippers mentioned in chapter 2 who, in order to avoid the law which forbade actual disrobing onstage, would exit into the wings, take off an item of clothing, re-emerge onstage, then repeat the cycle. The visual image in the Miss America Pageant of "girls" in "active wear," then evening gowns, then swimsuits, implicitly references the act of disrobing.

What a contestant "reveals" according to pageant coach Anna Stanley, is a "moral self" based on an appearance of "wholesomeness," proof of how "genuine" she is.[106] Yet what is actually being articulated is the codified *performance* of genuineness, and not the intangible and amorphous quality indicative of the moral center Stanley purports to discuss. The ascription by members of the audience of a performer's exposed "self," while integral to the intentioned performance, cannot negate its fictive foundation. As Goffman points out:

> While this image is entertained *concerning* the individual, so that a self is imputed to him, this self itself does not derive from its possessor, but from the whole scene of his action, being generated by that attribute of local events which renders them interpretable by witnesses. A correctly staged and performed scene leads the audience to impute a self to a performed character, but this imputation—this self—is a *product* of a scene that comes off, and is not a *cause* of it.[107]

A Miss Rhode Island contestant emphasizes the separation between presentation and person: "You're onstage, you're doing something for a different purpose other than something you normally do. You're doing it for the production."[108] The "production" is synonymous with Goffman's "whole scene of the action."

Laura Lawless, an Arizona State University law school student and Miss Arizona 2002, acknowledges her performance as a beauty contest title-holder at the Miss America Scholarship Competition as an institutional construct as well as an individual strategy. When the television camera crew arrived at her hometown to shoot the "up-close and personal" segment of the production, Lawless asked them to film her speech at the Capital on domestic violence. "So, why is it," she states, "that what ultimately got into my video is my sitting on a barc-o-lounger, playing with a puppy, pointing at a cactus?" Just as strategies of performance by strippers often leave out the realities of their personal lives, Lawless's composite performance of a beauty contest winner held no room for the less than "wholesome" aspects of her daily existence:

> I think that's why it took me so long to get to Atlantic City, because I've had judges over time tell me from the very first local pageant I ever did, never tell anyone about your history of mental illness, never tell anyone that you went to college at Harvard because it makes you seem unapproachable and cold, never tell anyone that you came from a broken home with poverty conditions because no one will be able to relate to you or hold you up on the pedestal that they expect Miss America to be up on.[109]

Miss South Dakota 2002, Vanessa Shortbull, echoed Lawless's description of the institutional fabrication of a beauty queen image, adding that the construction of her video revolved around her authenticity as a Native American:

> They were so focused on me being Native American, "please tell me the struggles that you've had of being an oppressed person," and I was like, I've been oppressed?

Where are my chains? Why didn't somebody tell me this? And they had this idea of . . . they wanted me to ride in a canoe across the lake and I can only think of the little Indian in Peter Pan as she's going across, you know, paddling.

Erika Harold, Miss Illinois 2002, laughingly remarked: "we're a reality show this year."[110] But Lawless was quick to point out that her "reality" bore no resemblance to the fiction presented onstage: "If you want to show what real women in the real world face, it's not living in a cornfield and playing with your puppy. For a lot of us it's going to work when you're 14 to support the family or trying to help a person who's, like my mother, dealing with cancer, that's what reality is." Not unaware of the irony in the marketing of the competition as "reality," Harold explained, "I see it more as a perform-ance, I don't see myself as, you know, Erika walking onstage in swimsuit. It's Miss Illinois competing to be Miss America. I grew up doing musical theatre and that's how I approach it." Harold's practical attitude is remarkably similar to that of stripper Riki Harte, who confesses to having "a few gimmicks. I do like a little girl show and a Valley Girl act. The Valley Girl show is my favorite. I'm not myself out there. I become Riki Harte, the actress."[111]

Scripting a personal "reality" to conform to a presentational image is a common theatrical device in both pageants and clubs. Just as exotic dancer Scotto states, "I have my set bio to protect my privacy and my safety. It's consistent for me, I tell everyone the same story, so that I don't forget," Erika Harold reveals, "In the past I had always had time to script my remarks, because I'm a perfectionist." In "Stripper Kung Fu," performers are advised to "be prepared. Know ahead of time how you will handle difficult or negative situations. Your most dangerous enemy when dancing is being caught unexpected and unprepared. All of these routines prepare you for your approach. Remember, repetition is the best form of emphasis. Practice your role."[112] Constructing a narrative of identity that isn't easily discernable as fraudulence requires skill, according to Vanessa Shortbull:

Oh, yes, there is a definite fine line and you can watch that with all the girls that, you know, come onstage, that they had that question before and [finger snap] right there, two seconds later they're like giving this answer and you know it's rehearsed, you know that they've said it a million times.

Apparently, for the beauty contestant and the stripper, there's financial danger in the too obvious script. "There is always one dancer who goes around to everyone saying, 'Wanna dance, wanna dance, wanna dance,' " explains Scotto, "why would I buy a dance from you? This is someone who is so focused on making money that she figures the way she's going to get more money is to ask everyone. The guys don't really like that."

Employing nearly identical acting rhetoric as the author of *Stripper Power*, pageant coach Anna Stanley advises, "The way to reach this level of preparation, is through having the right talent and having presented it before audiences so often that your body can do it on its own."[113] That rehearsing enough also allows disassociation as a performance tactic to mitigate the less desirable aspects of their work is clearly a part of the strategic arsenal of both beauty contestants and exotic dancers. "Lena," a carnival stripper, distances herself not only from the action of the performed event, but from the spectator as well: "I didn't get into them personally. I got into them as you would a piece of grass, 'How are you, grass, how are you today'—it's a protection from myself. You put up a wall between you and what's really going on."[114]

Other performers use less personal strategies of focus: "Sometimes I would even drop a thin veil in front of my eyes. It's easy to do. You glaze your eyes over by concentrating so much on one point that the background gets faded out."[115] It is a technique used by beauty contestants as well to combat the discomfort some contestants experience because of the required swimsuit costume. (When asked by an interviewer to name her favorite part of the swimsuit segment, one 2003 Pageant contestant answered unhesitatingly, "the exit."[116]) Miss Maine 2002 downplays it as a "speed bump":

> Being out in a swimsuit in front of the stage I think is not the worst thing that could happen to me and, you know, it's a speed bump in the road and it's only going to make me stronger in the end of everything . . . we all think about different things when we're on that runway and we're going down and we're wearing smaller pieces than we really want to.[117]

Erika Harold shrugs off the distasteful components of the competition: "We all came in here understanding what the rules of the game were, and if we were uncomfortable with that we wouldn't have competed."

Miss Arizona 2002 shares the pragmatic attitude, "You wear the jersey if you are gonna be playing on the soccer team, you wear the swimsuit if this is the competition." But Lawless also scoffs at what she sees as the naïve social equation of the contestants and any "truthful" self:

> I will never say that it's only a beauty pageant, but I'll never say that it's not. Because I got up this morning and I combed my hair and I put on makeup and I made sure that I was coifed to go out and record for the video today. When I go to my law classes, I come in my pajama pants, if I remembered to put them on

that morning, I'll have flip-flops on because it's in Arizona and it's 115 degrees and if I've washed my hair that week, I'm doing really well. So, I know that there's something that I'm doing differently because I'm in the middle of a pageant, so I would never lie, I would never say that it's not.

Similarly, the Miss Rhode island contestant who divulged, "I feel a lot more beautiful than I do in real life," was not negating the construction of the event. On the contrary, she explained that if your body is "all you have to show to the audience, then you want to use it to its fullest." That she felt "beautiful" doing it was, albeit pleasant, incidental. In the following comment, the contestant acknowledges the artifice employed in onstage presentation:

> And there was also an interview portion where you wore a business suit and you could see, like, the changes people made in between the categories. So, like, in the swimsuit you could be a little more playful, in evening gown of course you slowed down your walk, tried to, you know; very, very smooth movements and then when you get to the interview portion you're sitting on a chair, you know, you have your legs crossed, you're wearing a suit.

Institutional attempts to construct an image that will project a particular ideology are certainly not limited to beauty contests. At the Miss Exotic World contest in June of 2002, organizers at the meeting the day before the event were quick to define the acceptable parameters of display. "The judges are looking for who represents the ultimate burlesque girl. Classic striptease. Pasties, G-strings are required. No spread-eagle moves."[118] The five-hour event presented a shimmy contest, re-created burlesque comedy routines, showcased acts that were specifically designed for entertainment rather than competition, and the Miss Exotic World contest itself. "There's lots of strip clubs and competitions and that's fine," explains one event organizer, "but this is about preserving the tradition of burlesque, combining old style and new styles."

Echoing the attempts by the Miss America Pageant to distance itself from other similar forms of display by emphasizing tradition and education, the Exotic World event promotes itself as an institution dedicated to preserving a particular performance tradition, as well as an educational experience for up-and-coming burlesquers. With Dixie Evans, famous for her Marilyn Monroe imitation, Rita Atlanta, renowned for her champagne glass baths, Dusty Sage, widely acknowledged to have originated the topless go-go craze in San Francisco, and renowned stripper Tempest Storm performing the finale, the history of burlesque was well represented. Just as the Miss America Pageant and its numerous preliminary competitions bring onstage previous winners as exemplars of the organization's success, and Flo Ziegfeld brought together the "Peaches of 1918," a "crop" proving to be the "best aggregation of feminine loveliness in some years,"[119] the Exotic World contest seeks to legitimate its position as a contest "doing something completely different" from other strip events by virtue of its inclusion of legendary burlesque and striptease performers. That most of the acts by contemporary performers at the contest would not have been out of place in many exotic, bikini, and strip clubs nationwide was rendered irrelevant within the constructed context of the display, which was offered to a coterie audience of dancers, academics, fans, and locals.

In spite of the social designation of some forms of entertainment as more or less moral, the methodologies employed by female performers in their approaches to the work of display share remarkable similarities. Suzanne Yang has observed that "societal conventions and categorizations lead us to expect that appearances are tied to a stable truth beyond the surface."[120] That expectation is readily discernable by the 1930s as a performance tool utilized equally effectively by performers in culturally disassociated forms like beauty contests and striptease. In his 1923 book *The World in Falseface*, critic George Jean Nathan wrote: "A woman is charming in the degree that her body outdoes her mind in the manner of unsophistication."[121] Such a sentiment is as old as Ovid, who admonished women that their "artifice should go unsuspected."[122] To the contrary, Simone de Beauvoir has remarked that "artifice, like art, belongs to the realm of the imaginary," that the actor is "an agent through whom is suggested someone not there that is, the character she represents, but is not."[123] Perhaps ironically, the expertise with which both beauty contestants and strippers manage to perform their "authentic" selves abets the cultural separation of the forms. As Miss America 2003 divulged, "you want to be prepared, but you don't want to be so over-packaged that your authenticity is diminished."

Yet the construction behind the representation, the *acting*, remains relegated to the wings of public consciousness, as the "authenticity" of the image as a particular femaleness subsumes spectator knowledge of the skill required in the production. Paradoxically, in acting, progressing to the point where the "work doesn't show," means one has reached a level of professional proficiency. Unfortunately for the beauty contestant and stripper, that translates to an utter disavowal of any skill involved. According to Lee Mortimer: "It only takes a few months to put an 'exotic dance' together where the only thing you have to learn is how to walk provocatively across a stage and undress like you mean it."[124] Undressing "like you mean it" is as complicated an endeavor for the stripper as is the exhortation to the beauty contestant to just go onstage and "Be Yourself."

Arlene Francis in her 1960 educative manual for proper female behavior, *That Certain Something: The Magic of Charm*, actually used the metaphor of stripping as the means whereby one exposes one's true self:

> "Be yourself" is a phrase that has been bandied about since the days of Augustus Caesar, and everybody from the vicar to a psychiatrist tells you you've got to be that. But very few of them are able to explain just *how* to go about accomplishing it. Nearly all of us, from birth, seem to go through the years wrapping one suit after another of scratchy woolen [*sic*] underwear around our egos, when we should be putting on our bathing suits and getting some sun. The knack of being yourself is a process of peeling off the scratchy wool and daring to be spontaneous.[125]

While one presumes the imagistic parallels with the "strip-and-peel" professions resonating in Francis's advice to be unintentional, her use of "peeling off" as representative of exposing a "self" confirms the social presumption that, as Prus and Styllianoss state, "undressing in front of other persons is considered an 'intimate self-revelation.' "[126] Yet in the world of stripping and beauty pageants, authenticity *is* artifice, self-revelation is, in actuality, constructed self-repetition, scripted according to the requirements of the moment of performance and the potential for financial gain. "On Tuesday night," proclaimed a 1988 article in the *New York Times*, "Miss Gibbs will try to sell herself."[127] When it came to selling "herself" in performance, Miss Gibbs, who happened to be the reigning Miss Texas, might just as easily be replaced by Professor Susan Scotto, Gypsy Rose Lee, or Ann "Bang Bang" Arbor. As Mrs Malaprop observed in Sheridan's *The Rivals* (III.iii): "but, from the ingenuity of your appearance, I am convinced you deserve the character here given of you."

4. Performing Normalcy ✣

Strippers are no more aggressive or sexually disturbed than other women.
                                    Scott, *Behind the G-String*[1]

If it's not a beauty contest, how come I judged 150 women and not one of them had a pair of eyeglasses on.
                    Deford, "Confessions of a Miss America Judge"[2]

When asked why she enjoyed such phenomenal success as a burlesque stripper, Margie Hart answered: "Maybe because I'm just a wholesome, clean American girl trying to get along."[3] This response was only superficially flippant. Hart's declaration is both a separation of her "self" from her "act" and an ironic twist on the social definitions of "wholesome" and "American." Its insouciant humor relied on an assumption that Hart's professional activities embodied a provocative, even deviant, form of female behavior that another sort of "wholesome, clean American girl" would instinctively shun. "Embodied deviance" is defined by Jacqueline Urla and Jennifer Terry as "the historically and culturally specific belief that deviant social behavior (however that is defined) manifests in the materiality of the body, as a cause or an effect, or perhaps as merely a suggestive trace."[4] This idea is the major selling point of the business of stripping, dependent for its effectiveness upon a shared social vocabulary of image recognition. Whether it is understood as the "cause," the reason, the pathology, that underlies the stripper's actions; or, conversely, as her actions' inevitable result, the stripper's aura of social deviance codifies both occupation and the practitioner. As Urla and Terry argue, "subjects classified as deviant are essentially marked in some recognizable fashion."[5] In other words, society agrees upon a standardized, "normal," and recognizable definition of deviance that, in effect, renders the "deviant" conventional and clears the way for its productive commodification.

Beauty contests rely on the same sorts of "essential" markings, and for precisely the same reason, although, rather than "deviance," their productions and contestants market "normalcy," along with "morality" and "authenticity," as embodied conditions.[6] These approaches, while apparently oppositional, are in fact mutually dependent. In the same way that "the construction of deviance is always already also a process of constructing some model of the 'normal' body," the construction of the "normal" is predicated on a fabrication of the "deviant."[7] Additionally, a close analysis of beauty contests and stripping illustrates the ways in which classifications of normal and deviant are employed simultaneously as theatrical tools for success. The regularizing of specific images as "wholesome" or sexually "deviant" in pageants and stripping ratifies Roland Barthes's statement that "artifice aims at something common, not rare."[8] The necessity for both forms to adhere to specific social expectations of female behavior, whether naughty or nice, is a central reason for the rigid theatrical conventionality they share.

Scholarship has not traditionally supported this view. David Scott alleges that, "The stripper is a facade, a modification (if not a travesty) of natural human femininity in both form and substance."[9] Similarly, Robert Allen has stated that the "cooch dancer is not like a freak, she is one. Her exhibition is structured around the tension between her similarity to 'ordinary' women the male audience member sees and knows outside the tent and her fascinating otherness produced by her expressive and displayed sexuality."[10] But there is nothing "freakish" about such exhibition. The interplay that Allen correctly interprets as tension is a carefully constructed performance technique that, as previously explored, emerges as a theatrical response to the attempted moral bifurcation of the forms of female display. This chapter will argue that since there is no unified "natural human femininity," the stripper's use of her body in performance as a "text" (to be read as a familiar construct of "deviant" femininity) is no more a travesty than the beauty contestant's presentation of the "normal" feminine. More accurately, it is simply a variation.

Notwithstanding their aesthetic emphasis on meticulously structured facades of normative appearance and behavior, the presentation of "normalcy" as an entertainment draw is not limited to the realm of beauty contests, but has traditionally been employed with equal effectiveness by exotic dancers. Contrary to Katherine Liepe-Levinson's argument that "sexual desire in Western culture is, in fact, rarely represented through signifiers of the "normal,"[11] as early as the 1893 Expo, female performers (in the "Algerian Village") would "pantomime" their ordinary hygienic ablutions, thus positioning the audience as voyeuristic witnesses to a private, everyday ritual.[12] In the same way, Ziegfeld acts such as "Linger, Longer, Lingerie" in the 1909 *Follies*[13] functioned as promoters of a particularly "wholesome," that is, "normal," "homegrown feminine sexuality."[14]

Unsuspected surveillance has been a fundamental theatrical tool for many centuries. The pretense that no one is looking through the fourth wall, that actions are unintended for public consumption, allows for "normal," private behavior to be scrutinized by hundreds of onlookers shielded in the darkness of the auditorium, and the sexualization of such behavior by female performers occurred from the moment female display found its way to the American stage. Just as tableaux vivant presented programs like "Suzanna Surprised in the Bath" in 1855,[15] and the *Passing Show* of 1895 offered women scantily clad in negligees in "Chips that Pass in the Night,"[16] the American Wheel in burlesque staged "The Night-Gown dance"[17] and Earl Carroll in 1930 presented "Bridesmaid in Virtue's Bed."[18] As an extension of the burlesque, revue, and strip club bathing, boudoir lounging, and the ever popular "getting ready for bed" acts, the Miss America Scholarship Contest, in a contemporary version of televised voyeurism, has employed cameras backstage to observe and chat with the contestants. Presenting backstage behavior as "normal" and unaffected, in spite of the obvious presence of cameras and crew, supports the acceptance of a contestant's onstage behavior as equally "natural" by implying that audience members have been privileged to observe them in unscripted, "natural" situations.

Claims on normalcy are a varied but essential feature of all forms of female display. At the Ms. International Nude contest, in 1976, contestants were strategically presented as perfectly "normal" girls who happened to be naked at the moment of performance. As they paraded across the stage one by one, adorned only by the numbers on little cards hanging around their necks, the emcee noted their interests with comments such as "She likes to eat steak and her favorite pastime is knitting." When asked what winning the title of Ms. Nude International meant to her, the eventual winner mimicked standard beauty queen rhetoric in assuring the audience that she "would sincerely consider it a privilege to hold the title of Ms. International Nude and, also, for the fun and glory of achievement in competing."[19] She hoped the publicity "might win her a career in acting," following in the tradition of female nudity as a tool for career building.[20] The criteria by which the judges picked their winner is virtually indistinguishable from that of the more recognizable beauty contests: "I look to see if they have marks on their bodies, how their busts are shaped, their legs—and their smiles,' explained one judge, Barry Kravitz, a wholesale drug dealer."[21]

According to Robert Allen, Ziegfeld "managed to package feminine stage sexuality in such a way that his audiences connected the *Follies* not with the working-class sexuality of burlesque but with the cosmopolitan worldliness of Paris."[22] Yet in the same paragraph, Allen characterizes the Ziegfeld girl in starkly self-contradictory terms: "There was nothing sexually awe-provoking or threatening about the Ziegfeld girl. Hers was the contained, manageable, almost wholesome sexuality of the white middle-class girl next door."[23] Allen's descriptive schizophrenia is understandable if one bears in mind not only the early twentieth-century's growing social segmentation of entertainment forms focusing on the female body into binaried value systems, but also the inherent dependency that any performance of "normal" has on its inverse. "Worldly," that is, sexually knowledgeable, and "wholesome," that is, virginal, no matter how emphatically distinct they may claim to be in rhetorical or imagistic terms, cannot avoid definitional symbiosis in presentations whose governing premise is the display of the female form. As often as the pageant promoters in Texas insist that the "Miss Big Thicket" competition represents a particular wooded landscape, the parallels with entertainments like those of Nadja and her strategically placed fake fur are inevitable and, one must consider at some level, intentional.

"There's a little bit of Miss America in everybody, if they just apply themselves to bringing it out," insists pageant coach Anna Stanley.[24] Stanley's comment follows in the tradition of Florenz Ziegfeld, who in an endorsement of Ned Wayburn's training school stated, "I have seen the remarkable results of Ned Wayburn Training among the principals and girls of my productions. He can do the same for any woman. It is always a pleasure to use Ned Wayburn pupils because they are [. . .] physically fit—beautifully proportioned—and mentally alert."[25] (Ziegfeld's comment is also a reflection of the common conflation of female appearance with mental acuity, much like Stanley's: "The fact is, girls who feel smart usually enjoy looking smart."[26]) On the smaller, local scale, the democratic faith in the transformational potential of *all* young women is echoed in a Miss New Hampshire contestant's assertion that "there are so many deserving young women out there that could be wearing the title of Miss Lakes Region."[27] Positing the Miss America value system as an inherent quality, a dormant trait waiting to be released, further enables the public presentation—the supposed external revelation of the internal self—to be read as a "naturalized," "normal" state; a reading utterly at odds with the actual effort involved in achieving a successful beauty pageant façade.

Beauty contests also play on a social construct of competition among women as a "natural" process, one that plays its part in regulating appearance and behavior. Nancy Etcoff has argued that "every woman somehow finds herself entered into a beauty contest with every other woman"; that in our culture "women are always compared to one another and found wanting."[28] With axioms such as "Pageants offer them [contestants] insight into how well-prepared they are to face life,"[29] "A body that is physically well-conditioned reflects a woman's mental discipline,"[30] "God intended for us women to look graceful and beautiful,"[31] and, "Pageants teach women to project a professional image that allows them to get ahead while at the same time learning to be physically attractive,"[32] beauty contests insist (despite repeated assertions that contestants need only disclose their "real" selves) that being "natural" requires work, "learning," and preparation. "Despite the fact that each woman knows her own belabored transformation from female to feminine is artificial," notes Wendy Chapkis, "she harbors the secret conviction that it should be effortless."[33] This oxymoronic belief has endured for generations; early in the twentieth century Walter Kingsley stated it with particularly daunting succinctness: "The real thing has no off days—she is always enchanting."[34]

To approximate a socially regulated and recognizable embodiment of "beautiful" is to require artificial enhancement, guided and applied, ironically, with the objective of "naturalness."[35] In the 1920s "naturalness" served to distinguish a particular image of wholesome femininity from the iconic "Flapper Jane," disapprovingly described in a newspaper editorial of the period as, "frankly, heavily made up, not to imitate nature, but for an altogether artificial effect—pallor mortis, poisonously scarlet lips, richly ringed eyes—the latter looking not so much debauched (which is the intention) as diabetic."[36] Arguing against overt "artificial effect," but in favor of enhancement, Walter Kingsley ("About Beauties," 1920) wrote: "Give me the exotic, orchidaceous girl, of the conservatory type; the one who spends hours over her toilet and considers no trouble too great to present herself as a miracle of dainty preparedness." Kingsley offered no practical advice to women who sought to emulate miraculous orchids without any sign of "artificial effect."

Decades later, former Miss America Donna Axum (also a Miss America 2002 judge) would reinforce Kingsley's message: "The successful contestants do not acquire these skills overnight. These are young women who have brought themselves and their bodies into control through long hours of self-analysis and self-discipline, and who have trained with as much intensity as an athlete."[37] For young female contestants, bringing themselves "into control" through "a miracle of dainty preparedness" becomes the reductive visual signifier of the "successful" definition of the "feminine." Of course, as Susan Bordo points out: "Through the pursuit of an everchanging, homogenizing, elusive ideal of femininity—a pursuit without a terminus, requiring that women constantly attend to minute and often whimsical changes in fashion—female bodies become docile bodies."[38] For something to achieve "control," something else must always submit.

The meticulously practiced bodily restraint of beauty contestants supports Erving Goffman's assertion that "performers may even attempt to give the impression that their present poise and proficiency are something they have always had and that they have never had to fumble their way through a learning period."[39] Their tightly prescribed movements and gestural language express nothing so much as response to careful training. "What is more distasteful," asks Axum, "than to see a woman sprawled out?"[40] Axum's "distasteful" carries the distinct echo of exotic dancer Silver's characterization in chapter 2 of strippers as "less tasteful," or Grace Swank Davis's labeling of cooch dancers as "lowdown." Apparently, "dainty preparedness" and "sprawling" lie at opposite ends of the ideological spectrum of feminine attitudes.

Condemnation of physical "sprawling" as the exemplary antithesis of acceptable bodily deportment is but one indicator of a beauty contest value system that extends itself easily to behavioral regulation. Contestants "soon find that judges and pageant officials stress poise, speaking ability, goals and an amiable personality."[41] For some contestants, amiability is a "feminine" construct requiring the same rehearsal as the suck-and-tuck glide in order to achieve the appearance of effortlessness. Miss Arizona 2002 recounts her struggles with the concept:

> Well, I've been told in the past that I'm too much of a feminist and not enough feminine. And I'd like to know why there's a difference in the two words. Why can't one be graceful in an evening gown and still have strength in their convictions? So, I've been told "soften it up" a lot.

Amiability is an acquired skill presented as a normal aspect of femaleness, much like those skills considered acceptable for the talent segment in some pageant competitions: "The National College Queen pageant includes skills such as cake decorating, highway and safety practices, and color coordination in their eleven judging criteria."[42] Not surprisingly, feminine amiability also happened to be the publicly praised winning "trait" of Ms. Nude International, explicitly identified as a continuing sign of her worthiness for the crown:

> Winning hasn't changed Melanie [aka Corinne, winner of 1976 Ms. International Nude Beauty Contest] at all say her friends and neighbors, who thronged to her Arlington house to wish her well on learning of the win in Atlantic City. "She's the same sweet unspoiled girl we always knew."[43]

That "Melanie" remained "unspoiled" (a term redolent with virginal implications), throughout the Ms. Nude International Pageant was a testament to her feminine sincerity as powerful in its way as projections of contestant "amiability."

The construction of "BQI" (beauty queen image) presents a performance conundrum for practitioners. On one hand, pageant coach Stanley insists that "Niceness is your greatest asset,"[44] and on the other, "A swimsuit must be sexy enough to show off your assets."[45] The difficulty in presenting "niceness" and "sexiness" as simultaneous assets to be sold to the judges is that these constructed qualities need to be in balance, neither outweighing the other in emphasis. Andre Gide captured the essence of the problem with his observation that "One cannot both be sincere and seem so."[46] Sincerity, as a term carrying implications of purity, "entered discourse," according to Lionel Trilling, in the sixteenth-century. Its original Latin etymology, "sine cera" ("without wax"), referred primarily to things, not persons—to objects, not subjects. Yet the first-century Roman poet Martial expressed the outrage of an audience on discovering fraudulence in the composition of a female façade:

> You are but a composition of lies. Whilst you were in Rome, your hair was growing on the banks of the Rhine; at night, when you lay aside your silken robes, you lay aside your teeth as well; and two thirds of your person are locked up in boxes for the night . . . Thus no man can say, I love you, for you are not what he loves, and no one loves what you are.[47]

Nearly two thousand years later, male strip club spectators practice similarly suspicious scrutiny, as Katherine Frank notes:

> The customers I interacted with and interviewed made repeated attempts to secure what they described as authentic or "real" encounters with the dancers in the club. They also discussed the physical and behavioral cues that they used to determine whether a dancer was genuine or not; "fake" breasts or bleached hair was perceived as a sign of inauthenticity.[48]

Strippers, who feel an obligation, a "mandate," to have plastic surgery to enhance their breasts nevertheless must take care to present their artificial enhancements as "genuine." Such a requirement recalls the late nineteenth-century advertisements of George Lederer, who promoted chorus girls as "wholly feminine,"[49] as if to distinguish them from imposters whose femininity was merely partial.

The Miss America Organization's (MAO) reliance on a cultural memory of the unsophisticated, girl-next-door masks the artifice behind the every-girl image of the contemporary contestant with hazy evocations of the "natural" bathing beauties of 1921 and earlier. While such an approach may be profitable, it also reveals an inevitable dependence on the specious, for the natural "Golden Mermaid" is a fabrication. As early as 1922 pageant rules governing and orchestrating a "natural beauty" were in effect, decreeing among other things that "bobbed" hair was deemed an unnatural alteration of appropriate physical properties and ensured a contestant's disqualification.[50] The complex negotiation between the appearance of unsophisticated beauty and the actual efforts necessary to achieve a winning look have been an integral part of all beauty contests' performances of "normal" from their inception. Sarah Banet-Weiser has argued that "the Miss America pageant does not define itself in terms of sexuality, but rather promotes a self-production that relies on a more complex interweaving of two themes of femininity: typicality and respectability."[51] The point may be extended by noting that while "typicality" is an end result, "normal" is a standard by which others are expected to define and regulate their appearance and behavior. Additionally, while the MAO may not, for obvious ideological reasons, "define" itself rhetorically "in terms of sexuality," it unquestionably promulgates a definition of (hetero)sexuality as normative even as, by means of regulated appearance and physical movement, the organization insists on the control and containment of allowable sexual display. It was then, perhaps, not without irony that for the 2004 Miss America competition, executive producer Bob Bain "wanted the show to turn live to the set of 'Queer Eye for the Straight Guy,' for running commentary from the Fab Five." His suggestion was voted down by ABC because it was not in their best interest to advertise another network's product.[52]

"Normal," as defined by Harold Garfinkel in *Studies in Ethnomethodolgy*, means "in accordance with the mores."[53] In a perpetual "conumdrum of somatic femininity," beauty contestants reflect the societal suasion "that female bodies are never feminine enough, that they must be deliberately and oftentimes painfully remade to be what 'nature' intended."[54] Miss Arizona 2002 explained:

> It's been an extremely difficult thing for me to overcome my own self-esteem issues with walking in a swimsuit. I am naturally extremely thin, much thinner than I am right now. And I had to gain a considerable amount of weight to compete, which is the opposite that most people think you have to do to prepare for the swimsuit competition. But everyday I had to look in the mirror and had to scrutinize—do I look normal, do I look like the size 6 that they want me to be. I cannot be the size 2 that God intended me to be or that my metabolism allows me to be, and everything came down to counting calories and measuring and weighing and exercising and it becomes an obsession.

"Cover all scars, birthmarks, veins, and other imperfections," advises Anna Stanley.[55] Masking imperfections to conform to an ideological construct of normal and natural creates an unavoidable and unceasing condition of instability—there is always the risk that one will be discovered to be fraudulent. "The woman who checks her make-up half a dozen times a day to see if her foundation has caked or her mascara run, who worries that the wind or rain may spoil her hairdo," argues Sandra Bartky, "has become just as surely as the inmate of the Panopticon, a self-policing subject, a self committed to a relentless self-surveillance."[56]

The "Perfect Miss America" was defined by CBS, the network that broadcast the competition in 1958, with the following promotional blurb:

> Are you this girl?: Five feet, $6\frac{1}{2}$ inches tall, 124 pounds; 19 years old; blue eyes; brown hair; talented . . . *and* single. If you fit this description, YOU are the perfect all-time "Miss America." The figures above describe a composite "Miss America," with the statistical average of every Miss America since 1921, when the pageant began.[57]

But even the "perfect" Miss America described in the advertisement is a composite, a statistically averaged fantasy figure assumptively identified in the famous Bert Parks rendition of "There She Is" as "your ideal." Promoting a particular body type as the feminine ideal aided in the creation and success of the beauty business, which thrives by convincing women that they must alter their appearances. Paradoxically, women were also encouraged to become patriotic consumers, demanding their "natural right" to conform to a construct of beauty that could only be achieved through unnatural enhancements.[58] A 1970 *New York Times* article confirmed that, "although 'naturalness' is emphasized throughout the Miss America system, with artificial beauty aids grounds for disqualification, formal and informal ties with the beauty industry are strong."[59] As pageant coach Anna Stanley declares: "Contestants learn to present one look—their most beautiful one."[60] Naomi Wolf argues a broader, more complex view: "The qualities that a given period calls beautiful in women are merely symbols of the female behavior that that period considers desirable: The beauty myth is always actually prescribing behavior and not appearance. Competition between women has been made part of the myth so that women will be divided from one another."[61] Wolf's implicative assertion that women are more easily controlled when they are competitively isolated exposes another irony—that the competition which estranges them tends to erase individuality, ironically uniting women in a struggle to become identical.

"When women put on face makeup," notes Nancy Etcoff, "they are reworking their faces to approximate a shared ideal, in fact to replace their individual feature."[62] Institutional encouragement of such "approximation" is widespread, overtly evident in former MAO Chairman George Bauer's statement to the press, in September 2002, that the pageant was actively soliciting an un-named cosmetic company to serve as a sponsor. Nor is the impulse confined to beauty pageants. Lily Burana, explaining her adoption of the stage name "Barbie," puts it another way: "In creating this stripper persona, I strive for the blondest common denominator, and what's blonder than "Barbie?"[63]

Constructing an ideal image of femininity in America not only requires the homogenizing tools of makeup, but also the appearance of youth. Just as Walter Kingsley suggested in 1920 that "beauty should have [. . .] the slight suggestions of immaturity, for the full blown woman has her own special charm not so precious to the connoisseur," the feminine ideal presented in most beauty contests is confined within the 18–24 age range. Strippers have slightly longer careers, but even there, as Lily Burana recounts, "A thirty-two-year-old friend of mine was let go by a club manager who told her, 'We have to make room for the eighteen-year-olds.' "[64] That youth renders a female more "precious" situates women, once again, in a constant position of instability, forever pressured to alter their appearances in conformity with preferred feminine imagery, yet inevitably destined to be foiled by time and gravity. The latter decades of the twentieth century, however, have profoundly expanded the range of responses available to women in the face of this formerly intractable dilemma.

Urla's and Terry's argument that "the modern bodies we imagine today are in many ways the legacies of techniques of measurement, visualization, and classification that grow out of the powerful domains of scientific empiricism and medical treatment," is strongly supported by the overwhelming proliferation of techniques and applications in the business of plastic surgery.[65] Surgical alteration among strippers is so commonplace that enhanced bodies are now themselves designators of the "natural" stripper's desirable look. On the website "Strippers.cc" (characterized as "a resource where strippers can find industry information"), a link to a plastic surgery referral service lists the "most popular plastic surgery procedures for strippers: Breast Implants, Breast augmentation, Breast Enhancements, Liposuction."[66] Flashing banners inform the viewer that Liposuction can be had for $1999 and Breast Implants for $2999. Another website devoted to providing resources for strippers, "Stripper Power," explicitly states that "getting implants is not an option. If you want to be the top in this industry, it is mandatory."[67] Though less publicly acknowledged, "enhancements" have long been associated with beauty contestants as well. When Miss Brazil 2002, Juliana Borges, revealed that she had undergone nineteen plastic surgery procedures, a media frenzy occurred. Apparently, the viewing public had been unaware of the prevalence of such practices within the pageant industry. Borges provided details of the full year she had devoted to collagen injections, silicone implants, pinned-back ears and liposuction, arguing that the procedures amounted to a professional necessity: "The same way someone has to study to become a doctor, someone has to train. I have to work on my figure to get it where I want it. It's something I needed for my profession, for my work. I have a doctorate in body measurements."[68] Combining attitudes more familiarly associated with Svengali and Dr. Frankenstein, Borges's pageant trainer, Evandro Rossi, agreed that preparation and change were central to her success: "I took a rough gem that wasn't worked and created her. I made these small changes. She was a diamond that hasn't been worked and I brought her to life. I created Juliana and it worked."[69]

The accelerated commodification of "beauty" brought about by plastic surgery has affected female display as no other single development of the last half-century. Even its *possibility* can create news. In a 1984 article, a journalist recounted the following conversation with a young Miss America contestant:

> While flying last week, a plastic surgeon sitting in front of Miss Wood, after learning she was Miss Washington, offered her reduced rates on several cosmetic procedures. "He told me that he'll redo my face if I don't win and that I can come back next year and nobody will know." "I think I'll win without the surgery," Miss Wood said, "But he made my day."[70]

Apparently, in the event she did not measure up to the pageant's "natural" standards, knowing surgery was a back-up option and her face could be "redone" was enough to lift that particular contestant's spirits. But the surgeon's willingness to "redo" Miss Wood, Borges's pragmatic acceptance of the professional need for nineteen bodily alterations, and the stripper's belief that breast surgery is "mandatory," eerily evoke Susan Bordo's description of the "Reproduction of Femininity," as "the pathology and violence that lurks just around the corner, waiting at the horizon of 'normal' femininity."[71] One need only witness a single episode of Fox television's successful 2004 program *The Swan* to see how plastic surgery and beauty contests combine to offer the ultimate image of constructed beauty as normative.

Though she stopped short of surgical modification, the Miss Rhode Island contestant who considered her performance a presentation of who she "could be" exemplifies the studied construction behind the pageant contestant's onstage appearance. In a "Contestants Info Swap" exchange on the MAO webpage message board, a conversation between competitors at the regional and local levels featured a discussion of the "rules against attachable hair pieces" (echoing the 1922 rules governing "bobbed" hair) and the ways in which they rendered the embodied performance more or less authentic. Citing the efficacy of using a "hair piece" rather than her own hair to create a "curly romantic mess on the top of [her] head," as a way to convey a "natural" tousled look in the talent competition, one contestant offered insight into the widely acceptable use of embellishing tools as a means by which the performer's chosen image might become instantly recognizable. As further contestants' comments focusing on fake hair pieces prove, the "self" being sold to the judges changes according to the costumed contextual moment:

> I know a lot of girls here in Georgia use them! Everything from ponytail wraps to scrunchie like things made of curls. Area [*sic*] uses both at different times. Her hair is so thick she keeps it at shoulder length, but wants more when she puts it up. For interview sometimes she pulls it back into a tucked ponytail at the nape of her neck and uses a human hair wrap to cover the ponytail holder. For evening gown she puts it in a French twist and adds a glump [*sic*] of curls at the top to add height.[72]

Clearly the inventive contestants using "scrunchies" and "glumps" are under no illusion as to the importance of a "carefully calibrated degree of display and concealment."[73] In stating "I would have hated to judge this year—all 51 [contestants] projected a love for the system," one particularly astute competitor articulated two essential components for successful participation in a beauty pageant: "projection" of a carefully composed self and an understanding of the process as a "system" which must be negotiated ("system," defined by Webster's Dictionary, as a "plan of classification"). As Denise Gehman, Miss Michigan 1983, advises: "Don't ever cry onstage, never let the judges see you lick your lips, be concise, be prepared, believe in yourself and smile a lot—but naturally."[74]

The public announcement of female measurements in pageants has served to accentuate contestants' difference both from each other and from the male population. "Instead of granting an autonomous and active form of corporeal specificity," argues Elizabeth Grosz, "at best women's bodies are judged in terms of 'natural inequality,' as if there were a standard or measure for the value of bodies independent of sex."[75] While some pageants may have ended the tradition of announcing female measurements as individual contestants parade across the stage (there is no standardized equivalent for male measurements), the impulse to normalize female bodies that governed the tradition is still very much in evidence. It is perhaps worth mentioning here that "a Johns Hopkins study published a few years ago found that more than half of Miss Americas since 1970 have had a Body Mass Index below 18.5, placing them in the undernourished range according to World Health Organization criteria."[76] As one Rhode Island contestant admitted, "They do alter their bodies to look better on stage to conform to what people think is beautiful." In the 1930s, tape measurements were handed out at fairs with the reigning beauty queen's bust, waist, and hip size highlighted next to the promotion, "come see her at the fair," and newsreels ran shots of the young females lined up for a ritualized ceremony at which male judges determined their "official" measurements. The MAO continued with public announcements of body statistics up until 1986.

Today, in the absence of ordinal announcements, the visual images of contestants in swimsuits serve as their proclamations of worthiness. However, the normative swim-suited figure in the beauty pageant remains a carefully constructed paradigm. A *People Magazine* article reveals the secrets of Ada Duckett, a favorite pageant swimsuit designer and inventor of what came to be known as the "supersuit":

> "I'll tell you why the girls win in them. It's the fit. I alter them so they mold to the girl's figure." For each girl she alters the straps to widen or narrow the look of the wearer's shoulders, adjusts the neck and armholes to keep too much cleavage from showing and deepens or shortens the cut along the hips. The result, says Duckett: "no bouncing" of breasts, stomach or derriere. So that all goes as planned, Duckett offers two hours of instruction on the proper way to put on the suit. For example, the material is pulled forward at the crotch to give a snug fit across the buttocks.[77]

"The art of the costumer," observed one journalist in 1922, "may have as much to do as Mother Nature with the results."[78] Women whose figures deviated too far from the norm were accused of subterfuge, as in the case of Miss America 1953, who was "charged with illegal padding" by the mothers of other contestants because she appeared too amply endowed. In order to rebut the charge, the new Miss America's chaperone was forced to vouch for the authenticity of her breasts. Surveillance of appropriate body parts extended beyond breasts when pageant winner Lee Meriweather was trained by her director to "force her legs together to disguise their unique shape."[79] Notwithstanding the assertion of Shirley Cothran (Miss Texas, winner of her swimsuit competition) that the swimsuit segment "gives the judges a fuller composite picture,"[80] the technique of "forcing" a beauty contestant's legs together, irrespective of its stated intention to hide a flaw, offers revealing evidence of the contestants' rehearsed bodily control; a control designed to suggest normative female sexuality as a thing to be managed—the opposite of former beauty queen Donna Axum's image of the "sprawled" woman.

The methods by which the "feminine" is constructed and performed by beauty contestants are, in many ways, reiterated in the entirely different context of Harold Garfinkel's famous case study of "Agnes" in *Studies in Ethnomethodology*. Defined by Garfinkel as an "intersexed" person, "Agnes had an abiding practical preoccupation with competent female sexuality."[81] Note in particular his use of certain "normative" notions of the feminine in the following description of Agnes:

> Agnes' appearance was convincingly female. She was tall, slim, with a very female shape. Her measurements were 38–25–38. [. . .] Her usual manner of dress did not distinguish her from a typical girl of her age and class. There was nothing garish or exhibitionistic in her attire, nor was there any hint of poor taste or that she was ill at ease in her clothing, as is seen so often in transvestites and in women with disturbances in sexual identification.[82]

The cultural habit of assigning certain adjectives as designators of the more or less feminine—"garish" dress would function as an indicator of the less feminine—is evident even in the "objective" study of the subject. What is at issue is "identity and authorship in relation to gender,"[83] an issue equally at play in the assertion by the winner of a preliminary talent competition at the Miss America pageant in 1974 that, "Men and women are made to be different. God created them that way. Why can't people just accept that?"[84] For Agnes, "passing" as feminine *enough* involved "structured strain,"[85] a "rehearsed carelessness"[86] that belied the meticulous preparation for any appearance in public. As Kemp and Squire have argued, "the naturalness of the body is called into question by its inscription within a certain kind of performance."[87] Agnes's performance of femaleness had to be proficient enough to be accepted as natural in order for her to "pass" successfully. She "guaranteed for herself the ascribed rights and obligations of an adult female by the acquisition and use of skills and capacities, the efficacious display of female appearances and performances, and the mobilizing of appropriate feelings and purposes."[88]

Given that notions of the "normal feminine" are fictive constructs readily translated into a codified visual and gestural vocabulary, it is not surprising then that, in order to present a skillful and immediately recognizable composition of "real" femininity Miss Arizona 2002 turned to the entertainment field of female impersonation for training in the evening wear segment of the competition:

> I have a friend who's a drag queen, and I like to pretend that I'm a drag queen while I'm up there. Because I think they have more confidence in their walk than

anyone else and I know I'm very shy and I'm constantly thinking to myself don't fall, don't fall, just get down the steps, as long as you don't land on your rear end you did a really good job in evening wear, and then I said, no, just strut it, just be a drag queen walk out there with all the confidence, head held high and that is a kind of a performance, that's a strutting competition for me.

Gaston Bachelard's observation that the image carries its own *"exaggeration,"* is exactly what enables multiple representations of femininity, no matter the biological make-up of the performer, to be immediately socially recognizable.[89] As Laurence Senelick has noted, "gender exists only insofar as it is perceived."[90]

Agnes and beauty contestants share a similar necessity, and limitation—their constructed femininity is supposed to remain undetected, unlike many performances by female impersonators such as those at Ziegfeld's Club in Washington, DC. There, crowned title holder Miss Ziegfeld 2002 currently performs before an audience which, fully aware of the assumed gender as performance, judges her according to its perception of "appropriate" feminine display. "Gender roles performed by 'performers' never merely replicate those in everyday life," argues Senelick, "they are more sharply defined and more emphatically presented, the inherent iconicity offering both an ideal and a critique."[91] The critique of gender inherent in performances like those of Miss Ziegfeld is similarly evident at the Miss Gay America competition, an event that has been in existence for more than thirty years. The rules and regulation section on evening gown competition advises:

> A V-neck is fine but, if it is cut too low, it looks manly. Jewelry should accessorize and not be over-powering. Shoes should match the outfit and complement it [. . .] Hair should be appropriate for evening wear and style of gown.[92]

Again, the "appropriate" display of the feminine is presented as a normative standard, readily recognizable and thus appropriate for co-option.

In fact, links between female impersonation and beauty contests have been apparent for decades. In the 1970s, men in drag watching the Miss America Boardwalk Parade from balconies could see that contestants were wearing slippers and socks hidden from view by their dresses and the interior of the convertibles in which they rode. Thus began the pageant tradition of parade watchers yelling out "Show us your shoes." Following the Miss America Pageant each September is the celebrated "Miss'd America" pageant, also held in Atlantic City. "Miss'd America," "the wildest show this side of the Boardwalk," is an AIDS fund-raiser in which male contestants in drag compete in talent, eveningwear, and swimsuit competitions.[93] In 1999, "Miss Tenee" "a 6-foot-3 inch, 205-pounder," was declared the winner and "headed down the bulb-adorned runway as the crowd sang a reworked version of *There She Is*, the Miss America standard."[94] "Miss'd America" has been characterized as "a sarcastic antidote to the apple-pie sincerity of the real pageant."[95] Across the United States, as women compete in Miss America, Mrs. United States, Miss Sun Queen, Miss Rice Belt, and Miss Rural Electrification,[96] female impersonators compete in contests with the titles Miss Badlands, Miss Mid-America, Miss Gay Texas, Miss Gentry, Miss Gay Oklahoma, Miss Sweetheart, and, for the plus size impersonator, Miss Gay USofA At-Large. The contestant's performance in the Miss Badlands competition is judged according to his extraordinary grasp of a "feminine" gestural vocabulary in the same way that a Miss America contestant's presentation of femininity is adjudicated, along the way exposing social assumptions of gendered appearance as little more than artificially imitable fabrication.

Constructions of both femininity and female sexuality were reiterated, and in one case interrogated, at the Exotic World competition in Helendale, California, in June of 2002. One of the performers competing for the title Miss Exotic World was Selene Luna. With performance credits too numerous to list fully, Luna has appeared onstage as a model, burlesque performer, stripper, performance artist, cabaret performer, and film actress. She is also, as the burlesquers would say, a "pocket Venus," standing 3′ 10″ and weighing 67 pounds. Characterizing herself as "a media whore," Luna currently performs as a member of the "girl-gang" group Epiladies (a titular parody of a hair-removal product) in the Los Angeles area.[97] Her act for the Exotic World competition, a strip routine performed under the pseudonym "Starlet O'Hara," was a complex, parodic commentary on social norms of femininity and sexuality. Employing first a starlet's gestural vocabulary of controlled movement and stylized demure decorum, she then shed her stole (and the decorous behavior) to perform the traditional bumps, grinds, and shimmies of the striptease artist. Her act was a remarkable parallel to the theatrical technique of bait-and-switch utilized by MaryAnn Mobley in her winning performance at the Miss America 1959 pageant. Exploiting cultural norms, Luna offered a critique of socially accepted notions of feminine sexuality through the calculated use of her size and body type. Her performance inescapably exposed the intentional construction of staged feminine "normalcy," revealing it as narrow, confining, and stale.

While Selene Luna performed all the gestures considered "appropriate" to such forms, her physical "difference" asserted itself as a far more authentically explicit, and complex, image; an image that forced the audience to confront its own assumptions, not only regarding the constitution of a "normal" body, but also of the limitations imposed on vocabularies of sexual display for female performers of all kinds. As Nigel Rothfels has argued, the "precise cultural interpretation of an unusual person has a great deal to do with the historical moment in which that person finds himself or herself freaked by his or her own or another culture."[98] Luna's exceptional performance, a perform-ance that offered a simultaneous critique of standardized sexual display and the potential for acknowledging a wider representation of female sexuality in general, did not earn her a spot as one of the top three finalists. Even in the marginalized context of Exotic World, this was no surprise.

Just as Walter Kingsley insisted that the beauty must be, at all times, "enchanting," the stripper is expected to project a particularly recognizable, hence normalized, sexuality. In spite of the fact, noted in *Carnival Strippers*, that "The job demands that the girls be something that they really can't be, a sex symbol. No one can be a sex symbol all the time, not when they're up close. It's a contradiction in terms," social expectations demand that strippers operate within a narrow range of behavior, gestures, and even characters that can be instantly read as sexual.[99]

Constructing a socially acceptable display of female sexuality follows a similar path to that of the packaged femininity on the beauty pageant stage, both operating on standardizing principles. The carnival stripper "Lena," however, draws a semantic distinction between the construct of sexuality and the sensual, "We're not sensual when we're on stage. Sexy, maybe, but not sensual. Sensual is a beautiful word. Sexy is a plastic, phony, ugly word. When I'm not working, I feel sensuous. When I'm working, I feel sexy." She further argues against the notion of her status as a "sex symbol," insisting that "a sex symbol is someone who's set apart from everybody and is desired."[100] "Lena's" argument reflects the homogenization at play in performances by strippers who, like beauty contestants, offer the comfort of recognizable gestures that confirm the expectations of the audience. In this case, the expectation of a particular "tawdry" display of sexuality in the created context of the carnival tent is hardly distinguishable from the beauty contestant's canned interview response that thanks God for her success and hopes for world peace. "It's a lot more than being a sex symbol," insisted one Miss West Allis pageant winner, "You have to project personality."[101]

The range of accepted sexual display in strip clubs, like the range of "normal" femininities presented in beauty contests, is astonishingly narrow. As Jacqueline Rose has noted, "if the visual image in its aesthetically acclaimed form serves to maintain a particular and oppressive mode of sexual recognition, it does so only partially and at a cost."[102] For female performers, the cost is the extraordinarily limited range of gestures that are socially accepted as indicators of a "sexual" female. Bumps, grinds, pelvic thrusts, shimmies, and gyrations combine with scripted patter promising belief in the customer's sexual prowess and assurances of the performer's attraction. "The majority of female dancers," according to *Strip Show*, "improvise around the traditional pattern of disrobing."[103] Once again, as with burlesque disrobing acts, the imputation of voyeurism is repeated endlessly, exemplified by the standardized progression of one stripper's club audition: "first song in the dress, out of the top by the end of the second song, topless for the third."[104]

If, as Susan Scotto maintains, the commodity offered for sale in strip clubs is "attention," the limited range of performed sexual display can be ascribed to its fundamental nature as *pretense*. Suggestive representations of (potential) sexual adventure and normal femininity in both stripping and beauty contests take place in comfortable spaces where expectations are confirmed, not challenged. Thus, Professor Scotto's stripping repertoire is geared toward types, as were Ziegfeld's and Carroll's years earlier. "I have different personae depending on the costume I'm wearing," says Scotto, "Like I have my naughty librarian, or my naughty nurse." Katherine Liepe-Levinson suggests that such "everyday occupational uniforms" function as "a type of sartorial armor that refers to established class and gender norms which are highlighted and violated through the act of stripping."[105] Yet, because they are immediately recognizable and accepted as stereotypes, their power to "violate" social authority in any transgressive way is negligible. Occupational types function in the same way that the stage names "Jezebel" and "Lolita" served to categorize a dancer at Charlie's club and a first-time stripper or at Exotic World, respectively. In an ironic comment on the extent to which such types are ingrained in the American cultural landscape, "Jezebel" confessed ignorance of the origins of her stage name—she just "liked how it sounded."[106] One of her customers remarked on its significance, however.

The 1952 video *Striporama*, introducing the "G-String Quartet," instructs viewers that stripping consists of performative variations on one of four essential types: "the baby doll type, the slow and easy type, the wild and wooly type, and the literary genius." A stripper in 1938 broke it down into similar categories: "There's what we call the 'fast worker,' the 'slow worker,' the 'parade strip,' the 'society strip.' "[107] "Some women," she added, "do strictly a sex strip."[108] These familiar personae provide prefabricated characterizations within which individual performers can operate, but more broadly, the designation "stripper" itself has become an immediately recognizable performance type, just as has the BQI of the beauty contestant. The stripper is expected to perform the pelvic thrust and the shimmie as reliable indicators of her identity as a performer, just as contestants from New England in the 2003

Mrs. America Pageant were expected to don costumes featuring lobster claws and fall foliage as symbols of their regional origins in the pageant's opening-number.

The stripper as a type was even co-opted by one of America's icons of female wholesomeness, Marlo Thomas, in an episode of the 1960s television sitcom *That Girl* titled "The Call of the Wild."[109] Thomas entered the scene wearing a robe, with a towel around her neck, as though fresh from the shower. As if to drive home the metaphor of innocence-on-the-verge, she was eating an apple. Approvingly noting herself in a full-length mirror, she then began the predictable gestural patterns of a striptease—bumps, grinds, shoulder dips—as standard burlesque music crept into the soundtrack along with canned applause and male wolf whistles. As she dropped her robe to reveal a lacy slip, the door abruptly opened and her "transgressive" behavior was interrupted, to her horrified surprise, by "Daddy." Thomas's imperson-ation, while far less graphic than today's strip artists, nonetheless employed the precise movements found on countless club stages. Her character's ditzy wholesomeness embraced the stripper's traditional gestural vocabulary not as transgression, but inclusively. As if to paraphrase Anna Stanley's exhortation to potential beauty queens ("There's a little bit of Miss America in every girl, if she'll just dedicate herself to bringing it out"), *That Girl* seemed quite comfortable acknowledging the presence of her inner stripper. Her father's discomfiture notwithstanding, Thomas's presentation of "deviant" behavior relied on shared assumptions of its essential "normalcy."

As noted, striptease and beauty contests strategically, and often simultane-ously, deploy visual cues based on their perceptions of the audience's desires for a presentation of "normal" deviance and femininity. Capitalizing on the lingering nineteenth-century social fear (and hope) that "deviance could be masquerading under the guise of a 'normal' woman,"[110] exotic dancer and college professor Susan Scotto illustrates the performance potential when "normal" is worn as a costume:

> I love wearing gowns because it's this real perversion of a sort of socially acceptable moment. That's why I like wearing street clothes and taking them off, because guys really like that and they say, "Yeah, you know, I don't really want to see a girl come out there in a teddy because I can go home and see my girlfriend in that. What I really want to see is that girl who works in the mall." So, it's like somebody who looks like a regular person and then seeing her take off her clothes, pervert-ing something regular that you see every day.

"Perversion," while culturally accepted as "deviant," is also merely a variation. Because Scotto's perversion of the "socially acceptable moment" relies on the constructed image of "normal," it is always limited by its referentiality. Like Roland Barthes's discussion of "connotation" as a feature that "has the power to relate itself to anterior, ulterior, or exterior mentions, to other sites of the text," Scotto is cyclically reiterating another social norm of femaleness according to her understanding of the spectator's desire.[111] The strip club spectator who sits watching a girl who looks like she "works in the mall" is responding to the visual cues of "wholesomeness" in the same way that the beauty pageant viewer witnesses and interprets the staged performance of "every girl." Recognizable types are nonthreatening, as "Li'l Adams" rhetorically demonstrated in 1960 when she marketed herself as "naughty but nice."[112]

Historically, even civic organizations like the Jaycees, who play a major role in the volunteer effort that supports pageants on the local and national levels, have featured women who represented the antithesis of the beauty queen image at various functions. Shirley Jean Rickert, the one time child "vamp" star of *Our Gang* who later became the successful burlesque stripper "Gilda," was invited to a luncheon as an "honored guest," and Kathy Collins, famed stripper, provided the entertainment one summer at a Jaycee luncheon in Atlantic City. According to the organization's newsletter, " 'What's a nice girl like you doing . . .' was the question Kathy said is asked most of her, and we Jaycees were no exception. If you want the answer I suggest seeing her at the Capitol theatre."[113] Appropriating "deviance" as entertainment for the audience reaffirms both its own "wholesome" position and its social control over the stripper, neatly illustrating Jacqueline Rose's contention that "engagement with the image belongs to a political intention."[114]

The juxtaposition of "deviance" and "normal" as an operative tool is clearly indicated in Susan Scotto's description of another of her routines:

> One of my most successful sets is my *Mission Impossible* set—I have this leather sort of Dom bodysuit thing that laces up front, real Dom type stuff. So, I put that on with these black thigh highs then, over it, I put this black skirt and cream colored sort of business—like blouse, and then I put on my grey trench coat and I have my little briefcase. I come in wearing a hat and light a match and play the *Mission Impossible* theme. Then, in my briefcase, I have a little flail and some nipple clamps and some ropes. I like it because it's a three part costume, that once I've taken off the coat they think its just the business suit look, but then there's like the double whammy because they see something else under that. It's really fun to play with stuff like that.

Just as Lily Burana performs in what she refers to as "full Barbie drag," composed of "platinum hairpiece down to [her] behind. Hot pink gown and thong, clear Lucite platforms, rhinestone choker, and earrings [. . .] False eyelashes, frosted lipstick. The whole bit," Scotto peals off layers of different personae to enhance the dramatic appeal of the performance.[115] Each layer signifies to the spectator a particularly recognizable icon of femaleness— businesswoman, Dominatrix, or popular television character, even as it confirms social expectation of the roles, and the changeability, of women.

In practice, then, both beauty pageant and striptease not only employ, but rely on the apparent binary of "normal" and "deviant" for the successful establishment of their respective images. Once again, Scotto describes the technique: "One of the best things I have that people really like, is I take that colored Reynolds saran wrap and make a little costume out of that and they get to pull it off me. But in terms of personae, I really like to play up. I wear a lot of street clothes and like that idea of, I'm the regular person but whoa, look what's going on here." While acknowledging the role "normal" plays in sexualized display, one might be more likely to assume the performance of the antithesis of the genuine as visually absent from the beauty contest stage. And yet, as noted throughout these chapters, presentations of the deviant-Other-body proliferate across beauty pageant stages. Scotto's "whoa, look what's going on here" can, and should, be a response to beauty pageants just as it is to a strip act.

A message board on the MAO webpage illustrates the use of an opposi- tional Other as a foil for normalcy. In a discussion of one contestant's costuming for a monologue in which she assumes the aspect of a witch, another contestant offered her a prescription for "witchiness" that eliminates the use of an actual mask:

> Instead, you could use a lot of cheap jewelry and excess makeup (like rouge in circles on your cheeks), or over-extended lipstick, or a crooked crown, but I wouldn't cover my face.[116]

Astonishingly, the contestant conjures up a visual image not so traditionally witch-like as it is the imagined antithesis of a beauty queen, complete with drooping crown. Her description expresses an anxiety associated with excess, as well as an inability to appropriately fix facade to form. More significantly, her example immediately reinforces certain recognizable visual signifiers of a "fallen" woman, the moralistic antithesis of a pageant queen. Her suggestions accentuate, antithetically, the criteria by which pageant contestants are judged "appropriate" in terms of mutually constitutive, "natural," and "normal" presentations of female behavior, thereby endorsing the social sta- bility and mores promulgated by the MAO as implicit consequences of such behavior. "What we have to do," according to Leonard Horn (former CEO of the MAO), "is give them an opportunity to look more real and less plastic."[117] Horn's aim is complicated by the fact that, as beauty contestants have known for many years, the pageant world's idealized, asexual feminine composite is both performatively and conceptually at odds with its theatrical underlying principle, thus creating a situation in which opportunities to "look more real" are unlikely to proliferate.

As a result, gestural intimations of less than "wholesome" behavior can be perceived throughout every beauty contest, from the aforementioned "harem" dances to the swimsuit segments and torch songs. Unquestionably, Professor Scotto's intentional use of the ordinary, the "normal," in her stripping act as a tool for sexual enticement is founded on the same premise as the fabricated hyper-normal performance in a beauty contest. And even as the MAO disingenuously defends its use of the swimsuit as a means of conveying "fitness," it imbues its girl-next-door with hints of a sexualized body just out of reach. Sarah Banet-Weiser proposes that, "Surveying only the body in this competition [swimsuit] transforms each contestant into simply a body and not an embodiment of sexuality, moral transgression, or aggression."[118]

Yet it is arguable that, in American culture, there is no such thing as "simply a body." In the Miss America 2001 competition, when Miss West Virginia entered in her white swimsuit, a costume virtually indistinguishable from the lingerie worn by the Victoria's Secret catalog models, host Tony Danza garbled her name and then stammered jokingly, "I lost my concentration." Playing on an age-old social stereotype of the flustered male in the presence of the "bombshell," Danza effectively "sexed" Miss Virgina's body, irrespective of the contestant's actual intention to fulfill the chaste performative mandates of the competition. Like a number of Miss America's male hosts in the years since the forced retirement of the courtly, paternalistic Bert Parks, Danza proved unable to resist the impulse to enter the eroticized space the pageant trades on yet works so hard to deny. "Miss America has a new man in her life," he announced, "me." His contract was not renewed.

To presume that a female body onstage in a state of undress in front of millions of viewers is somehow *not* sexualized is to deny the evident iconicity in the visual image. Even when clothed, contestants in the 2001 competition were rhetorically linked to male desire, their sexuality and its reception by male authority expressed in "normal," hubba-hubba ways, as they once were in burlesque. (When the reigning Miss America was introduced as a teacher, Danza chuckled, "I would've never forgotten my homework.") While the contestants' projections of sexuality, if not altogether ingenuous, are at least as unselfconscious as they can be made to appear, masculine appreciation of the scantily clad female form as a sexualized display is acceptable within the confines of the patriarchal pageant structure. Two years later, the 2003 pageant emcee (Hollywood Squares game show host Tom Bergeron) quipped at the end of the swimsuit segment "Let's do that one again," and then commented on his own behavior with "that was such a guy moment, wasn't it?" ("Tom reflects the values of the Miss America Organization," stated George Bauer, former President and CEO of the MAO, in a September 2003 press release, "he is warm, engaging and genuine.") The telecast's backstage (male) commentator responded to a design detail of one contestant's dress during the evening gown segment with an enthusiastic "Viva le slit, Viva le slit." His comment was presumably intended to express appreciation for the contestant's clothing, rather than as an overt reminder that "slit" is a derogatory slang term for both vagina and whore. This normalized reaction is by no means confined to beauty contests. As Katherine Frank has remarked of strip clubs, "for many customers, then, heterosexuality could be comfortably secured, at least temporarily or in fantasy, through a public performance of desire for an obvious woman."[119] Frank's use of "obvious" linked to "woman" in the strip club would be equally apt as a descriptive of the codified appearance of the beauty contestant. What makes one a more or less "obvious" woman is exactly what strip clubs and beauty contests traffic in.

"Viewed historically," says Susan Bordo, "the discipline and normalization of the female body—perhaps the only gender oppression that exercises itself, although to different degrees and in different forms, across age, race, class, and sexual orientation—has to be acknowledged as an amazingly durable and flexible strategy of social control."[120] Ritualized reminders of this disciplined normalization abound in every form of female display, sometimes taking on quasi-religious overtones. In 1983, in an article titled "It's the Reenactment of the American Dream," Dan Wakefield observed:

> In the supercharged challenge of a world that often seems going down the runway to nuclear or social or economic destruction, the genuine innocence of the Miss America show is one of its persistent charms. Though last year's pageant was billed as "a tribute to 62 years of change in America" (from the time the first "bathing beauties" paraded down the Boardwalk), *its underlying appeal may be in how much remains the same.* The career goals and life styles of the contestants have inevitably altered with the times, but the basic ritual of the event—what the Pageant staff so correctly refers to as "*the liturgy*"—remains reassuringly traditional. They still come down the runway."[121]

The lack of multivalent images, the redundant performative definitions of what it is to be female, feminine, and sexual presented on the stages of beauty

5. Economics and Advancement: Or, Flesh-for-Cash Transactions and the Cinderella Myth ✒

The economics of being female are never particularly advantageous.

Etcoff, *Survival of the Prettiest*[1]

They said we were "using" women. I always thought we were using them right.

Bob Hope, host of 1970 Miss Universe Pageant[2]

At the end of the nineteenth century, typical wages for female employees in northeastern American cities ranged from $1.50 to $8 a week for factory operatives and department store salesgirls, to $6 to $15 a week for typists and stenographers.[3] According to Faye Dudden, as early as 1870, "the only profession that employed more women than the theatre [. . .] was teaching."[4] But by the 1920s, "theatrical choruses constituted the largest single category of regular employment for women in the entertainment industry,"[5] and for many young women represented a way out of what was increasingly becoming known as the "pink-collar ghetto of clerical work."[6] The gradual decay of Victorian social restrictions on women's activities outside the home certainly contributed to this shift but, in large part, the increasing acceptability of displayed female sexuality was made possible for potential performers by its promise of independence and economic success. Toni Bentley's characterization of such displays as a "flesh for cash"[7] transaction and her insistence that the act of exposing flesh for financial gain must be viewed as a commercial business transaction situates female bodies both as commodities for cultural consumption and as tools for the success of individual performers engaged in the business of display.[8]

Regardless of occupation, "regular" employment was a relative concept for women at the beginning of the twentieth century. A study of employment figures in Pittsburgh for women in 1907 and 1908 noted that, "Women remained at the lowest levels of "casual laborers," described as "temporarily permanent."[9] For many young female workers, previously held notions of the immorality of staged female display were rendered far more culturally palatable by the promise of monetary rewards, particularly in an economy that consigned them to a tenuously paradoxical position of temporary permanence. According to that same Pittsburgh study, "60 percent of twenty-two thousand women workers aged fourteen to fifty earned less than $7 dollars per week."[10] In a country increasingly oriented toward conspicuous consumption and a cultural atmosphere characterized by expanding permissiveness with respect to commodified images of women, the early twentieth-century reference to the *Follies* as "Life's Shop-Window" suggested more than mere audience voyeurism.[11] For many young girls, show business also offered a peek into a way of life that, in spite of its lingering disrepute, seemed to offer a promise of financial success.

As discussed in chapter 4, the business of female "show" was aided and abetted by the simultaneous rise of the beauty industry. With their commercialized promotion as exemplary beauties, women on the stage achieved status as a kind of aesthetic category and, as Kathy Peiss argues, "Aesthetic categories helped businesses define and build their markets."[12] The stage, far and away the dominant medium of public performance, offered an ideal marketplace for presentations that linked female display with contemporary notions of beauty and lure of personal profit. "The real value of a sexually attractive woman in a world which regards good looks as a commodity depends," according to Angela Carter, "on the degree to which she puts her looks to work for her."[13] Or, in the words of the famous stripteaser Lili St. Cyr, "Sex is a currency. What's the use of being beautiful if you can't profit from it?"[14]

As early as the mid-nineteenth century, "variation in pay" for the women entertainers on the stages of living pictures "was governed by the difference in good looks."[15] While the stage offered some real job advancement based on "looks," appearance also became a criterion by which women were judged hirable from the outset; thus, a particular, commercialized standard of beauty became mandatory as a job requirement and the path to social and professional success. As one 1932 article noted, "The cash customers didn't go to the *Follies* for laughs. They went for legs. And Ziggy knew it. He also knew how to pick girls who were charming and seductive and had that something or other which came over the footlights."[16]

The myth of monetary reward for comeliness was not confined to pay scales directly associated with stage work. Lois Banner contends, "The British

Blondes had turned immorality into glamour when they created the legend that beautiful women on the stage received large sums of money and jewelry from admirers who competed for their attention."[17] Notwithstanding the fact that the average chorus girl of 1910 "at the New York Columbia Theatre earned sixteen dollars weekly,"[18] the stage was seen by an infatuated public as "a world of glamour, where actresses from working-class background achieved fame and fortune, where chorus girls married millionaires and beauty contests gave hope to the ordinary woman that she, too, might be touched by such glamour."[19] "Working-class women in the early twentieth century," according to Susan Estabrook Kennedy, "were more involved in the struggle to leave the working class than in the development of an awareness of themselves as part of it."[20] Such an atmosphere, abetted by the myth of show business success, goes a long way to explain why so many thousands of young women eagerly sought to enter the profession. One need only look to *Cavalcade of Burlesque*, however, to see that the reality of a typical chorus girl's life was hardly a world of glamour:

> Most chorines work a seven-day week. The girls start work in the noon show, go through a matinee and after three hours off finish the evening performance at about 11. During the week there is usually one midnight show. The average show runs about 2 hours and 20 minutes; and this, plus rehearsal time, makes up the chorus girl's week [. . .] the gals usually have to make 27 changes of costume during a day's work—nine changes in each of the three performances.[21]

Working such a grueling schedule, H.M. Alexander notes, "They have about two hours of free time a day to raise all the hell that they're credited with."[22]

Moreover, the odds of getting hired were not favorable, as Ziegfeld remarked: "There were seventeen thousand candidates tried out here last season. Of these I took one hundred. This was a rather large percentage. As a rule, only one in a thousand is taken on."[23] Just as today the young stripper performing at the Miss Exotic World Contest 2002 under the stage name "Lolita" maintained that it was her desire to "be a star" that propelled her to the stage and stripping, in the early twentieth century the lure of a glamorous life compelled countless young women to line up outside theatres for auditions.[24] What they lacked in ability, they more than made up for in ambition. According to one *Saturday Evening Post* article, when Ziegfeld was casting,

> A call would be sent out for girls to appear on the New Amsterdam stage, say about eleven o'clock. Long before that all the streets leading to the New Amsterdam would be blocked with flocks of girls in all sizes, weights, and ages. Shopgirls and home girls, girls from small towns and big towns, chorus girls,

models, girls from burlesque, vaudeville and the movies, debs from Park Avenue homes and hostesses from taxi-dance halls—all the girls who ever worked for him before, and practically all the girls from all the shows then running in New York [. . .] They came in evening gowns and bathing suits, and fur coats and ballet dresses. Every kind of face, leg and head of hair known to anatomy.[25]

While the stage did offer some opportunity for economic gain, female performers' reputation for success grew with wildly disproportionate vigor in the public's imagination compared to the actual money earned by most women in the industry. In spite of journalist J.P. McEvoy's remark in 1932 that, "The story of the girls whom Flo glorified makes Harun-al-Rashid look like a Salvation Army Santa Claus," his later reference to Ziegfeld performers (such as Mae Murray and Martha Mansfield) as "twenty-two-fifty a week chorus girls" offers a less effusive, and more accurate, economic picture.[26] As Mort Minsky confessed, "Although our girls were paid better on the average than most, I do not kid myself that they were becoming wealthy."[27]

By comparison, a female garment worker in the early 1920s whose task was "finishing, buttonhole making and so forth," earned eighteen dollars a week.[28] A sixteen-year old taxi dancer working in a Chicago dance hall in 1926 (with the working strategy that "the first impression a girl has to make is that she is a good girl under hard circumstances") earned approximately thirty dollars a week.[29] In a push to unionize burlesque in 1933, it was discovered that "some chorines were earning $10 to $12 weekly and working seven days a week for 82 hours."[30] In 1934, female workers in the meatpacking industry employed at Swift and Company, earned "twenty two dollars a week, turning out a hundred and forty four packages an hour of bacon."[31] According to a 1946 article in *American Weekly*, Jessie Reed, a performer considered "the absolute top" as a Ziegfeld girl, was paid "$250.00 per week in her final years."[32] But, of course, by Reed's very characterization as the "absolute top," one understands that the majority of performer's earnings ranged somewhere below that amount. Most chorus, parade, and revue girls were not able to join the ranks of the "glorified" Ziegfeld girls. Nevertheless, the prospect of earning twenty-two dollars as a "glamorous" chorus girl or the equivalent as a factory garment worker propelled scores of women out the factory doors and into audition lines.

The principle of display as the means to legendary success was reinforced by popular groups like the Floradora Sextette, a group of female performers in the 1900 Casino Theatre musical comedy *Floradora* known for their good looks, if not their talent, all of whom were believed to have ended up marrying millionaires.[33] They were considered "goddesses, the first of their class to immortalize the chorus girl."[34] Marrying money as an attainable goal for performers and an indicator of personal success for women was also a part of the legend of the Ziegfeld girl, passed on without critical scrutiny by a cooperative press. In 1932, the *Saturday Evening Post* declared, "Glorification by the master showman meant, to a great phalanx of beauties, elevation to theatrical stardom and affluence and, to a great many more, marriage to multi-millionaires. No man in history, in the show business or outside it, ever raised as many girls to success as did Ziegfeld."[35] Even *Follies* star Will Rogers stated (though with his customary qualifying irony): "We have a hard time keeping our girls together, especially on tour. Every time we get to a new town some of them marry millionaires, but in a few weeks they catch up with the show again."[36]

In her analysis of beauty contests, former Miss America Jacque Mercer has also remarked that, contrary to the popular notion among contestants that the pageant will result in showbiz success, most Miss Americas, as well as those involved in the "hundreds of local contests that precede her selection," become "wives and mothers once their reign has ended."[37] Her assessment of the professional success of contestants in the entertainment industry is echoed in a 1970 article, "Miss America: Dreams and Boosters," which points out: "While few winners, even Miss Americas, later achieve real success in show business ('Most of them seem to marry well,' noted an Atlantic City spokesperson), the hope seems to persist that a break is just around the corner." Likewise, in 1951, *Cavalcade of Burlesque* noted that for burlesque performers, "their professional life span is not much more than 10 or a dozen years, after which most of them leave the theatre for domesticity, if, meanwhile, they have not graduated to the next step up to a job as Number Two stripper."[38] Jay Hornick placed an even shorter time limit on the chorine career: "The average life of a chorus girl in burlesque is about five years."[39] To the women who chose such a career path, few options were open to them when their five years were up. As early as 1904, "there were ten thousand unemployed chorus girls in New York City, and the *New York World* that same year gave even a gloomier estimate: for each opening, they contended, sixty thousand women applied."[40]

Increasingly, the boundary between displays of beauty and displays of flesh appeared a semantic one to the performers themselves, in spite of concerted attempts within the industries of beauty contests and striptease to promote themselves as oppositional foils. Irving Zeidman contends that "as the depression deepened, more and more girls turned to burlesque for a living, and the more competitive it got, the more they stripped."[41] Just as Miss Arizona 2002, noted that without the high heels and bikinis there would be no sponsors for the televised Miss America pageant, many female performers came to believe that "there was no answer to the fact that without stripping, there were no audiences, and hence no money."[42] "If a girl is in the chorus," states H.M. Alexander, "she hopes that next year she'll be a stripper. If she's a stripper, she hopes that some day she'll be making top money. If she's at the top, she hopes she'll stay there. Strippers usually know they're not going any place but where they are."[43] By 1953, one stripper interviewed in *Cavalcade of Burlesque* stated that, "Like many of her 'sisters of the flesh,' you pick it up as you go along." Once in show business as a chorus girl, she tried various things, finally getting a chance to strip. She adds, "Pretty soon, I began to realize that I'd probably stay in burlesque, and there's only one way to make money there, so I continued to strip, and here I am."[44]

While female performers successfully negotiated their way around cultural hierarchies of display, the industries promoting such display developed effective marketing strategies, as evidenced by the suppleness of one burlesque company's image policy: "Since, in the final analysis, Columbia's insistence on purity was not a crusade but a financial stratagem and, often enough, a publicity gimmick, there was enough flexibility to dirty a normally clean show if business warranted it."[45] Operating under the same principle at work in the cosmetics business, in which "the exact same product but in a different package," would be marketed to various segments of the public, beauty pageants and strip clubs found that categorization of forms of female entertainment aided in the defining of a specific commercial market.[46] The historical flexibility employed by beauty contests, revues, and striptease in marketing essentially the same sexualized female display as either wholesome or "dirty" (depending upon context and audience make-up), is epitomized in a typical mid-twentieth-century promotional fold-out for the Devani Bernae dancers which advertises the act as presenting a girl who "does a beautiful and graceful strip mid-air, with the trio doing sensational acrobatic tricks. Can be done without stripping for family audiences. For all-male audiences, the girl strips down to pasties or bare breast."[47] As one Minsky stripper phrased it: "If the crowd is cheap, we work cheap. If they're decent, we work refined."[48]

If press agents, often referred to as "tub thumpers," saw interchangeability as an effective marketing tool, they also employed paradox with equal zest.[49] The marketing of performers such as the Devani Bernae dancers as capable of changing, at a moment's notice, from strippers to acrobats according to the context of the venue assured that the promoters had more options when it came to booking acts. Constructing a flexible image, however, took some finesse. As Walter Kerr noted in a 1957 *Herald Tribune* article:

> To make a rather wistful and unconfident guess about the matter, I'd say that we may now have progressed to a point of theatrical sophistication where we want to

be entertained, all right, but where we don't want to catch the entertainers—or the management—flagrantly trading on our perfectly real appetites.

To appear less "flagrant," one of the most successful marketing strategies utilized by entertainments focusing on female display was the presentation of the performers as "All-American working women." Referencing early twentieth-century chorus girls, Lois Banner's comments might as easily be applied to the promotional verbiage used in pageants and strip clubs today: "That the chorus girl was basically a working woman was central to all the publicity about her. The emphasis was intended partly to counter the criticism of her supposedly libertine lifestyle—a charge that might inhibit attendance at her performances. But it also reflected the kind of woman the chorus girl was. All commentaries about her stressed her independence, self-assurance, even toughness."[50]

Whether or not the chorus girl *was* the image she projected, a cultural investment in the "amateur" status of the beauty contestant and the stripper as just a regular working girl (as opposed to a trained, coached, constructed image-maker) emerged as a potent marketing tool. Even at the 1922 Miss America pageant, there were two categories of competition—one for amateurs and one for professionals. The industry presentation of the performers as "normal" girls just trying to advance themselves enabled a gloss of motivational integrity to cover the organizations that promoted such female displays—they were able to present themselves as offering legitimate *opportunities*, paralleling "the cult of the beauty specialist," who promoted a "decent respect for oneself, of optimistic belief in one's heritage of beauty and a desire to come into one's own."[51]

Today, potential contestants are told to look to previous winners who overcame terrible odds to achieve their success: Miss Teen USA 1993, Charlotte Lopez, was a foster child who had lived with six families over thirteen years; Carol Gist, who was born out of wedlock and raised by her mother in Detroit's inner-city, became Miss USA 1990 and first runner-up to Miss Universe; Miss Universe 1970, Marisol Malaret, was orphaned at age ten and raised by an impoverished, elderly aunt.[52] The very real circumstances of these women's lives, and their sincere efforts to overcome obstacles, are not negated by the fact that such circumstances are also utilized as specific marketing tools, just as images of mothers stripping to support their children or pay for their college education abound in movies like *Striptease*, in which the film compels Demi Moore's character time and again to justify her stripping on the basis of her single mother status.

The "end justifies the means" argument has also played a vital role in the defense of beauty contests. In particular, the Miss America Organization

(MAO) has used its status as the largest supplier of scholarships for women in the world as a central marketing strategy, promoting the contestants as young women trying to get ahead, to better their lives and their communities through education. The organization specifically markets its commitment to "education for women" as that which sets them apart from other beauty pageants, as well as all similar events focusing on female display.

Yet education has also traditionally been appropriated as a promotional tool by stripteasers. While some female performers successfully adapted themselves according to assumptions like those of Earl Carroll, who adhered to the "concept that a beautiful girl does not have to know how to do anything except look attractive in as few clothes as possible,"[53] others, not the least of whom was Gypsy Rose Lee, were quick to realize the financial possibilities in capitalizing on a cultural attitude that proposed a "classic paradox: an intellectual strip-teaser."[54] While Gypsy may have been the most famous entertainer performing an ironic comment on social expectations of the intellectual merits of strippers, she was far from alone, as evident in the Minsky brothers' promotion of Eunice Jason: "the new stripper at the Carnival, received her B.A. from NYU last month (majored in sociology). The Minskys proudly consider her the most cultured stripper in burlesque today."[55] "In the so-called good old days, before pretty girls thought it was also necessary to have 'brains,' " complained one disgruntled mid-twentieth-century spectator, "the theatre, and its relatives of the variety stage and silent pictures, was an end in itself."[56] Apparently, in his opinion, by the 1960s: "Bust measurements qualify any blonde, no matter how dumb, to pontificate on international relations, whereas if she hadn't photographed so well, she'd still be working behind a beanery counter."[57] Similar comments have more than once greeted the pronouncements of beauty contestants, who are constantly encouraged to offer opinions on a range of topics for which their experience and education cannot possibly have prepared them to address.

Ironically, the MAO and strippers nationwide, both promoting their educated performers, have become de facto allies (at least in terms of marketing), aligning themselves against public attitudes like those expressed in the following statement from the 1960s: "I have yet to find a female of this generation in show business who does not think she is a minor-league Eleanor Roosevelt. Brains may be alright for someone who looks like Eleanor, but please, not for Marilyn Monroe."[58] Numerous stripper promotional blurbs market the performers as the "All-American girl" either working toward, or the proud recipient of, a degree. The 1955 December issue of *Modern Man*, "the man's picture magazine," features an article titled "Burlesque Intellectual," with an introductory paragraph explicitly marketing Lily Ayers as a beauty with brains:

> There are some strange, astonishing sights backstage at burlesque houses through the nation but none is stranger nor more astonishing than seeing a shapely blonde stripper reading poetry by Edna St. Vincent Millay and T.S. Eliot between the acts. She is luscious and literary-minded Lily Ayers, a burlesque intellectual with a penchant for poetry.[59]

The article offers the explanation that Lily's interest in poetry "began as a publicity lark both for Lily and a club of San Francisco poets. The poets thought Lily at a poetry reading would do the club some good."[60] While the poets packed the house, the return for Lily was somewhat less than satisfactory: "When I finished, the cheapskate poets even made me buy one of their books. Then I learned that they had charged a good, stiff admission price and made a gigantic killing on my appearance."[61] Recognizing the profitability in promoting herself as an anomaly—an intellectual stripteaser—Lily Ayers added an inclination toward poetry to her act, revealing in one poem her own beginnings as a baby beauty contestant:

> When I was just a little babe,
> As cute as I could be,
> They put me in a baby show
> Where everyone could see.
> I was just an innocent little tot,
> But I showed them everything I've got
> And the judge pinned a blue ribbon on me.[62]

Similarly, in a 1958 *New York Mirror* magazine article, "*Look* looks at Dorian Dennis," emphasis is placed on the fact that Dennis "holds a bachelor of science degree from NYU in chemistry."[63] In fact, Dorian Dennis was popularly dubbed "the stripperoo from NYU."[64] *Peep Show Magazine* promoted Lynne O'Neill, "the original garter girl," as a graduate of "Northwestern University with a major in drama."[65] A *Las Vegas Sun* article introduced "Nicole Debeers, 36, who will receive her masters degree in education from UNLV."[66] In the 1980s Brown University student Heidi Mattson marketed herself, in her book of the same name, as the "Ivy League Stripper," and *Playboy* produces an annual edition featuring college co-eds. The promotional hype surrounding Miss America 2003, Erika Harold, who is a Harvard law student, is a direct descendant of such earlier marketing techniques. That same year, a strip club promoter for Cheetah's and the Leopard's Lounge publicized his willingness to pay tuition fees for his performers, as long as they maintain a B average. The promoter said that the offer was meant to "upgrade our talent." A second-year communications major at an un-named university objected—on moral grounds—characterizing the offer as "disgraceful."

The link between educational achievement and show business success, as part of larger campaigns to legitimize female display and align it with upward economic mobility, has served the industry both straightforwardly and as innovative inversion. While some female performers trade on their intellectual attainments—or pretensions—others have exploited the contrived social binary between brains and beauty with equal effectiveness. The *Madison Square Garden Beauty Bulletin* of 1923 (not coincidentally sponsored by a cosmetic cream company) provided some journalistic justification for the *anti*-intellectual approach to show business success. "The Economic Interpretation of Beauty: Why Pulchritude Conquers Where Brains Fail" explored "the current phenomenon of the social ascendancy of the girl of physical beauty over the girl of brains." Sharp stripteasers immediately grasped the potential in capitalizing on such a cultural attitude, and the brainless blonde bombshell was born. "One of the smartest of the dumb-belles," according to Lee Mortimer, "was Sylvia McKaye, a slight blonde, who used to do nude dances. She was introduced thrice nightly as "Miss Unconscious."[67] Evelyn Moriarty, who retired to Hollywood and lived on her "rep and bank account," was another stripper who "billed herself as the 'World's Dumbest Dora.' "[68] The stereotypical dumb blonde and her intellectualized counterpart thus assumed their roles as primary marketing personae for women engaged in the business of female display.

Interestingly, strippers and burlesque queens have had a somewhat easier time negotiating variants of the dumb blonde/literary genius dichotomy. And while it is commonly recognized today that a number of strippers actually do finance their college educations by working in clubs, beauty contestants—whose prize money is often awarded exclusively in the form of scholarships—still struggle with the promotional juxtaposition of sexual display and educational advancement that is an inherent component of the current beauty pageant system. As Miss Arizona 2002 argued:

> I watched the promos, the commercials for the upcoming Saturday night finals, and the image that's the very last scene of the commercial is of a pair of lips, and I said to my traveling companion who was in the room with me at the time, 'Is that all I am? Is a pair of lips and a pair of hips?' Because there's a lot more to me. Under this blonde hair there's actually a brain and all I've seen in the promotional

videos is the women walking in their swimsuits and hugging each other and crying in their evening gowns.

The complaint by Miss Arizona recalls that of Lily Ayers who, almost fifty years earlier, looking back on her time as a showgirl at the Flamingo and Silver Slipper in Las Vegas, admitted that "even the glamour, the pretty clothes and good pay can be boring when all you are is an ornament."[69] Even so, for well over a century there has been no shortage of young women eager to take the places of Ayers and Lawless.

The Floradora Sextette, argues Lois Banner, "embodied a powerful American Cinderella myth—a belief system that was for women the analogue of the 'self-made man' myth for men."[70] It was a belief system predicated on beauty and display as a tool for the average American girl to gain financial independence and cultural admiration, one that became even more appealing during the Great Depression, when girls from rural towns arrived by the thousands in cities, anxious for work. For them, "showbiz" seemed to exemplify what Susan Glenn has characterized as the "two versions" of the Cinderella Myth:

> In one the chorus girl is released from her daily grind into the arms of a rich Prince Charming, or at least someone capable of satisfying her appetite for the finer things. In the other, her salvation is stardom.[71]

"Cinderella," or "Aschenputtel" in the Brothers Grimm's version, "originally designated a lowly, dirty kitchenmaid who must tend to the fireplace ashes."[72] For Cinderella, her way out of the ashes was through her beauty and desirability. "The key word is privilege," states Sara Halprin, "the privilege associated with beauty and not ugliness, the privilege of wealth, comfort, appreciation."[73]

Yet essential to the "Cinderella Myth," and absent from the myth of the self-made man, is the necessity of authentication, of proving oneself to Prince Charming. Only when Cinderella is made beautiful by the fairy godmother—groomed, coifed, bejeweled, and, thus, rendered acceptable for presentation to the Prince—does she have the opportunity to succeed. While the self-made man proves his worth to society at large through actions, usefulness, productivity, and innovation, Cinderella proves herself according to "fit"; the glass slipper symbolizing not only a suitably demure and transparent eroticism, but also her entry into a world of moneyed beauty, Prince Charming's world. That women should strongly desire to "fit" into that world is played out in earlier versions of the Grimm story, such as the Scottish "Rashin Coatie," mentioned as early as 1540, in which the stepmother cuts off the heels and toes of her own daughter's foot, producing a pool of blood and a violent image of mutilated virginity, to ensure that the slipper slides on.[74]

The Cinderella dream of being the chosen one is evident in Miss Ohio's 1969 statement, "Ever since I was four years old [. . .] I wanted to be Miss America. I knew that Bert Parks sang 'Miss America,' and when I would blow out the candles on my cake on my birthday, I always wished that someday he would sing to me."[75] The dream seems impervious to contradiction by even the most vexing social realities: even as she struggled to negotiate the tension between "desiring the recognition of winning the Miss America contest and accepting white standards of beauty" (as noted by Maxine Leeds Craig) Howard University student Mary O'Neal said, "I used to cry when they sang Miss America. I wanted to experience that. I wanted to be a winner. But I didn't want to look like anybody in that pageant. I would love to have had Bert Parks sing to me."[76] While a crooning Bert Parks may not be every woman's image of Prince Charming, he undoubtedly functioned on some level as a surrogate, the representative of those responsible for selecting the chosen one. Just as the Prince—or Flo Ziegfeld—embodied the power to "raise" girls to success, Park's warbling situated a winning contestant as the "ideal." As former Miss USA Emma Knight argues, young female contestants respond less to individual winners than to the iconicity encouraged by pageants: "it wasn't me the fans of Miss USA thought was pretty. What they think is pretty is the banner and the crown."[77] Or, in the words of an eight-year-old pageant parade viewer at Miss America 2002, "well you get to dress in high heels and you get to walk around the stage and everything . . . it's just cool."[78]

As if to corroborate Susan Glenn's "salvation by stardom" version of the myth, Ann-Marie Bivens 1995 pageant manual *101 Secrets to Winning Beauty Pageants* actually contains a subcategory in the chapter "Why Compete?" titled "Stepping into Cinderella's Glass Slippers," which states that "like a modern-day Cinderella story, a major pageant title instantly lifts a girl-next-door from obscurity into the celebrity spotlight."[79] In fact, the ancient tale is woven deeply in the fabric of pageant culture, even to the point of direct identification. A 1996 issue of *Pageantry Magazine* carries typical advertisements for the longstanding, nationally franchised "Cinderella Scholarship Pageants,"[80] founded in 1976 as a "division of International Productions and Publications, Inc."[81] The corporation produces its Cinderella Pageant in four age categories, beginning at age three and ending at seventeen. "With a strong belief that pageants without 'pageantry' are nothing more than contests," the organization "launched its first international finals in Dallas, Texas, at the famous Dallas Apparel Mart with a production budget of over $100,000."[82]

The pageant spared little expense in its effort to capitalize as fully as possible with the Cinderella fantasy. By the 1980s, it had "upgraded its international finals by designing three mammoth 'storybook sets' ":

> The sets included a quaint Cinderella's Village set for the sportswear competition, an elegant Cinderella Ballroom set for partywear and a 30-foot tall Cinderella Castle set for the grand finals.[83]

The influence of the Cinderella myth on the elaborate pageant system constructed by Miss America is equally pervasive, if somewhat less overt. As Roger Simon suggested in a 1976 issue of *TV Guide*: "The 50 pageants that are franchised to the states and are then franchised to the towns by the Miss America Pageant, Inc., are based on a dream. A dream made up not only of soft lights and silk gowns, but a dream made up of the belief that somehow, in some way, this . . . all . . . still . . . matters."[84] The "this" which must still "matter" refers to a lingering cultural suspicion, reinforced in countless ways, that the state of being beautiful ensures happiness and success because beauty causes one to be desirable, thus offering the only chance a woman has of being discovered and selected by her Prince; or, as the 1998 video *The Secret World of Beauty Pageants* phrases it, "elevated out of obscurity." Notwithstanding Simon's dismissive skepticism, belief in the myth remains widespread and enormously powerful. Speaking pseudonymously, former Miss USA "Emma Knight" described it as a cultural inevitability:

> If I could sit down with every young girl in America for the next fifty years, I could tell them what I liked about the pageant, I could tell them what I hated. It wouldn't make any difference. There're always gonna be girls who want to enter the beauty pageant. That's the fantasy: the American Dream.[85]

Knight's assessment was echoed twenty-two years later at the 2002 Miss America Scholarship Pageant by Miss Nebraska 2002: "I've grown up watching Miss America and that's such a dream." Staged rituals of female display that follow "set procedures," whether in the form of beauty contests or striptease, have, according to Lois Banner, "long existed to legitimize the Cinderella mythology for women, to make it seem that beauty is all a woman needs for success and, as a corollary, that beauty ought to be a major pursuit of all women."[86] "What I resent most," said "Emma Knight", "is that a lot of people didn't expect me to live this version of the American Dream myself. I was supposed to live it their way."[87] Knight's conflation of the Cinderella myth (success bestowed for being what you are) and the American Dream (success achieved for doing what you do) provides further evidence of the myth's tenacious ubiquity.

Although the social atmospherics of strip shows and beauty contests have been ideologically constructed to appear profoundly different from one another, the principal impulse for their creations of identity, in terms of both individual participants and the forms themselves, is rooted in monetary exchange, in the business of, as the *New York Times* bluntly phrased it in 2002, "trafficking in pretty women."[88] While the mechanics of particular cash transactions—or their possibility—may be ideologically camouflaged in some way, the reward remains the same. Sarah Banet-Weiser has argued of the Miss America Pageant that, "Ironically, the swimsuit competition serves as a crucial element of the pageant's moral structure, insofar as the emphasis is on the authenticity of this competition, as opposed to, say, bikini contests. In bikini contests, the contestants are competing only for cold 'hard' cash, whereas in the Miss America pageant, the women compete for a more 'refined' kind of cash: an academic scholarship."[89]

Banet-Weiser's ironic distinction between "hard" and "refined" cash highlights the way pageants legitimate their institutional ideologies with semantic sleight-of-hand. The appearance of legitimacy, as noted elsewhere, is critically important to both beauty contests and striptease, yet its parameters are often of little concern to practitioners whose gaze is fixed on more tangible goals. When exotic dancer Bel-Sha-Zaar's dancing was criticized for being less than authentic, she replied: "Is better eat, be commercial" [*sic*].[90] Her honest assessment of the "peel for pay art"[91] as a fictive construct produced for the express purposes of effect and profit is echoed in a statement by a former Miss Nebraska: "Hey, I'm in this to win money." "Gibby," the manager of a Pittsburgh strip club called *The Palace*, succinctly declared in 1977: "Money, that's all they're interested in. They're not going to stand out there naked for nothing."[92] It is doubtful that partisans of Miss America would bestow the same moral imprimatur on "Jezebel" (a stripper at Charlie's bikini club in Adelanto, California), as that reserved for Laura Lawless, Miss Arizona 2002, despite the fact that "Jezebel" is funding her Bachelor of Arts degree with the money she makes dancing. And Lawless's own argument for participation in the pageant system is notable for its hard-headed lack of any trace of moralistic motivation:

> I think of Winston Churchill when he said "Democracy is the worst form of government, except for all the others," well, when you think about pageants and scholarship programs, this is the worst way to get scholarship money except for all the other ways that are out there and I wasn't really eligible for a lot of others. So

unless they design one for educationally gifted, law aspiring children of single parents who happen to be white and not from a disadvantaged background, and just on the middle income median line, then I'm not going to be able to furnish the income for my education.

For Ms. Lawless, the pageant was a success: as one of the top fifteen contestants at Miss America 2002, she earned an extra five thousand dollars toward her tuition, over and above the money previously awarded to her at the local, state, and national levels of the competition. For her, highbrow/lowbrow distinctions between "hard" and "refined" cash meant less than pursuit of a personal goal, which required a realistic, not an ideological, assessment of the performance system in which she found herself.

Realistic assessment discloses yet another economic parallel between strippers and beauty contestants. In the mid-twentieth century, the columnist Bill Slocum wrote: "there are only 15 strippers making real, good money. All the girls hope to be another Lili St. Cyr."[93] In spite of the fact that real financial gains accrue to some beauty contestants, "every year at least 7,500 beauty pageants are franchised by either the Miss America Scholarship program or the Miss USA pageant."[94] The MAO, in promotional materials in 2002, stated that "more than twelve thousand women participate each year in the local and state events."[95] Many contestants expend far more capital on fees, costumes and travel than they ultimately recoup in earnings. Evening gown costs alone can range from "$1,500 to $5,000."[96] Even relatively successful contestants feel the pinch. In spite of the thirty five thousand dollars she collected in scholarship money, Laura Lawless admits:

I am in debt. I am on public assistance. I actually became Medicaid dependent. We are not provided with health insurance in our state pageant. There's radically different levels of pay that states get. And Miss Arizona is really to me like being in the peace corps for the year. Because you're doing a year of service for virtually no money. I don't even get out of pocket expenses for some things. I don't get my gas money to travel from one state to the other, I certainly don't get a car, I don't get an apartment paid for, don't get health insurance, I'm not in school full time so I don't qualify for the reduced cost health insurance from the school, so I had to lose that. It's a year of being in the trenches doing volunteer work.

Just as few strippers achieve the success of a Lili St. Cyr, few beauty pageant contestants enjoy careers that rival that of former beauty queen Cybil Shepard. Slocum's assertion that "stripping supplies jobs for more women than anything else in the night club business" is precisely the same rhetorical argument as that of the MAO, which insists that it provides more scholarships for women worldwide than any other organization. A Miss New Hampshire beauty contestant, emphatic that her winnings be recorded in specific detail, stated: "the more preliminaries you do, the more money you get; winning Miss Derry [a qualifying competition] paid for my textbooks for the year [eight hundred dollars]. My winnings paid for at least a quarter of my college."[97] In three years, without being named Miss New Hampshire or appearing on any national stage, she claimed to have earned at least fifteen thousand dollars toward her education. But she provided no details of her expenses over that time. As Dawn Perlmutter insists, "One needs to question the amount of money women spend on all the contests they have to win to get to the Miss America Pageant and weigh that against the amount of funding given out."[98] Given the sheer numbers of pageant aspirants at all levels, the ratio of participants to big money makers must be taken into consideration.

While the MAO is quick to point out that it does not charge an entry fee, the vast majority of pageants across the country do so, to the tune of over one hundred dollars per entry on average. The Miss Mountain State Pageant in West Virginia asks one hundred and fifty dollars (with a discount for siblings who compete together);[99] and the Miss Georgia Forestry pageant demands one hundred and seventy five dollars plus a "mandatory" twenty dollar T-shirt fee (in addition to these fees, the contestants are required to sell four "good luck" ads at twenty-five dollars apiece[100]). The Majestic Beauty Pageants invite contestants to purchase a "Grand Supreme Package" for two hundred and ninety five dollars—with an additional twenty-five dollars for consideration in each of several "optional" categories of competition, such as "Best Personality, Best Dressed, and Overall Most Beautiful."[101] The Miss Baltimore Teen All-American Pageant, which emphasizes its evening gown competition as promoting "Elegance, Fashion, and a Sence [sic] of class," charges a fee of three hundred and twenty-five dollars plus an additional twenty-five dollar "application" fee.[102] Additional, often hefty, fees are disbursed to pageant coaches, wardrobe advisors, and choreographers. One particular coaching operation offers a range of services including a one-day seminar—the "Princess Training Package"—at a cost of one hundred forty dollars per person. At a minimum class size of fifteen, the package consists of "Continental Breakfast, Her Heighness [sic] Training Manual, Her Heighness [sic] 'Pretty In Pink' T-Shirt, a Framed Training Certificate, Make-up *or* Bath & Body Products, and a $20.00 gift certificate (good for any product on the organization's logo page)."[103]

In addition to requiring substantial direct outlays, the pageant industry maintains a long tradition of unsalaried employment of its contestants in the production of the pageant itself. Candidates have frequently assumed mandatory responsibility for the work of gathering a minimum number of paying customers, or the selling of ad space in programs and other media. As Maxine Leeds Craig found during her research for *Ain't I a Beauty Queen: Black Women, Beauty, and the Politics of Race*, the pageant-sponsoring African-American newspaper *The Oakland Western American*, trumpeting "the noble rhetoric of racial pride to generate interest in the competition"[104] of 1927, blatantly manipulated its contestants to ensure its own financial profit:

> The winner of the popularity contest would be the young lady who could get her supporters to buy the greatest number of votes. Two dollars and fifty cents bought three hundred votes and a year's subscription to the *Western American*; nine dollars procured nine hundred votes and a four-year subscription.[105]

The charging of fees for participation in certain competitive events is a common fundraising practice among nonprofit organizations, which include many of the pageant-sponsors. Yet access to the spaces designated for female display seems to come only at a price, irrespective of the presenter's corporate status. Profit-driven strip clubs do precisely the same thing. In 1991, Lily Burana paid a stage fee of "twelve dollars for the day shift, seventeen for the night [. . .] payable at the beginning of the month when you pick up your schedule, and the fees are nonrefundable. If you cancel your shift, you don't get the money back."[106] Dancers at Charlies in California pay fifteen dollars per shift for the use of the stage, and at many clubs dancers must also tip the deejays and the bouncers on a regular basis. Burana states, "the fees serve no clear purpose—all we know is that we have to pay them."[107] Perhaps one "purpose" shared by both beauty contests and strip clubs is the continued reinforcement of the notion that the participants owe financial and symbolic fealty to the organizations for the sanctioned space in which they present their displays.

Miss Maine 2002 admits, "I'm going to walk away in debt." She adds, "I know the larger states do have sponsors, but where I'm from, Maine, I had to go out and find my own sponsors. I do receive twenty-one hundred as the state winner, but that doesn't go very far when you're talking about extravagant evening gowns and talent costumes so . . . everything does add up." Even though the debt she accrues essentially renders moot any scholarship award she wins, the money she, and her parents, expend in order for her to compete and earn the pageant title "is well worth it. I couldn't even put a price on this. This is definitely priceless." For Miss Maine, the willingness of her parents to fund her preparations to compete enabled her to hire additional coaches and designers:

> I actually did get a coach, I visited a few times in New Jersey, my coach does live down here, I took the train down. And I have a designer in Rhode Island, and

I have a choreographer in New York City. This was something my parents made available to me. This was something I had to do for myself and I talked it over with my family, and I knew that this was something we could do if we really sat down and budgeted everything because it does get expensive.

Mary Morin, Miss New Hampshire 2002, considers herself lucky to be competing in one of the more heavily sponsored states: "we are fortunate in New Hampshire. I had seven-thousand dollars for wardrobe plus about a thousand from Miss America, so I spent very little out of my own pocket that I saved through working."[108] A previous Miss New Hampshire, Tami Jean Brisebois (Miss New Hampshire 1985), saw the system differently, confessing, "It seems like a funny kind of game to me—to go into debt for the sake of earning scholarship money."[109] As Miss Arizona 2002 points out, there is certainly the potential for inequities within the pageant system:

> If you're from one of the states that has an additional wardrobe allowance of ten thousand dollars or great donations, then you're going to be on a different playing field when you get here than if you're the person who's trying to get everything that they need for three weeks plus a year's worth of appearance clothes, business suits for the year, on eleven hundred dollars. You know, it's the difference between shopping at Target and shopping at designers. We don't have the luxury of doing that.

In the opinion of another contestant, pageants "offer lots of promises. But everyone really needs to read the fine print. If you are only after the scholarship money, you really won't even come out even."[110] Additionally, because contestants are technically "volunteering" their time as state representatives, they are unable to deduct the costs of their preparations, leaving them without the compensating satisfaction available to stripper Lily Burana, who, after spending nine hundred dollars on costumes, concluded: "It takes a lot of money to look this cheap. Not to worry [. . .] costumes are tax deductible."[111] Nonetheless, contestants like Miss Maine hold onto the hope they will emerge with a win that somehow justifies the expense: "I've worked so very hard and this would be the time to show that everything is paying off."

Ensuring that the work "pays off," financially as well as figuratively, has always been a fundamental concern for female performers engaged in display. Ann Corio, in her salad days in the burlesque business, asked a theatre manager in Cleveland, Ohio, for a salary of five hundred dollars a week. When he balked at that amount, Corio instructed her personal manager to negotiate a percentage of the take at the door instead of a fixed salary, then proceeded to hire someone to stand at the door and count every ticket sold, to prevent any "misunderstandings." At the end of the week, Corio had earned ten thousand dollars.[112] The always-inventive performer Rita Atlanta, mentioned earlier as the innovator of the onstage champagne glass bathing act, incorporated and sold pieces of herself on the stock exchange. At the end of her act, Rita would announce to the audience that anyone who wished could go to the "Lichtenstein Stock Exchange" and ask for a "few shares of Rita Atlanta prfd." [preferred].[113] David Scott has argued "the strip joint is clearly an erotic domain for most of the audience," but these performer strategies make it clear that, for the stripper, as for the beauty contestant, the stage is "a place of work."[114] "To the girls," wrote Mort Minsky in *Minsky's Burlesque*, "it was all business. It was not a question of holding back on grounds of modesty. It was how to get the biggest hand and, of course, the biggest paycheck."[115]

Though major stars like Rita Atlanta, Ann Corio, and earlier headliners such as the Floradora Sextette found profitable and imaginative ways to market themselves, most performers engaged in displays of constructed femininity struggle to find steady income and make a livable wage. Dixie Evans, whose burlesque act played upon her resemblance to Marilyn Monroe, points to the inclusion of "amateur nights" at clubs for putting professionals out of work:

> Then one day you go to the theatre and there's a big sign out front, "Amateur Night." . . . Oh, oh . . . Now here's a bunch of real young gorgeous girls backstage. [. . .] They're really movin' and shakin' and the bosses are checking us out and saying, "Look at these real young beautiful girls . . . 19, 20." You know. "Well, we gave them 75 dollars a week." It happened all the time.[116]

"Most strippers start out as go-go girls" (the equivalent of today's bikini club girls), remarked 1970s strip club manager "Gibby," "then graduate to the bigger pay of stripping."[117] But in the business of female display, the equivalent of Ziegfeld's "twenty-two-fifty a week" chorus girl of the 1920s had only managed to garner a ten dollar wage increase by the year 1952: Virginia Kinn is said to have earned "32.50" a week as an "exotic dancer."[118] By 1962, theatrical booking agents were complaining that they were unable to convince exotic dancers such as "Sarovya" to leave their jobs in New York to accept temporary work out of town. John Leslie, a personal manager, remarked in a letter to Paul Jordan, a prominent theatrical agent of the mid-twentieth century, that he "tried to get another one yesterday who was highly recommended [but] she has a steady three-day week-end that pays her 150.00 close to New York—on L.I."[119]

The business of "bookings," where a centrally located office coordinates and matches performers with events, is commonplace in many theatrical entertainments even today (although webpages, such as that of Abbie Rabine, Miss Massachusetts 2001, are quickly becoming the first point of contact between a performer and a hiring venue).[120] The large national beauty pageants also operate as booking agents for their winning contestants, most often scheduling them as motivational speakers or ribbon cutters for civic events. According to a *New York Times* article, "The corporation [Miss Universe Inc.] charges a fee for every appearance by Miss USA—and by Miss Universe and the nearly 100 winners of national pageants that compete in the Miss Universe Pageant."[121] As Miss South Dakota 2002, Vanessa Shortbull, explained, "we have a booking agent who books appearances for us and we get appearance fees which goes [sic] back partially to the organization, but we get paid. And we can do as much as we want or as little as we want." Shortbull's autonomy as a reigning pageant queen was emphatically not a feature of former Miss USA, "Emma Knight's" experience, however: "The minute you're crowned" she said, "you become their property and subject to whatever they tell you."[122] According to Knight,

> You immediately start making personal appearances. The Jaycees or the chamber of commerce says: "I want to book Miss USA for our Christmas Day parade." They pay, whatever it is, seven hundred fifty dollars a day, first-class air fare, round trip, expenses, so forth. If the United Fund calls and wants me to give a five-minute pitch on queens at luncheon, they still have to pay a fee. Doesn't matter that it's charity. It's one hundred percent to Miss Universe, Incorporated. You get your salary. That's your prize money for the year. I got fifteen thousand dollars, which is all taxed in New York. Maybe out of a check of three thousand dollars, I'd get fifteen hundred dollars.[123]

"After six weeks, according to Kellye Cash, Miss America 1987, "your eyes are opened. You realize, 'Hey, this is a job. A seven-day-a-week, 12-hour-a-day job.' "[124] As *The Secret World of Beauty Pageants* explains, "the women are really applying for a job to promote the sponsors for a year." Not all the employees find the arrangements salutary. Miss USA 1990, Carole Gist, filed an eighteen million dollar lawsuit against the Miss Universe Organization citing "unfair labor practices." According to the suit, Gist stated "she had to work seven days a week, with no overtime or holiday pay, and that she did not receive all the prizes she was promised."[125] Gist further complained that she had not even been reimbursed for such necessities as pantyhose and makeup used at scheduled public appearances. Miss USA 1988, Carole Gibbs, was said to have remarked of the lawsuit, "She's not overreacting and it's not an isolated incident."[126]

When Miss Ohio 1969, Kathy Baumann, failed to achieve her "dream" of having Bert Parks sing to her (she finished as first runner-up), she nonetheless "was considering finding a booking agent." "I had hoped to fill in on more appearances than I was able to," Kathy told an interviewer, but "it just didn't work out that way."[127] In order for the booking agent to get an engagement contract for the performer, one crucial component of the negotiation had to be in place—the buyer's interest. As Kathy Baumann soon learned, being a Miss America runner-up carried little marketing cache in the real business of entertainment. As one former state title holder, Sharon Singstock, Miss Wisconsin of 1965, remarked with an air of practical cynicism: "I used the pageant, and it used me. I got to travel. I went on the Miss America-Pepsi-Cola tour of Vietnam. But you learn how to use it. Sometimes I put it on resumes and sometimes I don't. Some doors it opens and some people it offends. You just have to know which is which."[128]

Historically, the lower echelons of the stripping business have been no more lucrative than the also-ran ranks of the pageant business. On March 25, 1962, Paul Jordan booked three exotic dancers into the Lebanon (ME) Elks Lodge for a 4:30 p.m. show. The take was two hundred dollars for all three dancers. After Jordan's fee was deducted (the usual agent fee is 10 percent), each female performer would have earned in the neighborhood of sixty dollars. That same year, on March 28, the Maine Plumbing and Heating Salesman's Association hired three exotic dancers for the apparently standard fee of two hundred dollars, but gave them free food as a bonus. According to Paul Jordan's bookkeeping records for the year 1969, fees listed for now-legendary female performers ranged from $1,607 for Tempest Storm to $850 for Irma the Body and $321.42 for Lola Montez, to lesser amounts for the lesser known commodities such as Raven Blue at $214.28 and Sugar Sweet at $28.56.[129] While it is unclear from the records exactly what was being recorded—income for the individual performers or Jordan's yearly percentage of the take—what is evident, even by 1960s standards, is that stars like Tempest Storm fell far short of fulfilling the Floradora myth of millions. Additionally, while it has tended to get lost in the haze of history, it is worth remembering that the Floradora performers did not earn their millions, but married them.

In 1974, the Portland, Maine Elks Club paid three hundred and thirty dollars for three dancers. In a negligible improvement after six inflationary years, when the Maine Plumbing, Heating, and Air-Conditioning Show took place on April 10, 1980, three "exotics" were paid a total of three hundred and seventy-five dollars (minus the agent percentage) for their 7:30 p.m. show.[130] For some performers, bookings like this served as a way to keep work-ing, to stay afloat, even if the actual income received for the effort amounted to little or nothing. In a December 14, 1976, letter of intent-to-hire from

Michael G. Hayashi to her personal manager Leo Grund, Darlene Prescott (the "Pocket Size Venus") was hired to perform ("topless in some numbers but NEVER bottomless"—emphasis Mr. Hayashi's) in Japan at the redundantly named "Green Green Hotel" as the "American star." For this engagement, Prescott would have a ten-day rehearsal period with "a room and three meals a day but no salary."[131] One assumes that she was paid for her actual performances, but the books provide no evidence of such remuneration.

The income earned by strippers who worked in clubs often closely resembled that of itinerants who operated through booking agent. According to Lily Burana, "there are two classes of stripper—the house dancer and the feature entertainer. House dancers (or house girls) typically work in one club for a six-to eight-hour shift. Some clubs pay house dancers a nominal hourly wage; however, most dancers are treated like independent contractors and work only for tips."[132] While occasional strippers such as Cara Lott (according to a 1987 letter from her agent to Paul Jordan) might earn as much as two thousand dollars at a venue like Show World in New York,[133] club manager "Gibby" points out that a stripper's expenses must to be taken into consideration when figuring out her income: "her agent gets 10 percent, she's got to pay for transportation, gowns, music, food. She ends up taking home about $200 a week."[134] Riki Harte, interviewed by *The Las Vegas Sun* in 1977, discovered that although "top professional strippers may earn close to $1,000 a week," many "take home only $300."[135] Even "Gibby's" more generous estimate that the "average girl makes $500 a week" is tempered by his addendum explaining that such compensation comes after "working thirty shows."[136] Lily Burana's winnings for first runner-up and Best of Show in the Miss Topless Wyoming contest were "two honkin' big trophies, a half-dozen roses, and $225—two hundred for first runner-up and twenty-five for Best of Show."[137] In Burana's memoir *Strip City*, a colleague named Scarlett, who worked from 1975 to 1986, recalled of her employers that "they used to pay seventy-five dollars a shift."[138] Yet, in the end, she confesses, "I didn't have anything. I didn't travel anywhere. I didn't have any jewelry. I made a thousand dollars a week, my rent was only two hundred a month, and when I finally got out, I had eight thousand dollars in credit card debt."[139]

Even today, a house dancer who moves up to feature status, booking into clubs for limited engagements rather than staying put in one location, has the potential to earn more money. But as Burana points out, "her initial investment in costumes, props, and merchandise is much greater."[140] Considerable numbers of strippers, like many beauty contestants, have short professional lifespans. Many retire after years of earning little more than enough to get by in rent, food, and costumes, perhaps with an education along the way, and maybe even health insurance (although as Laura Lawless pointed out, even winning the title of Miss Arizona did not guarantee having medical coverage). Very few make significant amounts of money and even fewer enjoy what, by society's standards, might be considered substantial careers. In Jim Rattray's profile article "Playpen," the "Texas Playmate" Dior Angel, when asked "why so many strippers stay in the profession," succinctly observed: "There's no market for secondhand G-strings."[141] This assessment was also expressed (somewhat more sentimentally) by Brook Lee, Miss Universe 1997, who tearfully remarked in an interview toward the end of her reign that the "charity of choice for the outgoing Miss Universe would be creating a halfway house for beauty queens on their way out."[142]

Processions of half-dressed and undressed women assembled and presented for purposes of commercially qualitative judgment and vicarious eroticism offer an inescapably consumerist experience. Thus, the stage on which exotic dancers and the beauty contestants perform is at once a frame for social discourse on composed and imposed images of women, and a marketplace devoted to the sale of those images. But the images themselves are never the sole, or in many cases even the primary, product up for sale. At strip clubs, real profits are generated not by the dancers, but by the sales of alcohol that their performances are carefully designed to encourage. In the world of pageants, profitability is possible only because of corporate sponsorship. Mr. Guy, a successful coach with the Miss Texas USA pageant, notes that, ideological aims aside, "The sponsors want someone who can sell their product, and the judges want someone who can sell the sponsor's product."[143] In addition to its iconic cultural impact, the pageant business has traditionally served as a potent advertising medium for American businesses large and small. "Companies and corporations that provide the necessary sponsorship for needed elements such as televisual production costs, the rental of Convention Hall, and judge's fees," according to Sarah Banet-Weiser, "are well-established, reputable organizations such as Clairol, Chevrolet, and Cheer."[144] Their investment, far from being altruistic or ideological in any way, carries with it contractual expectations and responsibilities meant to create the strongest possible link between the beauty queen's wholesome, attractive image and the corporations' products and services. *The New York Daily News* described one version of this relationship in 1965:

> She [Miss America] will tour the country as spokeswoman for such gigantic business corporations as Toni, Oldsmobile, Pepsi Cola and the textile firm of Bancroft and Sons. According to a recent survey of the "Miss America" setup made by the Associated Press, these companies underwrite an annual budget of $500,000

spent by the New Jersey-chartered non-profit corporation which conducts the national pageant.[145]

Contestants may not merely be required to participate in advertising campaigns for sponsors, but to become consumers of the sponsors' products themselves. In the early days of the Miss Universe pageant, every "U.S. entrant—33,000 in 42 states—was required to purchase a Catalina [swim]suit."[146] The privileges of sponsorship include access even to the performance event. At the Mrs. America 2002 pageant, the sponsor Carol Wior and her patented "Slimsuit" were prominently marketed as part of the pageant itself. The "Slimsuit," which "guarantees an inch or more off the waist and stomach, and comes with a tape measure so the customer can see the measurable difference," was modeled by contestants during the telecast in an infomercial format.[147] Arrangements like these did not appear with the television age, however. From its inception, long before concepts such as the "civic platform" and the "role model" entered pageant discourse, the Miss America Pageant was conceived as an openly commercial venture specifically designed to extend the Atlantic City tourist season. To this day, Miss America employs its contestants as representatives of that city's recreation industry.

Even at the level of local pageant sponsorship, businesses that sign on "want to be sure that the person crowned queen will reciprocate by advertising for them in the community."[148] As a 1970 *New York Times* article noted:

> The Miss America "farm system"—disposing of millions of dollars each year and drawing on some 7,000 girls whose dreams of a show business career will almost surely never come true but who may win a college scholarship or a successful husband—has become a national industry, perhaps the biggest fount of small town boosterism in the land.[149]

Unquestionably, "small town boosterism" still attracts commercial support in states such as New Hampshire, where sponsors of the Miss New Hampshire 1999 pageant were announced at regular intervals throughout the evening's competition, simultaneously enlisting new customers and promoting the civic-mindedness of the business and its proprietors. According to *The New York Times*,

> It is largely on the strength of the Miss America image—the girl next door sponsored by the druggist down the street—that local pageants have quietly grown to the point that their costs this year [1970] will total over 26 million, with a promotional spin-off that will run into millions more [. . .] Despite costs, most of the pageants—all of them non-profit—are expected to earn enough from ticket

sales to bolster local civic projects, a Jaycee park, for example. Increasingly, however, some of the excess is simply plowed back into the business in an effort to make next year's pageant more elaborate.[150]

Aiding and encouraging the style of local pageants, the previously mentioned Cinderella Pageant not only promotes itself as a platform for the self-improving contestant, but also markets its pageant-producing kit, "the most complete pageant staging kit in the industry, making the pageant an excellent fundraising project for civic and service organizations."[151] "The staging kit included in-depth instructional materials," according to the Cinderella webpage, and contains "the pageant's own line of custom trophies, crowns and banners, 4-color entry blanks, program book covers and posters which standardized preliminary events across the nation."[152] Just as Jane Bebita, 1998 Director of Personal Appearances for the Miss Universe Pageant, openly acknowledged, "We're obviously a for-profit company and we're in this to make it bigger and better," individual and franchised pageants nationwide, no matter their promotional rhetoric (i.e., giving women opportunities) never lose sight that they are in the pageant *business*.[153] A 1965 *New York Daily News* article argued the same point:

> What is behind such a pageant as Miss America? Big business, money, publicity— that's what. Despite the hullabaloo of the stage show, the surface varnish of devotion to education, art and high ideals, it should be remembered that this, and all other such spectacles, are basically commercial enterprises.[154]

Since its television debut in 1954, when 75 percent of American households watched Bert Parks crown Lee Meriweather, the Miss America Pageant's commercial fortunes have been irremediably dependent on ratings and revenue generated by its single September broadcast.[155] As long as ratings remained high, this dependency produced little discomfort. But the ratings have not cooperated. In the twenty years from 1954 to 1974, they dropped by more than half, to about 30 percent. Ten years later, they were down to 20 percent, and they have continued to decline.[156] The 2003 pageant produced a new record low, a fractional whisper compared to Miss America's former numbers.

Since other, less ideologically aggressive televised beauty pageants (Miss Universe, Miss USA, etc.) have maintained considerably healthier ratings profiles, it's tempting to blame Miss America's troubles on the disconnection between its rhetoric and its actuality, which has attracted accusations of hypocrisy, irrelevance, and exploitation since at least the 1960s. Whatever the reason, however, the result of the pageant's decreasing power to attract consumers has effectively transferred much of its governing authority from the organization's nominal directorate to the network executives who oversee its broadcast. In recent years particularly, their influence has produced significant alterations of the event itself.

At the 2002 Miss America pageant, in an attempt to address lingering issues of social relevance and the perceived demands of a televisual culture, the program's executive producer, Bob Bain, specifically cited the network's desire to develop a wider audience for its commercial sponsors as a primary reason for changes in the competition's format. The swimsuit and evening gown segments swapped positions, a move that allowed more contestants (15) to appear in swimsuits in a more prominent portion of the evening's lineup.[157] Encouraged by the success of programs like *American Idol* and *Survivor*, the production staff added an online audience participation component, extended the onstage quiz portion, and allowed the 46 non-finalists to cast a vote worth 10 percent of the final score. Miss South Dakota, Vanessa Shortbull, viewed the changes as unfortunate, but unavoidable:

> We heard from the production staff that when they were watching the ratings that the places where the ratings actually dropped were during talent and during the interview portion of it. People really, honestly, when they watch this program on television, really don't want to hear what we actually have to say, they don't. They want to be entertained.

Unfortunately for Miss America, these alterations did not result in higher ratings. Early in 2004, the Associated Press reported that ABC, the pageant's presenting network, planned to cut the broadcast time of the 2004 pageant from three hours to two, and was considering the elimination not only of the entire talent competition, but also of any mention of the contestants' cherished civic "platforms."[158] In late July, 2004, it was announced that the talent portion (which once counted for 40 percent of the total score) would remain in the preliminaries, but would be reduced to a montage for the two-hour televised event. In a head to head event, only two contestants would be allowed to perform talent before the TV audience. In spite of such efforts to modernize the pageant format, the 2004 competition produced the lowest ratings in the program's history, with 500,000 fewer viewers tuning in than the year before. Following the 2004 competition, ABC declined to renew its contract as the Pageant's presenter. As this book goes into press, the Pageant has yet to be picked up for broadcast by any other network.

Even as the MAO struggles with the complex negotiations required to preserve its production's financial viability for sponsors, it continues, as Sarah

Banet-Weiser points out, to work toward "obscuring the commercial structure of the pageant."[159] This obscurantism most often takes the form of announced support for the organization's nominal goal—the raising of scholarship money for its contestants. The tactic appeared in exemplary fashion in 2002, when the pageant, not without controversy, unveiled the Miss America Slot Machine. The designer of the machine, Jerry Seelig, of AC Coin & Slot, explained how it operated:

> Well, it's a slot machine that you put your money in, you pull the handle and if you get lucky you get a special bonus symbol that will activate the Miss America bonus [. . .] there's six contestants lined up. Each one of them is worth different coin amounts and as the reels spin they line up, and when they match you win money.[160]

Getting "lucky," to borrow Mr. Seelig's terminology, meant successfully manipulating the Miss America icon's body parts, an objectifying technique borrowed from the successful world of advertising female images. According to a study on the marketing of images of gender such techniques are "analogous to striptease in this sense, as the exposure of successive body parts distances the erotogenic object, making it untouchable so as to tantalize the drive to look."[161] Or, in this case, the drive to spend hundreds of nickels trying to line up the female body parts. Some members of the press, as well as Miss America contestants and their supporters, balked at the blatant link to gambling, but former Miss America Heather French argued that the MAO image was not tarnished because the money earned from the machines (minus a percentage taken by Harrah's Casino), would assist the contestants in fulfilling their educational goals.[162] According to a spokesman for Harrah's, "The money generated could be in excess of millions of dollars. Over the years, and time will tell, obviously, when the machines start to move to other properties and more people have an opportunity to play those machines, that money could double, triple, quadruple."[163] Although the MAO has calculatedly situated itself as a nonprofit corporation motivated by civic and educational altruism, its dependence on symbiotic relationships with sponsors and on financial arrangements like those established with Harrah's Casino and the Miss America slot machine have done little but complicate the organization's efforts to regain its former popularity. Much of this failure can be traced to the mutual antagonism of impulses within the organization itself, which has never satisfactorily reconciled its contradictory missions: to succeed in the commercialized business of female display while simultaneously veiling its actual agenda in self-ennobling rhetoric and a veneer of moral uplift.

According to *The Secret World of Beauty Pageants* (1998), "3 million women compete annually in America alone" and the beauty pageant industry grosses "5 billion dollars a year." Clearly, while individual participants may incur debt and go on government assistance in order to compete, for the pageant industry at large the payoff is more than satisfactory. Precisely the same condition exists in the world of the stripper. Just as sponsoring groups and franchise owners are the true financial winners of beauty pageants, strip clubs (more popularly known these days as "Gentlemen's Clubs") earn millions of dollars for their owners. That the industries are the actual recipients of any large amounts of money to be made is a fact often lost in the murky world of statistics. Yet, "according to *Stripper Magazine*, a New York publication, there may be as many as 3,000 strip clubs in the United States and Canada. The average audience on any given day may be conservatively estimated to be about 200 (coming and going). That translates into over 600,000 viewers per night, over 3.5 million every week."[164] If each of these customers spends just $30.00 (an extremely conservative sum), the *weekly* take at North American strip clubs rises to over 100 million dollars. Meanwhile, at bikini clubs like Charlie's in California, dancers work only for tips, not a salary, and are required to pay a "stage fee" each night they perform. Countless beauty contestants pay large fees and solicit sponsors for program ads in order to be allowed to compete. The profits achieved by beauty contestants and strippers in their quest for the Cinderella dream are miniscule compared with the profits made by the organizations that promote and sponsor their performances.

In the business of staged female display, beauty and desirability are synonymous, and Rebecca Schneider has written that desire is a commodity that must be continuously re-circulated to stay in the market.[165] Similarly, the Cinderella Myth declares that beauty is a requirement for desirability, and desirability, continuously re-circulated, is the way to success in a gender economy. Nancy Etcoff rightly argues that the pursuit of beauty is not, in and of itself, the issue, but rather asks the more pointed question: "Isn't the problem that women often lack the opportunity to cultivate their other assets, not that they can cultivate beauty?"[166] The description of early twentieth-century female workers as "temporarily permanent" serves equally well for strippers and beauty contestants, who respond by the thousands to a cultural myth of Cinderella success based on beauty and desirability, committing themselves to the acquisition of characteristics that in our current cultural landscape are inseparable from youth, and to an economic environment that insists that the possession of those characteristics will increase the odds of career success.

One pre-teen pageant contestant, interviewed on the Atlantic City boardwalk as she waited for the Miss America parade to commence, likened the pageant experience to suspension in a permanent childhood—a female version of Peter Pan's "I won't grow up":

> Like every girl's dream who does pageants, the rush of just being here, seeing all the girls and seeing how their family supports them, it's something that even though I think it's something I might outgrow, I hope I don't because I want to do it forever. It's just something . . . you don't want to grow old, I don't want to grow old enough that I can't do pageants.[167]

The young contestant's friends who surrounded her, wearing the crowns and sashes that pronounced them winners, solemnly nodded in agreement. The image of the beauty queen suspended in time, forever young and lovely, is simply another version of the "temporarily permanent." If, as Lois Banner has argued, a large proportion of working-class women at the turn of the century "found their values within the commercial pleasure culture,"[168] they also found their *value* (their "shelf-life," as one pageant executive phrased it) presented in the performances on popular stages.[169] "Girls are a commodity the same as bananas, pork chops, or a lot in a suburban development," said Earl Carroll. "They are the most fundamental of all commodities."[170]

6. Naked Politics: Regulating and Legislating Female Display ᴐ·

Legal rules—like other cultural mechanisms—encode the female body with meanings.

Johnson, *The Feminist Difference*[1]

I nstitutional rules governing the behavior of female performers, onstage and off, are readily found in beauty contests, revues, burlesque houses, and strip clubs. Early on in the business of entertainments with a particular focus on women's bodies, elaborate rules (both established and unspoken) controlled female display even as they exploited the very notion of such surveillance. Just as a "sensational march through the streets became a commonplace adjunct to model artists' arrests,"[2] ensuring a big crowd in the house the following evening, the years following the 1893 Expo saw "Coney Island sideshow operators [going] out of their way to have their dancers arrested. The resultant publicity guaranteed ticket sales."[3] Nineteenth-century theatrical developments characterized by Olive Logan as the "leg business" had, in fact, become in many ways the thing she had warned against—a business in which women onstage wore as little "as the law would permit."[4]

"Conditions of embodiment," notes Kathy Davis, "are organized by systemic patterns of domination and subordination, making it impossible to grasp individual body practices, body regimes and discourses about the body without taking power into account."[5] Davis's patterns of power account for the complex tension between acceptable display and unacceptable spectacle that constitutes the subtext of a broadly understood cultural demand that all female performance be held to certain "standards." These standards, however rigid they may appear at any given moment, have historically been neither fixed nor stable, but rather subject to revision and recalibration on the basis of decisions made, as Lawrence Levine has noted of cultural categories, "by the few for the few":

> There is, finally, the same sense that culture is something created by the few for the few, threatened by the many, and imperiled by democracy; the conviction that culture cannot come from the young, the inexperienced, the untutored, the marginal; the belief that culture is finite and fixed, defined and measured, complex and difficult of access, recognizable only by those trained to recognize it, comprehensible only to those qualified to comprehend it.[6]

Such a cultural mandate has been legitimated by "law's promise of order, of security and of identity for those who are both eligible for and willing to accept membership of its community—those who know where to *draw the line.*"[7] But, as Nicola Lacey argues, the law's "hidden face is its power to silence and exclude those who insist on reading between its lines or who live in the wrong side of its tracks, whilst effecting the discursive alchemy of nonetheless *including* them in the universal reach of legal subjectivity."[8] The unstable space between "community membership" and "the wrong side of the tracks" has traditionally been the site of female display's contested claims on legitimacy, as entertainment, as business, as art, and even as speech.

New York Mayor Fiorello LaGuardia's campaign against burlesque's "G-string morality" in the 1930s, a campaign based on an ideological agenda tied to his bid for re-election,[9] and Cardinal Haye's plea for censorship laws against the "slop-jar theatricals,"[10] were calculated attempts to rein in "disreputable" displays of female sexuality. Yet as Andrea Friedman has astutely observed, "Much of the testimony [against burlesque] concerned not disorderly *behavior* but a kind of disorderly *status.*"[11] By this standard, burlesque's presentations of women situated it in the ranks of the socially delinquent ipso facto, without evidentiary support. Censorship and obscenity laws aimed at particular expressions of sexuality have often been allowed by the Courts "merely because of [an] alleged tendency to undermine community morality, without any evidence of any direct or immediate harm."[12] "Because the obscenity laws allow—indeed, *direct*—the majority in any community, and the members of any jury," explains Nadine Strossen, "to criminally punish sexual depictions that they dislike or disapprove, these laws squarely violate the viewpoint neutrality principle that the Supreme Court has called the 'bedrock' of our proud American free speech tradition. If the expression concerned any other subject, First Amendment law would protect it against majoritarian sanctions, no matter how hated it might be."[13]

Nevertheless, the societal belief that standards regulating female display needed to be in place became a governing principle linked to all such entertainments by the end of the nineteenth century. That the body *was* regulated became more important than the terms of the regulation. In 1908, when a "cooch dancer," named "Chooceeta," was arrested for "indecent wiggling," she was "found guilty and fined ten dollars," yet only a few years before when brought before the court, her dance had been interpreted as "cute, graceful, and artistic."[14] If community standards are the measure by which laws are introduced and upheld, they are, nonetheless, as changeable as the makeup of communities themselves. Once again, according to Nadine Strossen:

> The unpredictability of whether a given work will be determined "obscene" is heightened by the Supreme Court's rule that the "prurient interest" and "patently offensive" criteria are to be weighed in light of "community standards" in each particular locale where the work might be prosecuted. Consequently, even if the work might not be deemed "prurient" or "patently offensive" in one place, it could well be found to satisfy these criteria in another place.[15]

Apparently for "Chooceeta" and her dance, even a change of place was not necessarily required for a change of standards. Occasionally, however, regulation had an unexpected, and undesired, benefit for performers. As Irving Zeidman points out, "The censors made it worse for themselves by prescribing explicit rules and regulations of undress and behavior. This resulted merely in sanctioning what was not expressly prohibited. By defining the length of time a girl could undress on a public stage, the reformers condoned, by inference, the actual stripping itself."[16] Such unintended encouragement was likewise offered by an 1890 ruling in Minnesota "prohibiting women from wearing tights on the stage," but neglecting to include naked limbs in the decision.[17] For the most part, however, the legislative system in the United States has responded to staged female sexuality with limitations that amount to embodied gag rules, mitigating display with restrictions such as pasties and g-strings (known in burlesque as "gadgets"), and often adding performance guidelines or explicit proscriptions against certain kinds of bodily deportment.[18]

The industry's response has been nothing if not creative. Earl Carroll "designed, and was the first to use, what he humorously described to the girls as 'pasties,' also nicknamed 'Carroll's Chastity Belt,' " as a way to skirt indecency laws.[19] A G-string soon became iconic as the social "patch of respectability between the strip-teaser and the audience."[20] Burlesque stripper Dixie Evans negotiated the line between "respectability" and giving the audience its money's worth of display by following on the heels of Nadja's earlier use of fake fur: "A lot of girls liked to use moleskin for pasties and put rouge on the end so it's look like your real breasts. Sometimes we'd get a couple of hairnets, whatever color we were down there, wad them up and sew them on the outside of the g-string. It kept the cops on their toes."[21] (In a contemporary parallel, according to Lily Burana, at the strip club Cheetah's in Las Vegas, "dancers at this open-24-hours establishment have to wear two g-strings, to keep errant pubic hairs from peeking out and giving pissed-off vice cops an excuse to yank the club's liquor license."[22]) While beauty contestants scotch-taped their breasts together to create cleavage, stripteasers applied pasties to circumvent obscenity laws.

In her discussion of Patricia Williams's work, Barbara Johnson has stated that the " 'intersubjectivity of legal constructions' is based not on a model of transitive communication, but on a dialogue of profound discontinuity."[23] Such a discontinuity is equally apparent in a cultural climate that renders the ceremonial announcement of a beauty contestant's measurements socially acceptable yet insists on the symbolic covering of nipples, or a regulatory atmosphere in which "the authorities tolerated cooching, but nudity was likely to bring the police."[24] The trend of discontinuity continues today. According to Lily Burana, "The only hitch at Baby Dolls is that you can't wear a t-back or thong; you have to wear a tanga-cut bottom, which still shows the entire behind, but is about two inches wider across the top. It seems a silly distinction, but local municipalities are always forming ad hoc committees to dicker over what constitutes a buttock or a breast or a nipple, and how much—down to a fraction of an inch—a dancer can show."[25]

Regulatory efforts to define acceptable limits of female exposure were by no means confined to the stage. Early in the twentieth century, "Municipalities in which beaches were located passed ordinances regulating the extent to which arms and legs had to be covered. In 1913 a woman at Atlantic City wearing a short bathing suit was assaulted by an outraged crowd."[26] In a famous incident, Annette Kellerman was arrested in Massachusetts in 1907 for posing on the beach in a one-piece bathing suit. The suit was Kellerman's own design, and posing in it a marketing strategy to promote sales.[27] The notoriety occasioned by her arrest undoubtedly proved no impediment to Kellerman's commercial objective.

Inconsistencies of both definitions and enforcement have taught those in the business to cultivate a certain performative flexibility. As Strossen points out, because obscenity laws are based on subjectivity, they "offer a license to the police and prosecutors in any community, or the members of any jury, to punish sexual expression that they find distasteful."[28] A 1958 Dorian Dennis interview discloses that the subjective nature of legislation requires a constant renegotiation by performers:

> Regulations concerning stripping vary from community to community. Dorian usually gets a briefing from the management when she reaches a show date. This involves information on how "strong" or "rough" a performer can get without inviting the police, and it also involves the degree of permissible nudity. In Las Vegas, for instance, minimum apparel is merely a G-string. In Philadelphia or Detroit, a beaded fringe and a beaded brassiere are required.[29]

In addition to the control they exerted by designing bodily coverings of various kinds, revue producers Ziegfeld and Carroll closely monitored the behavior, onstage and off, of their "girls." Ziegfeld was even referred to as the "bailiff of glorification of the American girl."[30] According to a 1934 *Collier's* article, "No seminary students were ever under closer surveillance. When the girls went on the road [Ziegfeld] would get detailed reports about all of them from his company manager and then wire each according to her transgression, "Don't get fat . . . Don't stay up late . . . Don't go to wild parties."[31] Ziegfeld was a "hard taskmaster," insisting his chorines be "well-groomed in the streets, hotels, restaurants or wherever they were seen by the public. He insisted upon gloves, hats, high heels and stockings at all times."[32] "Too much rouge, mascara or lipstick off stage was as forbidden as wearing a costume with the slightest variation from his dictates."[33] Carroll was no less an offstage martinet, even going so far as painting above the dressing room door at his theatre: "I would rather you were less talented than less loyal."[34] Believing that "beauties run in schools, like fish," Carroll added, "At times, the fishing is fine and a lot of beauties are caught. And at other times, the only thing a man can do is get a couple of finnan-haddies and hope for the best."[35] According to Carroll's biographer, Ken Murray, "every night before bedtime he would gather all the girls around him in a circle, like Campfire girls, and would give them pep talks and lectures [. . .] He had them behave exactly as well-trained soldiers."[36]

Throughout their history, beauty contests have been governed with similarly elaborate strictness. As early as the 1888 Rehoboth Beach Miss United States Contest, rules extended from personal behavior to personal attributes. Not only were contestants required to be single, they had to be "no more than twenty-five years of age, a minimum of five foot four inches tall, and a maximum of one hundred and thirty pounds."[37] It was required that Miss America contestants be single as well, with no annulments or divorces in their histories. Contestants in the early Miss America pageants were scored on their individual body parts (construction of the head, worth 15 points; the eyes, worth 5 points, etc.) and their legs were inspected by officials to make sure they weren't using body makeup.[38] While, as Angela Latham has stated, "entertaining women were allowed to display their bodies in ways that were otherwise considered immodest," it must be noted that parameters of display were always carefully constructed and enforced.[39] For beauty contests the "primary purpose in the past, as in the present, was social discipline and not social advance."[40]

While obscenity and indecency laws obviously apply to men as well as women (and today male strippers are required to wear specified apparel), the vociferous call for regulation of the female form has often centered on issues of contagion, an argument remarkably absent from debates surrounding male nudity.[41] As one anti-burlesque newspaper editorial railed, "Only by closing up these plague centers and keeping them closed [. . .] can the city cure itself of the moral leprosy which they spread."[42] As noted in chapter 1, nudity in tableaux vivant became an issue of moral corruption when promoters began staging displays of (seemingly) naked women. Implicit in the copious regulations aimed at "peel for pay" entertainments is a conceptual link to the female form as a site of contagion, and its representation of corporeal toxicity is a crucial concept informing attempts to legitimize containment. "Burlesque's shows defining attribution," according to Andrea Freidman, "was not exhibitionism per se but sexual suggestiveness."[43]

Pathologizing performers as potential carriers of moral contagion gave plausibility to the authoritative notion of quarantine. For legislators and reformers, that suggestiveness amounted to, as Elizabeth Grosz has pointed out, perceptions of women's corporeality "as a mode of seepage."[44] Unable to adequately quarantine the ambiguous "suggestiveness," legislators resorted to a strategy of regulating through masking, by focusing on brassieres and panties (or "nets" as they were known in burlesque[45]), as if in the hope that if spectators were unable to actually see the offending female body parts, they might forget they were there. In an application of the strategy of legislatively approved fabric swatches, "when Sally Rand appeared in the New York Paramount Theatre, she was ordered to wear panties."[46] Mocking the cover-up tactics, "The fan dancer donned long flannel underwear, receiving some excellent publicity and a good week's gross at the box office."[47]

In spite of performer circumnavigation of legal constraints, efforts at containment continued. Somewhat prematurely, *Variety* asserted in 1932 that "The strippers and shakers of burlesque have stripped and shaken for the last time."[48] But by 1933 Commissioner Geraghty of New York had issued more sweeping rulings "forbidding female performers to remove any part of their costumes offstage or to touch them while onstage."[49] A New York Magistrate in 1935 dismissed charges against two strippers, stating "nudity is no longer considered indecent in uptown nightclubs and theatres," but Mayor LaGuardia remained undeterred.[50] "There is no constitutional right to be immoral," he argued, "and filth, vulgarity and immorality do not come with constitutional provisions for the freedom of speech."[51] Eerily prescient, LaGuardia's position that "vulgar" female display was not protected under the first amendment would resurface nationwide in courts of law time and again, most recently, and tellingly, in a 2000 U.S. Supreme Court case. Additionally, female display became situated as antisocial, responsible for the deterioration of the community's fabric, for "rampant sex crimes."[52] From 1932 to 1942, argues Freidman,

> Opponents of burlesque articulated a logic of male sexuality that reflected the economic conditions and political imperatives attending the Great Depression and the wartime boom. During times of economic crisis they described an escalating trajectory of male sexual danger, as they moved from asserting that burlesque *attracted* men who were likely to harass female passersby to arguing that it *incited* them to rape and murder.[53]

For a while, the vitriolic anti-burlesque publicity drew crowds. Newspaper headlines read: "BURLESQUE GOES ON AS LAW CHIEFS ARGUE."[54] Following testimony before Congress by the Minsky brothers, "everybody in town toned down their act. We had the girls wearing heavily beaded fringes on the G-strings instead of the usual flesh-colored elastic ones. But there was standing room only. Most of the customers had never seen a strip before. They were there because of the publicity."[55] The boom was not to last. As reformers tried new suppression strategies, producers attempted to strike a balance between appeasing the censors, toning down the "cacky" presentation (the burlesque term for smutty), and appealing to the public.[56] Theaters such as Chicago's Star and Garter "advertised that it now featured 'Censored Burlesque' and 'Clean Entertainment for Self-Respecting People.' "[57] Even the Minsky brothers made an effort but, according to Mort Minsky found themselves trapped in a "damned if you do, damned if you don't" conundrum: "our problem was that trying to walk the tightrope between the city's oppressive minions and popular taste; we had apparently leaned a little too hard in the direction of good taste."[58] As one reviewer noted, the show "unfortunately failed to reach the usual high standard of lechery which is associated with the name Minsky."[59]

"In 1932 municipal officials and antiburlesque activists turned their attention from criminal law to the licensing process as a means of controlling burlesque."[60] It was to prove their most successful strategy. Burlesque strippers remained on New York stages, but the stages were increasingly located in dimly lit dives and private clubs. And even there, for a time, antsy owners responded to the climate by dropping "the strip like a hot stove-lid," fearing the State Liquor Commission. As H.M. Alexander remarked, "No one's taking chances with his liquor license."[61] As early as 1909, theatres were expressing anxiety about the link between censorship and license control, according to *Variety*, "May 1, the time for the renewal of theatrical licenses, is approaching, and this is said to be the reason for the renewed strictness of the policy in enforcing Sunday Laws."[62]

In a 1932 hearing, Commissioner Geraghty had decided that withholding theater licenses was acceptable "if it could be proved that a theatre attracted a class of disorderly person."[63] But it was not until later, when then Commissioner Moss actively applied the ruling, that its full impact registered. If Moss's application of license control as a censorship strategy was not original, it was highly effective. "As burlesque's defenders argued that its audience of 'average citizens' had the wherewithal to control their responses to its provocations, their foes reciprocated with the assertion that burlesque's incitements led inexorably first to disorderliness, then to violence, and finally to debility."[64] The anti-burlesquers found company in organizations such as the 42nd Street Property Owners' Association and the Catholic Church. "When on April 30, burlesque-theatre licenses expired for the year, Catholics demanded that renewals be denied. [. . .] After a police raid on three Brooklyn houses had hauled 11 strip-teasers into court, Commissioner Moss padlocked the city's 14 shows."[65] Soon, Moss decided, "even ninety-day licenses were too long. He cut down the period to sixty days, then thirty, and even on a week-to-week basis."[66] Burlesque lacked any legal recourse in the face of this new assault.

The control of female display through licensing has proven permanently useful as an expression of subjective community standards, even when such standards lack legal foundation. In Gilford, New Hampshire, in 2002, Darlene Sherman, the owner of the King's Grant Inn, a local lounge, requested permission to present weekend shows featuring exotic dancers. Sherman had previously been granted a license by the town selectmen for mid-week performances, but hoped to expand to five nights a week. Zoning laws in Gilford characterize exotic dancing as "unusual entertainment," warranting the issuance of thirty-day permits only. Month to month approval had been forthcoming for Sherman until she requested the weekend shows.[67] Chairman Larry Routhier blocked approval by abstaining from the vote. "As a selectman I can't vote no, he stated, "as a parent I didn't want it to seem

I was . . . sanctioning exotic dancing."[68] Fully aware that he was manipulating the system, "if he had voted no based on his moral beliefs, Routhier said, he would have been violating Sherman's right to free speech."[69] Mayor Fiorello LaGuardia's stated "desire to be the Mayor of a clean American city and protect its morals," is reincarnated, though less forthrightly, in selectman Routhier's attitude toward Darlene Sherman and the King's Grant Inn.[70]

While Ziegfeld, Carroll, and Vice squad superintendents jostled for position in the wings of burlesque, "hostesses" for the Miss America pageant acted as a morality squad in their own venue, enforcing the offstage organizational rules that banned all contestants from night clubs, bars, inns, and taverns, and forbade the contestants from having conversations with any member of the opposite sex during competition week—including their own fathers.[71] Contestants are still discouraged from frequenting businesses which serve alcohol, perhaps a theatrical carryover from an unwanted association with earlier concert saloons in which female performers and prostitutes shared the same space, if not the same customers. At the Foxy Lady in Providence, Rhode Island, regulations apply not just to performers but also to female patrons, who must be escorted by a male companion or they are denied entry. Once admitted, ladies must even be escorted to the bathroom—by security guards—ostensibly to prevent unauthorized sexual transactions. The behavioral proscriptions that strip clubs impose on women (whether customers or performers) are connected not only to the entertainment itself, however, but to the club's other primary business, the sale of alcohol. Alcohol and female display have a longstanding but uneasy relationship—considered volatile enough in some quarters to require mitigation on one side or the other. New York State protects its citizens from their combined effects with legislation that, in effect, declares the absence of alcohol in "strip clubs is the trade-off for no nipple pasties and no G-strings. Full nudity must be taken sober."[72] In the West coast equivalent, a full nudity club is defined as a "juice bar."

But strict behavioral regulation is by no means unique to the clubs. At beauty pageants, the ubiquitous male emcee functions as an onstage monitor in much the same way Ziegfeld and Carroll once performed behind the scenes. The male authority figures utilized at specific moments in the competition provide constant symbolic reminders of containment and control. In a pattern remarkably reminiscent of traditional wedding ceremonies (in which her father "gives away" the bride), men escort their daughters down stairs, kiss and embrace them, and then direct them with a gesture to walk alone toward the audience. The use of this familiar visual signifier of patriarchal transfer from father to husband, following on the heels of a previous spectacle in which the contestants appeared in white gowns, resonated with ancient attitudes toward the female body as a commodity in the ritual of male gift-exchange. Additionally, in the 2001 Miss America competition, a huge screen behind the exchange featured larger-than-life pictures of the contestants as babies and children, images that suggested not only the women's essential powerlessness but also their potential reproductive capabilities. The beauty contest rule that contestants' ages fall within the range of eighteen to twenty-four is neither random nor insignificant, and in this case, the handing over of nubile, reproductively ripe women by fathers to an enthusiastic, cheering crowd carried within it performative vestiges of a fertility ritual, even if only ostensibly for entertainment purposes.

At the 2002 Miss America competition, it also betrayed the organization's intentional control of the contestants. The gendered tradition of fathers escorting daughters (considered a sentimental moment by contestants such as Mary Morin, Miss New Hampshire 2002, who remarked, "I was so proud to have my Dad escorting me, it was such a proud moment for him to escort his daughter on the Miss America stage, so I was happy . . . I have no regrets") was proven far more actual than symbolic when Miss Arizona asked to be escorted by her mother. The request was denied. For Laura Lawless, the insistence on patriarchal symbolism clashed with the pageant's assertion of belief in the value of women role models:

> It was an extremely difficult decision for everyone involved and I'll tell you, it was very hard for me all day yesterday in rehearsal and actually walking out on that stage because my mother is my world and she always has been. She was penniless, she was homeless, and she was pregnant. And my own biological father walked out of my life. [. . .] And in an ideal world we wouldn't just have to look for the pretty picture of a woman being escorted by a man. A woman should be able to be escorted by anyone. It doesn't matter her gender, it should be the role she plays in her life.

The hypocrisy that rhetorically promotes the advancement of women yet disallows a woman to take her rightful place as the most significant figure in a contestant's life is emblematic of the double standard inherent in the event. Just as at the strip club Cheetah's in Las Vegas, it would seem that at the Miss America pageant, "there are two sets of rules—those that they tell you and those that you actually work by."[73] As a response to public criticism following the 2002 pageant (almost unquestionably due to Lawless's efforts), the MAO now permits contestants to be escorted by their mothers.

Protestations against the rigidity of regulations governing symbolic or behavioral contents in female display are largely fruitless, however, and outright defiance is punished with banishment and public shaming. In a vernacular iteration of policies employed by beauty pageants nationwide, a manager at The Lodge, a Dallas strip club, insists: "Don't even think about bending the rules here, 'cause that dawg don't hunt."[74] "No lie," confirms Lily Burana, "they have a corkboard filled with Polaroid photos of women they've fired, some with the word *lewd* scrawled, Prynne-like, under their names."[75] Such *Scarlet Letter* labeling echoes that often found in negative reactions to burlesque, as one newspaper reader noted, "There are pictures of strippers going to jail, holding gloved hands, newspapers, make-up boxes in front of their faces. There are full-page spreads illustrated with half-nude chorus shots. There are headlines with the words 'smut' and 'sex' in 54-point caps."[76] Though somewhat obscured by irony, the internal and external effort to confine strippers within acceptable boundaries of "lewdness" remains and issue of control, not content.

Beauty contests are no less zealous in this regard. Situating her as a metaphoric sister to the burlesque performer with the word "smut" or "lewd" plastered on her photo, the Miss America Pageant "asked" its 1983 winner, Vanessa Williams, to renounce her title when it was found she had posed nude in photographs prior to her entry into the contest. The photographs were published in *Penthouse* magazine. As columnist Brendan Gill dryly observed at the time, the Penthouse publisher "announced that he had only been doing his duty by his readers, whose need for nude photographs was evidently of a heart-rending intensity."[77] Williams' dethroning was inevitably justified on moral grounds. Yet as Brook Lee, Miss Universe 1997, has said "you win a pageant and the next morning you give up your whole identity for a year. You become a copy-righted trademark."[78] The incident was characterized as a reflection of the Miss America Organization's (MAO) commitment to rectitude, in spite of the fact that Ms. Williams had not disobeyed the rules of the organization while a participant in the pageant. Apparently, the MAO believed the nude photos of Williams amounted to at least a symbolic, albeit retroactive, copyright infringement. The point did not escape public notice—numerous newspapers, such as the *Daily News*, wondered aloud about the furor when "the pageant is in the same business as Guccione, showing off pretty girls for money."[79] The MAO's institutional reaction seemed intended to forestall potential contagion from the exposure to an illegitimate embodied performance, paralleling Goffman's assertion:

A false impression maintained by an individual in any one of his routines may be a threat to the whole relationship or role of which the routine is only one part, for a discreditable disclosure in one area of an individual's activity will throw doubt on the many areas of activity in which he may have nothing to conceal.[80]

That Ms. Williams' behavior might discredit the entire organization was the apparent fear motivating her removal. By disassociatively quarantining themselves from Vanessa Williams, the performances of other contestants could retain their status as legitimate signifiers of more seemingly positive values. A similar incident occurred when Jill Nicolini was named Miss Long Island 2002. She had previously been featured in *Playboy's* 2001 issue *College Girls* Special Edition (for which she was paid five hundred dollars.[81]) According to *Playboy*, Nicolini "graduated at the top of her class as a broadcasting major and maintains a 4.0 GPA while studying for her master's."[82] As Ms. Nicolini recalls the incident, "The director of the Miss Long Island pageant said he heard I was in Playboy. An anonymous caller called him. He asked me if I posed and I said yes. He said that *Playboy* wasn't something that the Miss America organization approves of." According to Nicolini, under pressure, she relinquished her crown.[83]

The MAO contract for contestants states that they are prohibited from "engaging in any activity that could reasonably be characterized as dishonest, immoral or indecent and from conducting themselves in any manner that is inconsistent with the standards and dignity of the Miss America Program."[84] Such an intentionally ambiguous "morality clause" has precedent in the U.S. Supreme Court's Miller decision of 1973, which established three criteria for decreeing a work obscene. Nadine Strossen has argued that all three are "inescapably vague": (1) the "average person, applying contemporary community standards, would find that the work, taken as a whole, appeals to the prurient interest" in sex; (2) "the work depicts or describes, in a patently offensive way, sexual conduct specifically defined by the applicable state law"; and (3) "the work, taken as a whole, lacks serious literary, artistic, political, or scientific value."[85] The MAO relies on a similarly vague set of conditions by which it judges a contestant's behavior "inconsistent with the standards and dignity of the Miss America Program." Once again, as with the cooch dancer "Choceeta," elusive "community standards" define the limits of acceptable display. According to the pageant world's understanding of those standards, the photographs of Vanessa Williams and Jill Nicolini rendered them incapable of representing the MAO because of the overt sexuality of their published images.

The MAO labels of "indecent" and "immoral" seem an assumptive reflection of the Supreme Court's definition of "prurient" as an interest in sex that is a " 'sick and morbid' one, as opposed to a 'normal and healthy' one."[86] "Imagine yourself," asks Strossen, "sitting as a judge or a juror attempting to determine whether a particular sexually-oriented work appeals to a 'sick' interest or a 'healthy' one. Can you honestly imagine doing anything other than invoking your own tastes and preferences? Do you want other individuals to judge by their own standards a work that you find exciting?"[87] Williams' photographs, in addition to being considered "indecent" by the MAO, also flew in the face of the organization's hyper-heterosexual image. With their depiction of a lesbian encounter, the photographs offered the image of a Miss America not just openly sexual, but potentially homoerotic (although they might also be read as performances of a familiar male fantasy). Thus, the pageant response to the photographs was consistent with its insistence that performances by beauty contestants serve as indicators of their "genuine" natures. The fact that Vanessa Williams's personal morality is no more determinable on the evidence of a photo shoot than from her onstage performance in a pageant was not taken into consideration.

Williams's expulsion, despite its ultimate failure to tarnish her image or damage her career, demonstrated the pageant system's willingness to enforce retroactive behavioral standards on its contestants. Such enforcement has been developed subsequently to include not just deliberate acts like Williams's, but also inadvertent ones. In addition to establishing criteria for the "decent" and the "moral," there is also a clause in the MAO North Carolina franchise's contract which stipulates that its state representative must promise she has *never* done anything in "bad taste."[88] Unfortunately for Rebekah Revels, the act of getting dressed one morning constituted just such a lapse. Revels resigned her Miss North Carolina title on July 23, 2002, because of two nude photos taken by her former boyfriend while she was dressing for work. According to Revels, "The Miss America Pageant was not going to let me compete because they feel I breached the moral clause of their contract, after my ex-boyfriend e-mailed them and said, 'Ask her about two nude photos.' "[89] While one might argue that Revels was guilty of bad taste in her choice of boyfriends, the MAO chose instead to name the first runner-up, Misty Clymer, in Revel's stead. Much to the dismay of the MAO, Revels defiantly decided to contest its action by filing a breach of contract lawsuit. (Wendy Chapkis has noted "The defiant woman's real failure is not that she isn't trying hard enough for the title of 'crowned beauty' but that she seems uninterested in the competition for Miss Congeniality."[90]) The MAO brought the full weight of its legal apparatus to Revels's case.

Upon hearing of Revels's contestation, Misty Clymer also hired a lawyer, who happened to be a former Miss North Carolina herself. Janet Ward Black argued that the contract between the reigning queen and the MAO is about "turning the business relationship over to be managed by the pageant. They would not want somebody arranging on their own for inappropriate appearances." She added that "similar contracts have helped protect the reputations of other beauty pageants under the Miss America umbrella."[91] What is clear from the MAO's actions, and from Black's statements, is that the "reputation" of the Miss America pageant is a carefully policed construction. "Inappropriate appearances" in Revels's case not only referred to the photos of her bared breasts, but the logical inference that she had chosen to put herself in a compromising position that allowed a male spectator (i.e., boyfriend) to snap the shots. The photographs broke the illusion that the MAO works diligently to present, an image of their contestants as wholesome (read virginal) role models. According to findlaw.com, the legal effort to maintain its "reputation," in the Revels case cost the Miss American Organization a "1.4 million dollar loss due to the expenditure of the proceedings."[92]

What was at stake was not the alleged moral turpitude of Rebekah Revels, who had after all won her state title outright under the same sort of intense scrutiny aimed at Misty Clymer and every other contestant, but rather the protection of a lucrative brand name. In a different lawsuit centered on the erroneous claim by a radio talk show that the pageant is "fixed," the MAO asserted:

> The continued public support of the Miss America program and continued success of the Miss America Organization in its philanthropic efforts are dependent upon Plaintiff's ability to maintain its good name, integrity, and reputation in the minds of the American public and in the perception of businesses that purchase advertising and pay licensing fees for the right to use the Miss America name and marks in their sales of goods and service.[93]

The MAO's investment in the perpetuation of its image as beyond reproach extends from control of its contestants' behavior to control of their public rhetoric. Specific prohibitions sometimes approach the realm of the absurd. Miss America 2003, Erika Harold, was told by pageant officials "not to talk publicly about sexual abstinence, a cause she has advocated to teenage girls in Illinois" (her home state).[94] "Quite frankly, and I'm not going to be specific, there are pressures from some sides to not promote [abstinence]."[95] One would assume that the MAO would find nothing morally objectionable in a platform of abstinence, but as one news article understated, "the pageant has traditionally been skittish about sexual subjects."[96]

Institutional pageant rules share remarkable similarities with countless other regulations surrounding female display in all forms. The contract signed by MAO contestants in North Carolina explicitly stipulates, among other things, *when* she is allowed to wear her crown, that she "always has been female," "how fast she has to write thank-you notes," that she will maintain medical insurance and "turn over medical records if requested," and requires her to check her phone messages "every morning and evening and return all calls."[97] The contract also stipulates that she is not an employee of the pageant, but "only an independent contractor."[98] (Thus allowing the pageant to avoid financial and other obligations of an employer.) Arcane details do not escape regulatory scrutiny in the world of stripping, either. At The Lodge in Dallas, Lily Burana explains, "your nails have to be perfect (they checked mine), your costume formal (evening dress—prom queen style, not street-walker), and your heels a certain height (nothing less than three inches)."[99] In the same way that Earl Carroll and Flo Ziegfeld enforced the rules contrived for their chorus girls, the manager of The Lodge insists that "the music women can dance to is restricted to selections that will 'be pleasing to their demo-graphic—affluent men age thirty-five to fifty-five.' "[100] At the previously mentioned King's Grant Inn in New Hampshire, the owner "attached a list of self-imposed regulations" to her application for a permit, stipulating that dancers "are not permitted to touch or solicit any customers. There is no drinking while performing, and all tips must be taken in the garter belt."[101] In an expression of continued fear regarding "ocular decorum" and contagion, one strip club goes so far as to dictate the duration of eye contact: "when giving couch or lap dances, they must not make eye-contact with their client for more than 5 seconds."[102]

Regulatory interest in the business of female display is habitual at every official level, from individual presenting organizations to the municipalities that host their venues, from law enforcement agencies to state legislatures to the Supreme Court of the United States. Nadine Strossen argues, "The First Amendment's broadly phrased free speech guarantee—"Congress shall make no law . . . abridging the freedom of speech"—contains no exception for sexual expression. Nevertheless, the Supreme Court has consistently read such an exception into the First Amendment, allowing sexual speech to be restricted or even banned under circumstances in which it would not allow other types of speech to be limited."[103]

In March 2001 a short Reuters news article reported that Leilani Rios, a sophomore at the State College in Fullerton, California, had been forced to leave the college's track team because of her part-time job as an exotic dancer at the Flamingo Theater. The coach of the team justified his disciplinary action by declaring that "her decision to remain an exotic dancer would detract from the image and accomplishments of her teammates, the athletic department and the university."[104] Mimicking Mayor LaGuardia decades earlier, the coach, John Elders, also explicitly positioned himself as the team's (and the college's) moral guardian, stating, "I have to protect the kind of image that we represent."[105]

Leilani Rios's job was discovered when members of the Cal State Fullerton baseball team (who remained anonymous) patronized the Flamingo Theater and subsequently reported her employment to the track coach. Although Rios herself had not been wearing any item that might have publicly indicated her affiliation with the college, the baseball team members were all outfitted in Titan caps and sweaters. Their "image" apparently remained unsullied, however, for no disciplinary action was taken against them for their attendance at the Flamingo, whereas Rios, who was using the money earned at the club to pay for her Cal State education, was summarily dismissed from her team.

Elders's paternalistic belief that, as track coach, he wielded both the power and the responsibility to define the off-field activities of his female student-athletes as either appropriate or deviant is clearly revealed in his comment to the college's newspaper. "I had to really do some soul searching," he declared, "about what I really felt was the *right* thing . . . what's best for Leilani and what's best for our program."[106] His dismissal of Leilani Rios, and the language he used in its justification (remarkably similar to that of the MAO), simultaneously infantalized Rios's capability to choose what is "best," and declared a policy prohibiting performative expressions of female sexuality (if not their appreciation by customers), a prohibition enforceable by means of banishment. Coach Elders's assumption—unstated but explicit in his actions—that there is nothing wrong with *seeing* an exotic dancer but something unacceptable about *being* one, is a familiar anomaly in the American attitude toward stripping. Briefly stated, this assumption exonerates exotic dancing's spectator as an innocent observer of performance, yet denies similar recognition to the performer, whose routine is taken at face value as lewd and suggestive *conduct* rather than a theatrical expression invented for the entertainment of the observer. Such an inference naturally calls the moral character of the exotic dancer in serious question, so the retributive action of expelling Rios from the track team might thus be construed as an attempt to avoid an apparent source of contagion. Coach Elders's assumption that exotic dancing reveals and promulgates an immoral and contagious self whose pathogenic effects require containment might be dismissed as unexamined reactionism rooted in a familiar double standard. Yet his behavior finds precedent—one might even say sanction—in the judgment of the U.S. Supreme Court, which, only a year before the Rios incident at Cal State, used similar language and similar logic in its own struggle with the issues raised by performative female sexuality.

In February 2000, the Court upheld previous appellate rulings in what had become known as the Kandyland Case, concurring with "the acceptability of the traditional judgment [. . .] that nude public dancing *itself* is immoral."[107] The Court further upheld that such display "had negative secondary effects on the community" and, as "expressive conduct" was considered on the "outer ambit" of the First Amendment and thus subject to a "less stringent standard" of scrutiny.[108] The Cal State Fullerton track coach was in heady company in his marginalization of Leilani Rios. Just as Commissioner Moss had fought to contain burlesque stripteasers, the City of Erie, Pennsylvania, had sought to regulate the performances of exotic dancers at the Kandyland Club, all of whom were female, by banning complete nudity and insisting that dancers wear a minimum of pasties and a G-string, thus ostensibly protecting the community from the "harmful secondary effects associated with nude dancing."

The remarkable similarity of the decisions by the Supreme Court and John Elders, grounded in assumptions of contagious negative secondary effects as well as a deliberate misreading of exotic dancing's theatrical basis, can be read as symptomatic of an authoritarian attempt to use the fringe positioning of exotic dancers as a means by which particular moral boundaries might be delineated and enforced. As Patricia Williams has noted, "the extent to which technical legalisms are used to obfuscate the human motivations that generate our justice system is the real extent to which we as human beings are disenfranchised."[109] The telling use of the phrase "outer ambit" in the Supreme Court ruling solicits the "disenfranchisement" of exotic dancers in two ways: metaphorically, as deviants who act without regard for culturally sanctioned norms of behavior; and concretely, as virtual scofflaws who teeter precariously on the edge of legal protection.

The Supreme Court's insistence on hearing *Erie, PA v. Kandyland Club* as a case of conduct perpetuated a socially mandated hierarchy of appropriate female behavior on the stage, a hierarchy rooted in the imposition of an extralegal moral code of bodily deportment. Having accepted the legitimacy of such a code, prima facie, the Court found itself obliged to justify its ideologically dependent decision in law, a process which led it to ignore or deny significant historical, legal, and performative evidence against the Erie case, and, conversely, to assert, inflate, or distort the value of statutes and precedents interpretable as favoring that case. A review of *Erie, PA v. Kandyland Club* suggests that a majority of the U.S. Supreme Court, like Coach John Elders, was prepared to resort to any available shelter, in rhetoric or in law, in order to protect the rights of communities to suppress what they perceive as affronts to "decency," specifically in the regulation of exotic dancing. This impulse rests far less on legal or community standards of conduct than on a deep and amorphous anxiety regarding the public display of the female body, and it was this anxiety, not legal or statutory suasion, to which the Court ultimately responded in upholding Erie's censorship of Kandyland's exotic dancing.

This particular Supreme Court case will be explored here in detail because it is now the "standard" by which other court cases involving female display are decided, and, as such, is essential to understanding contemporary regulation of women engaged in sexualized display. In fact, the Court agreed to hear the case in order to render more specific certain points previously legislated in the *Barnes v. Glenn case* (a case which focused specifically on adult entertainment zoning). The Kandyland case is fraught with issues of theatrical misapprehension and ideological hegemony in the legal interpretations of [im]morality, historical precedent, conduct versus speech, and the constituent aspects of protected performance. The case is also illustrative of how past legislative actions in our theatrical heritage, such as those employed against burlesque, continue to haunt present day jurisprudence in spite of their assumptive notions of morality.

"The culture of any society at any moment," according to Victor Turner, "is more like debris, or 'fall-out,' of past ideological systems, than it is itself a system, a coherent whole."[110] The historicity of the policing of the female body on the stage in the United States may or may not be traceable as a "coherent whole," but it nonetheless reflects a system of patterns, or "debris," that continually reiterates a calculated attempt by various factions of society to curtail and contain public expressions of female sexuality. Because the Erie statute purportedly aimed at nudity *in general* and was "not specifically directed at expression," it was deemed by the Supreme Court to be neutral, and therefore constitutional.[111] One of the arguments emphasizing the "neutrality" of the Erie statute held that it was simply an update of one provision of an "Indecency and Immorality" ordinance that purportedly had been on the city's books since 1866, "predating the prevalence of nude dancing."[112]

Leaving aside for the moment considerations of how one might possibly characterize the labels "Indecent" and "Immoral" as in any way "neutral," it is worth remembering that the year 1866 arrived during a period of exceptional public outrage—and titillation—over the exposed female form on the American stage. As early as 1860, the actress Laura Keene had startled the public with a production of *Seven Sisters*, prompting one reviewer's notice of the "hundred miscellaneous legs in flesh-colored tights."[113] As discussed in chapter 1, in 1861, Adah Issacs Menken scandalized audiences in *Mazeppa*, when she emerged onstage astride a live horse, clad only in a pink bodystocking and tunic. She reprised the role five years later, in 1866. While each of these events attracted its own notoriety, the hyperventilated media coverage of the musical extravaganza *The Black Crook* could not possibly have gone unnoticed even in Erie, PA. During the 1865–66 season at Niblo's Garden in New York, this "melodrama in spectacle form" immediately incited a volatile public debate concerning women, performance, and morality.[114] Newspapers described the female performers as "demons" with "scarcely a rag left upon them to take off" and the *Times* reviewer noted the women wore "no clothes to speak of."[115]

The year 1866, when Erie, PA, put into effect its "neutral" "Indecency and Immorality" ordinance, therefore witnessed silent, barely clothed female performers become the talk of the country. In this light, the City of Erie's 2000 attempt to cite an 1866 statute as an example of political neutrality with respect to the female form onstage was ill-informed at best. At worst, it was simply false. Erie's effort to substantiate its argument historically was rendered an absurd charade when, as the Supreme Court's Justice Stevens noted in his dissent, the cited 1866 ordinance was found not actually to exist in the city's books. In other words, the City of Erie used a *cultural memory* of a particular ruling that could not be tangibly produced, a spurious reliance that seems to justify Roland Barthes' appealingly cynical notion that "the retrospective is never anything but a category of bad faith."[116]

The acceptance of content neutrality by the Supreme Court was possibly the most significant turning point in the case. Webster's definition of *neutral* that would seem to be the one drawn on by the Court reads: "without strongly marked characteristics; indefinite, indifferent, middling"; in other words, not strongly expressive of any one thing in particular. In effect, the Court's decision relegated the case to the "outer ambit" of First Amendment issues, in that "what level of scrutiny applies is determined by whether the ordinance is related to the suppression of expression . . . If the government intention is the regulation of conduct and not a deliberate attempt to suppress expression, the ordinance need only satisfy the 'less stringent,' intermediate O'Brien standard."[117] This crucial distinction, imposing standards of conduct rather than speech on the Erie case, was rooted in a precedent involving the burning of a draft registration card. In that case, the "Court rejected [the] claim that the statute (prohibiting the destruction of draft cards) violated his [O'Brien's] First Amendment rights, reasoning that the law punished him for the *noncommunicative* impact of his conduct, and for nothing else.' "[118]

Under this "intermediate" standard, the Erie ordinance might be viewed as one that regulates conduct alone and does not specifically "target nudity that contains an erotic message." Therefore, *all* public nudity is banned. On the surface, such an injunction might seem plausible, particularly in a community willing to argue that it perceived an actionable threat to order from random displays of the naked human body. Yet during the same year that it sought to impose this ordinance on the dancers and proprietors of Kandyland, Erie, PA, played host to stage productions of *Equus* and *Hair*, both plays in which female (and male) nudity occurs. Additionally, at the trial court proceeding, counsel for the city said, in reference to the ordinance: "to the extent that the expressive activity in [such] productions rises to a higher level of protected expression, they would not be covered."[119] Counsel also stated that the city was not "aware of the nudity" and had not enforced the ordinance because "no one had complained."[120] Justice O'Connor, delivering the opinion of the Court, asserted that "one instance of nonenforcement—against a play already in production that prosecutorial discretion might reasonably have 'grandfathered' in—does not render this ordinance discriminatory on its face."[121]

This extraordinary section of the Court's opinion is worth further analysis. Why should a single production of a play warrant "grandfathering" when an entertainment form that can arguably be traced back at least as far as the early 1860s does not? Is lack of complaint a measure by which laws are enforced? Is it possible that a production of *Hair* could be running in Erie and not be noticed by anyone serving as an official of the city? Perhaps the answer lies in the ordinance's preamble, almost an exact replica of the argument used by the anti-burlesquers, in which the city council found that "certain lewd, immoral activities carried on in public places for profit are highly detrimental to the public health, safety and welfare."[122] Still, the "group nudity and simulated sex" in *Hair* was "protected speech," as Justice Scalia imagined Erie had concluded. Clearly, a particular kind of cultural discrimination was at work in the Court's reasoning, one that positions exotic dancing as "lewd" (the exact word scrawled under the photographed faces of dancers at The Lodge in Dallas), yet finds that *Hair* rises to a standard worthy of being "protected."

A judicial distinction separating legitimate from illegitimate culture was evidently anticipated in one Erie Council member's refusal even to categorize exotic dancing as entertainment, a classification that might be construed as a protected form of speech: "We're not talking about nudity. We're not talking about the theater or art . . . We're talking about what is indecent and immoral . . . We're not prohibiting nudity, we're prohibiting nudity when it's used in a lewd and immoral fashion."[123] If, however, as the Council member asserted, the issue at hand was not "nudity," not "theater or art," but morality, it becomes increasingly difficult to recognize in the court transcripts exactly where the critical concept of "neutrality" can be applied. Throughout the text of the delivered opinion, and certainly in the City of Erie's preamble to the ordinance, there resides a consistently moralistic assumptiveness that can only be characterized as at best condescending, and at worst stigmatizing (and legally prejudicial) to exotic dancers. Still, the case against Kandyland required as much assistance as possible in order to sidestep the difficulties presented by the U.S. Constitution's guarantee of freedom of speech. The acceptance of content neutrality and the application of the O'Brien standard not only allowed Erie, and the Court, to avoid the inconvenience of the First Amendment, but also to take full advantage of a rich lode of historic and cultural antipathy toward sexual display in women, and even toward women themselves.

According to the Supreme Court: "the ordinance is within Erie's constitutional power to enact because the city's efforts to protect public health and safety are clearly within its police powers."[124] This conceptual tactic finds correspondence in Coach John Elders's action, which emphasized the expulsion of Leilani Rios from his track team as a result of his responsibility to "protect" the team. For the "safety" of the community, monitoring and regulation of the nude female body is therefore justifiable. Such monitoring, as a hedge against the threat of moral condemnation based on appearance only, recalls Great Britain's Contagious Disease Act of 1864, under which women suspected of prostitution were hauled off to the police station for inspection.

The second O'Brien criterion is actually an extension of the first, bolstered with important references to evidentiary precedence:

> the ordinance furthers the important government interests of regulating conduct through a public nudity ban and of combating the harmful secondary effects associated with nude dancing. In terms of demonstrating that such secondary effects pose a threat, the city need not conduct new studies or produce evidence independent of that already generated by other cities, so long as the evidence relied on is reasonably believed to be relevant to the problem addressed.[125]

The precedent cited for such an "evidentiary foundation"[126] had nothing to do with exotic dancers and their nudity, but rather was a case involving issues of zoning: "secondary effects are caused by the presence of even one adult entertainment establishment in a given neighborhood."[127] This liberal use of precedent regarding the dispute between the Kandyland Club and Erie, PA, was foregrounded in Justice Stevens's dissenting opinion (joined by Justice Ginsburg). Stevens argued that "dramatic changes in legal doctrine" were being "endorsed" by the Court in this case.[128] He specifically pointed to the use of evidentiary material that had previously been accepted only with regard to zoning, to the regulation of the location of adult entertainment *buildings*. "A dispersal that simply limits the places where speech may occur," argued

Stevens, "is a minimal imposition whereas a total ban is the most exacting of restrictions."[129] Notably, there already existed in Erie an ordinance that dealt with zoning restrictions. That ordinance, however, according to one council member, had simply "never been enforced." In Justice Stevens's and Justice Ginsburg's opinions, the Erie ordinance sought to ban the *message* being conveyed by nude dancing, and so was unconstitutional in light of the dancing's entitlement to protection as speech. The intentional conflation of the female body with the space it occupies, as indicated in the language of the majority opinion presented by Justice O'Connor, at once dehumanized its targets (hence erasing any concern for speech), and continued the judicial attempt to fix boundaries whereby contagion and its mobility might be minimized. As Elizabeth Grosz has remarked, "The city is one of the crucial factors in the social production of (sexed) corporeality: the built environment provides the context and coordinates for most contemporary Western [. . .] forms of the body."[130]

Of course, the cross-referential imagery of women as buildings (and buildings as women) evident in the Court's focus on zoning has an extensive history. In the fourteenth century, Mondeville characterized bodies as houses, and a woman's body in particular as that which could only "be maintained as such by constant surveillance of its openings."[131] Leon Battista Alberti's fifteenth-century treatise on *The Art of Building in Ten Books* warns that buildings should not be "colored and lewdly dressed with the allurement of painting . . . striving to attract the eye of the beholder, and divert his attention from a proper examination of the parts to be considered."[132] The Supreme Court's ruling once again imagined the female body as an architectural space subject to regulation by zoning, a structure whose facade or frontal appearance can be legislated—in this case by the application of a pastie. The ruling is, therefore, essentially a way to "house" particular perceptions of women, and in a larger sense to inhibit the mobility of female sexual expression, with the object of preventing its escape from the bounds of societal control. Perhaps even more illuminating than the Court's employment of the woman-as-architecture metaphor is the absence of any distinction between exotic dancers and prostitutes noted in the Erie preamble, which stated that it sought to adopt the regulation:

> for the purpose of limiting a recent increase in nude live entertainment within the City, which activity adversely impacts and threatens to impact on the public health, safety and welfare by providing an atmosphere conducive to violence, sexual harassment, public intoxication, prostitution, the spread of sexually transmitted diseases and other deleterious effects.[133]

As if aware of the air of irrationality surrounding the City of Erie's stance, one Council member made an attempt to minimize the effect of the ordinance by acknowledging that "the girls can wear thongs or a G-string and little pasties that are smaller than a diamond."[134] As Justice Stevens asserted, however, "To believe that the mandatory addition of pasties and a G-string will have *any* kind of noticeable impact on secondary effects requires nothing short of a titanic surrender to the implausible."[135] Still, the "less stringent" standard of O'Brien "requires only that the regulation further the interest in combating such effects."[136] One can only infer that the Council's wish to enforce its gesture of authoritative control, rather than the intention to secure any actual reduction in "deleterious effects," was the impetus behind the city's suit. In any case, Erie's judicial right to regulate entertainment on the basis of its presumed effect on public morality was affirmed by Justice O'Connor in her statement:

> The council members, familiar with commercial downtown Erie, are the individuals who would likely have had first-hand knowledge of what took place at and around nude dancing establishments there, and can make particularized, expert judgments about the resulting harmful secondary effects.[137]

In O'Connor's phrasing, the Council members were intriguingly positioned as "experts" on the threat to their city's commercial prospects and, simultaneously, as spectators with "first-hand knowledge of what took place." The inference suggests an ambivalence in which the members sought the knowledge to be gained from their exposure to the contagion of the naked female, while alternately desiring, and exercising, the power to proscribe the message conveyed by her nudity. How "first-hand" their knowledge may have been remains a matter for speculation, but apparently (in the spirit of Alberti) they gave "a proper examination of the parts to be considered."

The Supreme Court's assertion that this particular case be tried as the "regulation of conduct" rather than a case directly aimed at the "suppression of expression," is much too readily dismissive of the freedom of speech protection normally afforded entertainment. If, as Strossen notes, "the Supreme Court long held that the First Amendment extends to all forms of art and entertainment," the *Erie, PA v. Kandyland club* case appears to constitute a refusal on the part of the Court to recognize exotic dancing as performance.[138] "Censorship," states Judith Butler, "is not merely restrictive and privative, that is, active in depriving subjects of the freedom to express themselves in certain ways, but also formative of subjects and the legitimate boundaries of speech."[139] In denying the dancers their rights as performers, the Supreme

Court sought to ratify society's stigmatic assessment of exotic dancers as deviants rather than professional entertainers. By identifying them as engaged in conduct, the Court created a legislatively permissible category of exclusion for nude dancers, within which they may be viewed as exhibitionists who display themselves for the sake of display, rather than as performers who convey meaning through a constructed event.

Exotic dancers do not practice a uniform method of conceiving performances, and not all performances are constructed linearly, or in terms of recognizable narrative. Nonetheless, communication through gestural patterns is an essential attribute of the event. Random, unchoreographed physicalization is the exception in exotic dancing, not the rule. Implicit in the judgment of the Court, however, with its insistence on references to "the" erotic content of the Kandyland dancers' performances, was the assumption that exotic dancers are performatively indistinguishable from one another, merely repeating a message of universalized, monochromatic eroticism in their individual routines. Rhetorically, such an assumption de-individualized the dancers, establishing their assignment to a classification or grouping more easily subject to codification and subsequent regulation. The Kandyland dancers were thus perceived as belonging to a category that Fredric Jameson refers to as "minor," a "fringe group separated from the 'dominant' by its participation in sexual practices that, to the extent that they are recognized as belonging to a 'type' [. . .] are deemed pathological."[140] The reductionism that defined nude dancing in terms favorable to its moral antagonists—as a single-message signifier—rather than in more objective terms—as an expressive conduit for multiple meanings—was additionally notable as an effective attempt to ignore the cultural (and in this case judicial) contradictions attendant on public displays of the female body. These contradictions asserted themselves nonetheless, for what the female bodies on stage at the Kandyland Club may have been *articulating* was precisely what compelled the City of Erie to pursue its program to render those bodies silent, an objective the city eventually achieved by proving, to the Supreme Court's satisfaction, that the dancers' performances did not constitute speech, but conduct. Metaphorically, the court-ordered pasties became, in effect, an attempt to consign particular bodies to a state of muteness.

"The regulation that *states what it does not want stated*" argues Judith Butler, "thwarts its own desires, conducting a performance contradiction that throws into question that regulations capacity to mean and do what it says, that is, its sovereign pretension."[141] The Supreme Court's ruling in favor of Erie, PA, in spite of its apparent impartiality, succeeded in exposing the Court as a judicial body rife with contradictions, assumptions, and prejudices, ultimately committed to the imposition of a particularly moralistic agenda.

By agreeing to consider the case under the O'Brien framework of content neutrality, while simultaneously declaring "nude public dancing *itself* is immoral," the Court, to borrow from Judith Butler, "stated what it did not want stated," namely, its own cultural bias. In so doing, the justices symbolically sanctioned the exclusionary behavior of Cal State Fullerton's track coach, and others, while ratifying the primacy of societal mores that proclaim overt displays of sexuality disruptive, regardless of their arguably protected legal standing. Thus, the Court approved the Erie community's attempt to maintain a position of hierarchical cultural stability through enforced behavior.

Unquestionably, regulations against striptease performers and beauty contestants are tied to cultural notions of "a woman's place," whether zoned to a city's fringe, banished from the track team, or front and center on high-school auditorium stages. In the mid-nineteenth century, Olive Logan asked the public to consider the "nude woman question." Rather than addressing the pressing issue of why women remain "the question," legislative bodies such as the Supreme Court, institutional organizations such as the MAO, and individuals such as Coach John Elder attempt to fabricate an answer by regulating the parameters of female display and imposing ideologically based definitions of morality. Through such gendered directives, they perpetuate the societal imposition of a particularly narrow definition of "place" for women. In the end, an investigation of the sociohistoric relationship between female display and regulation confirms Stuart Hall's belief that "Every regime of representation is a regime of power."[142]

Afterword ∾

"I don't know what'll come next, but there will be girls in it. There always is girls"
Boston Herald, 1919[1]

When Olive Logan asked the public to consider the "nude woman question" in the mid-nineteenth century, it is doubtful even she could have predicted how culturally entrenched the issue would become. In July 2003, more than 100 years after Anthony Comstock's rhetorical rant, "Why is it that every public play must have a naked woman?,"[2] the New York Times' Jesse Green remarked: "These days, there's always some excuse for nakedness onstage."[3] The institutionalization of fleshly display in American popular entertainment is an old story, yet what seems peculiar is that there remains, after 150 or so years of staged female nudity, a taut cultural tension between display and morality necessitating "some excuse."

The nearly nude or overtly naked female form is relentlessly present—not merely in beauty contests and stripping, but in everything from the television dating programs *Joe Millionaire, The Bachelor, Who Wants to Marry My Dad,* and *For Love or Money,* to the game shows *Fear Factor* and *Dog Eat Dog* (in which famed burlesque stripper Dixie Evans, in a nod to the theatrical heritage of such forms, made an appearance in May 2003). Every program has a woman stripping (under the pretense of dressing or undressing) and a scene where she appears in a bikini and "gets wet." Moreover, the recent television competition (2003) to crown the definitive *All-American Girl* confirmed that overtly sexual images are becoming more culturally accepted as an integral aspect of female competitions based on display.[4] The program, which promoted itself as a search for the young woman who would "really" represent America, required its contestants to run an obstacle course in tiny bikinis, breasts bobbing as they worked their way through a maze of tires, and bottoms rocking as they squirmed on their bellies through a tight tunnel. In its premier episode, the show featured a dancer from Las Vegas who performed an exotic dance routine replete with the mimed phallic image of a smoking gun. One very appreciative judge, former basketball star John Sally, strongly advocated for "his chickadee from Vegas" throughout the competition.

Given the diverse proliferation of sexualized images of women in popular entertainment, the show's marketing strategy (a "beauty" contest) as the pretext for displaying such images might seem superfluous. Yet the producers of the contest utilized its pageant format quite explicitly to play upon the audience's expectation that the All-American Girl was ipso facto wholesome, ensuring that few would question why the clothing requirement for the obstacle course was a bikini; or, why nearly naked contestants were, quite literally, jumping through hoops, compelled to endure the ever present possibility that a hook or snap would come undone and they would be "exposed." The continued insistence that productions such as *All-American Girl* are about something, anything, other than display is directly tied to society's sustained belief in female performance as revelatory of a moral, or immoral, self.

Performing women have been corseted for centuries with cultural theories of appearance, morality, stability, deviance, and pathology, resulting in, as Jacqueline Rose has commented, the "constant pressure of something hidden but not forgotten."[5] "Acting female is what traditionalists and reactionaries prescribe for women," states Faye Dudden, "but an 'acting female'—a woman who plays roles—reveals the possibility of escaping that imperative."[6] Still, as I have argued, the inherent problem for women who participate in the entertainment forms of stripping or beauty contests is society's refusal to accept the illusive craft in their performances, clinging instead to a cultural misapprehension that performers "are what they do." This perception situates these performers at opposite ends of an assumptive moral spectrum. We have a cultural investment in perpetuating and controlling the images of women on public stages, using their bodies as maps in order to discover or affirm our own moral bearings and to establish rules for public female behavior. Thus, beauty contests have always been, in spite of pageant organizations' rhetorical objections to the contrary, a performance of "social discipline and not social advance."[7] Similarly, strip clubs offer a highly regulated environment where performances of allowable female sexuality, within a very narrow range, are enacted.

Because we have become so culturally inured to openly displayed images of nude women in the United States, it is often easier to recognize ideologically based regulatory control at work in other countries. In 2002, the Miss World Pageant gained unanticipated notoriety when it was forced to move from the Nigerian capital Abuja to London after rioting left more than 200 dead and well over 500 injured. Newspapers announced that angry mobs "rampaged through the streets stabbing, bludgeoning and burning bystanders to death. Shops were looted, cars were overturned and scorched while makeshift barricades were set alight. Fires also burned in mosques and windows were smashed. Shehu Sani of the Kaduna-based Civil Rights Congress told the Associated Press he watched a crowd stab a young man, force a petrol-filled tire around his neck and burn him alive."[8] According to a news article, "hordes" of men were heard shouting "Down with beauty" and "Miss World is sin."[9] "Critics said the show should be abandoned. 'These girls will be wearing swimwear dripping with blood,' British writer Muriel Gray said."[10] Allegedly, the "violence erupted when a Nigerian journalist wrote an article claiming the Prophet Muhammad would have approved of the contest and might even have taken one of the contestants as his bride. The result was the deadly rioting in the northern city of Kaduna."[11] The paper that issued the article printed three apologies and, according to Reuters, said the story "went out in error."[12] Perhaps it is possible to read the journalist's offending news article as an (ill-conceived) attempt to legitimize the pageant, to make it more culturally palatable through the hypothetical sanctioning of Muhammad. In any event, the riots were a tragic reminder that female display carries within it a political component irrespective of region or culture.

The prevailing sentiment that the riots occurred because of the news article linking Muhammad to a beauty contestant masks the much deeper root concern over the destabilizing influence of women on a given social order. The fact is Miss World 2002 was a locus for societal controversy before the offending news article ever went to press. "The controversy began when a number of contestants boycotted the competition after an Islamic court in Nigeria condemned a woman to death by stoning for having a child outside marriage. The Nigerian government promised the sentence would not be carried out, and Morley [the Miss World organizer] pressed ahead."[13] The two seemingly diametrically oppositional events, a beauty pageant and a capital punishment case, became linked by violence and their relationship with governmental regulation of female visibility and behavior. Only the most idealistic would interpret the Nigerian government's suspension of the death sentence as a direct result of the resistance by beauty contestants. The patriarchal policy did not change, only the press release. The Miss World furor and the death sentence case reflect continued preoccupations with parameters of female autonomy. Additionally, cases of rioting at previous Miss World competitions would seem to confirm (without denying it may have played some role) the link to Muhammad as something of a red herring. At the 1996 Miss World pageant, "when the finals were held in the Indian city of Bangalore, police fired tear gas and rubber bullets at rock-throwing protestors, and one man committed suicide by self-immolation."[14] Such actions echo and reinforce the arguments made by anti-burlesquers and the U.S. Supreme Court that sexualized female display is the cause of "harmful secondary effects," leading the population to lose all sense of social order.

In the United States, where Miss America beauty contestants thank God for putting them on the stage, and a bikini-clad Mrs. America Pageant contestant proudly announces her status as a minister's wife,[15] female sexuality and ideological notions of value and morality are intentionally conjoined to market a particular image of socially acceptable femaleness. That the naked woman is endemic to American entertainment should not obscure the fact that the performing women in question are just as subject to systematic control as were the participants in the 2002 Miss World contest. To look at the Miss World chaos and segregate it as an occurrence only possible in some "Other" (read less civilized) country, is to align oneself with the promoter of the dubious (and now urban-legendary) entertainment "Hunting for Bambi," a Las Vegas enterprise that purported to offer men the opportunity to shoot naked women with paint guns for $10,000. The game's impresario, when confronted with criticism from women's groups, remarked that "the women who think this is abusive and degrading need to put their attention where it should be, and I think that is Afghanistan. We love our girls."[16] While the actual existence of the "hunt" has been declared apocryphal by Las Vegas officials, the governing attitude expressed by its promoters most certainly is not.

The issue is still one of a woman's "place." For many female performers in the United States, "place" signifies an embodied condition dependent upon, to reiterate Geraldine Maschio's definition used in the Introduction, a culturally "verifiable image of woman."[17] Cultural verification of "appropriate" female conduct, whether in entertainment or elsewhere, need not be defined or explained, only referenced, to be understood. When candidate Mitt Romney, in the 2002 Massachusetts gubernatorial race, referred to his opponent Shannon O'Brian's debate conduct as "unbecoming" (a phrase remarkably absent from the lexicon of male descriptives), his remark may have provoked outrage, but required no clarification. Precisely the same sort of received cultural definitions of "becoming" behavior for women are daily exhibited on strip club and pageant stages. They, too, require no explanation.

The societal compulsion to assign forms of female display to so many discrete value systems has masked the overriding truth of beauty contests and striptease—that both forms are ultimately conservative confirmations of our social expectations. In spite of individual accounts of "empowerment" by some strippers and pageant contestants, and academic assertions of the social "transgressivness" of female disrobing in front of male paying customers, nothing happens in a strip club that one has not thought about, read about, or done. As Roland Barthes remarked of stripping, "the props, décor and stereotypes intervene to contradict the initially provocative intention [. . .] eventually to bury it in insignificance."[18] Governed by economics and social myths of deviance, strip clubs are, to borrow from Terry Eagleton's description of carnival, in the end, "politically ineffectual spaces."[19] Such a description applies equally well to beauty pageants which simply invert the strip club's myth-making strategy, positing and marketing a variant social construct—"normalcy" rather than "deviance."

Undressed for Success is an attempt to explore Judith Baer's imperative that we "inquire not how women fit theories, but how theories fit women."[20] As long as theories of morality are branded across the bodies of performing women, the potential for expressing what it is to be both female and a performer will be necessarily constrained and profoundly misunderstood. The rising field of feminist geography, which interrogates the situating of women within controlled social space, has pointed out that with regard to women and place, "men acting in the context of geography are the fieldworkers, [with] the Woman appearing as landscape."[21] Until ideologically based assumptions of morality cease to function as criteria by which performers in strip clubs and beauty pageants are socially recognized, these performers will continue to serve as cultural markers, and marketers, of a rigidly standardized definition of the American Female in popular entertainment.

Notes ∾

INTRODUCTION

1. "Striptease" is used throughout the book as a general category of female display, encompassing subcategories such as stripping, bikini dancing, and exotic dancing. The distinctions between such subcategories are detailed within individual chapters. Likewise, relevant differences in individual beauty contests are addressed in specific chapters.
2. Personal Interview, Susan Mills, May 1, 2001. All subsequent references to remarks made by Ms. Mills are excerpted from this same interview.
3. Read, *Theatre and Everyday Life*, 11.
4. Maschio, "A Prescription for Femininity: Male Interpretation of the Feminine Ideal at the Turn of the Century," *Women and Performance*, 42–49. Although it refers to female impersonators, Maschio's "verifiable image of woman" carries the inherent understanding that any cultural image bound by accepted standards of "authenticity" is a fictive construct.
5. Felski, "The Dialectic of 'Feminism' and 'Aesthetics,' " *Feminisms*, 425.
6. In particular, Sarah Banet Weiser's *The Most Beautiful Girl in the World* and *Beauty Queens on the Global Stage* (edited by Colleen Ballerino Cohen), have focused on the role beauty contests play in gendered constructions of nation-ness and political control. Katherine Liepe Levinson's recent book *Strip Show: Performances of Gender and Desire (Gender in Performance)* explores the potential for the transgressive and the "wielding of power" in the act of striptease. Additionally, Lucinda Jarrett's *Stripping in Time*, David Scott's *Behind the G-String*, Katherine Frank's *G-Strings and Sympathy: Strip Club Regulars and Male Desire*, and Lily Burana's *Strip City* offer glimpses into performance, presentation, and social response in the realm of exotic dancing. *Female Spectacle* (Susan A. Glenn), *Ziegfeld Girl* (Linda Mizejewski), *Rank Ladies* (Alison Kibler), and *Posing a Threat* (Angelea J. Latham) have also made significant contributions to contemporary discussions of female display and social agency. Finally, in an unpublished 1991 dissertation (*Fashion Shows, Strip Shows, Beauty Pageants: Theatre of the Feminine Ideal*) that is unavailable from UMI, Tara Maginnis conducted an exploration of some of the links between forms of female popular entertainment. My interdisciplinary study was, in part, made possible by the hard work and scholarship of the aforementioned academics.

7. Kirshenblatt-Gimblett, <www.nyu.edu/tisch/performance/pages/essays/bkg. html.>.

8. Mankowitz, *Mazeppa*, 20.

9. Logan, *Before the Footlights and Behind the Scenes*, 587.

10. Quoted in Allen, *Horrible Prettiness*, 153.

11. Bentley, *Sisters of Salome*, 34.

12. Zeidman, *The American Burlesque Show*, 157.

13. Johnson, *The Feminist Difference*, 22.

14. Zeidman, *The American Burlesque Show*, 38.

15. "Miss America Pageant Cans Talent Spots," July 30, 2004, CNN, <http:// www.cnn.com/2004/US/Northeast/07/29/pageant.talent.ap/>.

16. Eaves, *Bare: On Women, Dancing, Sex, and Power*, 268.

17. Ibid., 288.

18. "Warren G. Harding calls for a Return to Normalcy, Boston, MA, May 14, 1920," <http://www.pbs.org/greatspeeches/timeline/w_harding_s.html>, accessed June 15, 2003. Thanks to Martin Marks at MIT for pointing out the relevance to this project of Harding's definition of "normalcy."

19. Etcoff, *Survival of the Prettiest*, 84.

20. Banner, *American Beauty*, 183.

21. *City of Erie v. PAP'S A. M.*, 529 US 277, 120 S.Ct. 1522 (2000) at 6.

22. Alexander, *Strip Tease: The Vanished Art of Burlesque*, 43.

23. *Miss America*, written by Michelle Ferrari, Dir. Lisa Ades and Leslie Klainberg, Narr. Cherry Jones, American Experience, PBS, WGBH Boston, 2002.

1 "STRIPPING THE LIGHT FANTASTIC": HISTORICAL CROSS-POLLINATION IN STAGED FEMALE EXPOSURE

* Lee Mortimer, *Daily Mirror* clipping quoting Winnie Garrett, uncatalogued loose papers, Paul Jordan Collection, Harvard Theatre Collection, Box 3.

1. Early-twentieth-century popular Burlesque song title, quoted in Zeidman, *The American Burlesque Show,* 139.

2. Mankowitz, *Mazeppa*, 20.

3. Ibid.

4. Quoted in Mankowitz, *Mazeppa*, 20.

5. Logan, *Before the Footlights and Behind the Scenes*, 587.

6. Russo, "Female Grotesques," 213.

7. Rose, *Feminism and Geography*, 6.

8. Hornick*, Cavalcade of Burlesque*, Vol. 2, No. 3, 15.

9. Quoted in Mankowitz, *Mazeppa*, 136.

10. Davis, *Actresses as Working Women*, xvi.

11. Logan, *The Mimic World*, 565.

12. Quoted in Fraser's, *The Weaker Vessel*, 28.

13. Allen, *Horrible Prettiness*, 108, emphasis mine.

14. Whitton, *The Naked Truth! An Inside History of The Black Crook*, 5.
15. Banner, *American Beauty*, 255.
16. Quoted in Gilbert, *American Vaudeville*, 243.
17. Wilmeth and Miller, *Cambridge Guide to American Theatre*, 79.
18. Ibid., 390.
19. McCullough, *Living Pictures*, 16.
20. Ibid., 17.
21. Quoted in McCullough, *Living Pictures*, 19.
22. Ibid., 81.
23. Ibid., 84.
24. Zeidman, *The American Burlesque Show*, 36.
25. Hearn, "Tips on Tables," uncatalogued loose papers, n.d., Paul Jordan Collection, Harvard Theatre Collection.
26. Nathan, *The World in Falseface*, 151.
27. McCullough, *Living Pictures*, 104.
28. Stencell, *Girl Show: Into the Canvas World of Bump and Grind*, 51.
29. Ibid.
30. Gilbert, *American Vaudeville*, 190.
31. Quoted in Minsky, *Minsky's Burlesque*, 83.
32. Wortley, *A Pictorial History of Striptease*, 83.
33. Zeidman, *The American Burlesque Show*, 84.
34. Unidentified publicity material, Paul Jordan Collection, Box 5, Folder O, Harvard Theatre Collection.
35. Wigley, "Untitled: The Housing of Gender," *Sexuality and Space*, 358.
36. Montrelay, "Inquiry into Femininity," *M/F*, 89.
37. Liepe-Levinson, *Strip Show*, 155, emphasis mine.
38. Carlton, *Looking for Little Egypt*, 19.
39. Terry and Urla, *Deviant Bodies*, 9.
40. Carlton, *Looking for Little Egypt*, 23.
41. Unidentified promotional materials, Box 5, Folder D, Paul Jordan Collection, Harvard Theatre Collection.
42. Carlton, *Looking for Little Egypt*, xi.
43. Ibid., 57.
44. Zeidman, *The American Burlesque Show*, 60.
45. Carlton, *Looking for Little Egypt*, 51.
46. Liepe-Levinson, *Strip Show*, 113.
47. Carlton, *Looking for Little Egypt*, 63.
48. Ibid., 93.
49. Zeidman, *The American Burlesque Show*, 13.
50. Peiss, "On Beauty . . . and the History of Business," *Beauty and Business: Commerce, Gender, and Culture in Modern America*, 15.
51. Farnsworth, *The Ziegfeld Follies*, 21.
52. Bentley, *Sisters of Salome*, 19.

53. Ibid., 39.
54. Glenn, *Female Spectacle*, 100.
55. Ibid., 101.
56. Bentley, *Sisters of Salome*, 30.
57. Buckley, "The Culture of 'Leg-Work': The Transformation of Burlesque after the Civil War," *The Mythmaking Frame of Mind: Social Imagination and American Culture*, 117.
58. A *Hartford Current* review, quoted in Bentley, *Sisters of Salome*, 39.
59. Glenn, *Female Spectacle*, 103.
60. Bland, "Trial by Sexology?" *Sexology in Culture: Labeling Bodies and Desire*, 185.
61. Rosen, *Popcorn Venus: Women, Movies, and the American Dream*, 19.
62. Zeidman, *The American Burlesque Show*, 61.
63. Promotional 8×10s of female performers, Box 5, Paul Jordan Collection, Harvard Theatre Collection.
64. Kinetz, "Do a Striptease, Sing a Big Aria, All in a Night's Work," *New York Sunday Times*, March 14, 2004: 26.
65. Carlton, *Looking for Little Egypt*, 59.
66. Fish, *Blue Ribbons and Burlesque: A Book of Country Fairs*, 236.
67. Ibid., 204.
68. Ibid., 248.
69. Hornick, *Cavalcade of Burlesque*, Fall 1951, 18.
70. Ibid., 24.
71. Ibid.
72. Ibid.
73. Osborne, *Miss America: The Dream Lives On*, 55.
74. Banner, *American Beauty*, 257.
75. "Days When the Black Crook was Daring," *New York Times,* March 10, 1929.
76. Gypsy Rose Lee Collection, Box 79, Folder 2, anonymous newspaper clipping, Billy Rose Theatre Collection, New York Public Library at Lincoln Center.
77. *The New York Woman*, 1936, Billy Rose Theatre Collection, New York Public Library at Lincoln Center.
78. Ibid.
79. Zeidman, *The American Burlesque Show*, 142.
80. Quoted in Latham, *Posing a Threat*, 107.
81. Cantor, "Ziegfeld and His Follies," *Collier's National Weekly*, January 13, 1934, 9–10.
82. Murray, *The Body Merchant*, 42.
83. Ibid., 43.
84. Ibid., 238.
85. Rogers St. Johns, "The Girls Who Glorified Ziegfeld," *American Weekly,* 1946 (n.p.).
86. Earl Carroll *Vanities* program, 8th Edition, 1930.
87. Farnsworth, *The Ziegfeld Follies*, 156.
88. Earl Carroll *Vanities* program, 8th Edition, 1930.

89. Associated Press news photo and blurb, 1926.
90. Earl Carroll *Vanities* Program, 8th Edition, 1930.
91. Rogers St. Johns, *American Weekly*, 1946 (n.p.).
92. Minsky, *Minsky's Burlesque: A Fast and Funny Look at America's Bawdiest Era*, 231.
93. 1922 Ziegfeld *Follies* program, Harry Ransom Center, Ziegfeld Collection, Box 1.17.
94. Zeidman, *The American Burlesque Show*, 119.
95. Eddie Cantor, "Ziegfeld and His Follies," *National Weekly*, January 13, 1934, 8.
96. Nathan, *The Theatre, The Drama, The Girls*, 290.
97. Farnsworth, *The Ziegfeld Follies: A History in Text and Pictures*, 11.
98. Percy Hammond, reprinted in the *Dallas News*, November 4, 1923, Ziegfeld Collection, Box 1.18, Harry Ransom Center.
99. Zeidman, *The American Burlesque Show*, 140.
100. Nathan, *The Popular Theatre*, 86.
101. Woolcott, *New York Times Theatre Reviews 1920–1926, Volume 1*.
102. Ziegfeld Collection, Box 4.24, Harry Ransom Center.
103. Nathan, *The Theatre, The Drama, The Girls*, 147.
104. Banner, *American Beauty*, 152.
105. Quoted in Farnsworth, *The Ziegfeld Follies*, 40.
106. Ibid.
107. *Cavalcade of Burlesque*, Vol. 2, 15.
108. Reid, *Dramatic Mirror*, 5.
109. 1924 Ziegfeld *Follies* program, Ziegfeld Collection, Box 1.19, Harry Ransom Center.
110. Mrs. America Pageant, PAX Channel, October 12, 2002.
111. Quoted in Allen, *Horrible Prettiness*, 233.
112. Ibid., 245.
113. Nathan, *The Theatre, The Drama, The Girls*, 293, emphasis mine.
114. Tony Pastor Collection, 1893 Theatrical Broadside, Harry Ransom Center.
115. Louis Reid, "Vaudeville in Many Cities," *Dramatic Mirror*, July 3, 1920.
116. Quoted in Minsky, *Minsky's Burlesque*, 231.
117. Zeidman, *The American Burlesque Show*, 137.
118. Ibid., 43.
119. Levine, *Highbrow/Lowbrow: The Emergence of Cultural Hierarchy in America*, 7.
120. Zeidman, *The American Burlesque Show*, 142.
121. Etcoff, *Survival of the Prettiest*, 44.
122. Quoted in Chapkis, *Live Sex Acts*, 211.
123. *World Telegraph* (n.d., n.p.), Paul Jordan Collection, Box 5, Folder E, Harvard Theatre Collection.
124. Quoted in Meiselas, *Carnival Strippers*, 113.
125. Alan Carter, "Hey Big Spender!: Spend a Little Time Getting to Know Janette Boyd," *New York Daily News,* January 30, 1986, Paul Jordan Collection, Box 3, Harvard Theatre Collection.

126. Franklin L. Thistle, "The Off-Stage Shenanigans of Strippers," <www.javabachelor.100megs4.com,> Vol. 3, No. 8, February 1959.

127. Burana, *Strip City*, 257.

128. Quoted in Scott, *Behind the G-String*, 229.

2 "IT AIN'T WHAT YOU DO, IT'S THE WAY WHAT YOU DO IT": SEGMENTING FEMALE SPECTACLE ON THE BASIS OF CONSTRUCTED MORALITY

* 1930s popular song title quoted in Minsky, *Minsky's Burlesque*, 231.

1. Quoted in Allen, *Horrible Prettiness*, from an 1871 *New York Clipper* editorial.

2. Minsky, *Minsky's Burlesque*, 197.

3. Corbin, "Puritan Attacks on the Stage and Its Clothes," 1919, Black Crook Collection, Box 1, Harry Ransom Center.

4. Schneider, *The Explicit Body in Performance*, 7.

5. Goffman, *The Presentation of Self in Everyday Life*, 251.

6. Quoted in McArthur, *Actors and American Culture, 1880–1920*, 129.

7. Mankowitz, *Mazeppa*, 20.

8. Roach, *The Player's Passion*, 41.

9. Ibid.

10. Allen, *Horrible Prettiness,* 50.

11. Stratton, *The Desirable Body*, 101.

12. *Star and Garter* Souvenir Program, 1943.

13. Quoted in Crary, *Vision and Visuality*, 41.

14. Kott, *The Memory of the Body*, 93.

15. Terry and Urla, *Deviant Bodies*, 7.

16. Douglas, *Purity and Danger*, 4.

17. Logan, *Before the Footlights and Behind the Scenes*, 576. It should be noted that Olive Logan herself did not lack for detractors. Mark Twain wrote of her "oddly created notoriety" that "she was merely a name and some rich and costly clothes, and neither of these properties had any lasting quality" (Quoted in Kurt Gänzl, 106).

18. Allen, *Horrible Prettiness*, 264.

19. MacKinnon, *Only Words*, 33.

20. Quoted in Bentley, *Sisters of Salome*, 79.

21. Quoted in Glenn, *Female Spectacle*, 89.

22. Ibid.

23. Quoted in Bentley, *Sisters of Salome*, 80.

24. Grosz, "Bodies-Cities," 243.

25. Johnson, *The Feminist Difference*, 22.

26. Quoted in Latham, *Posing a Threat*, 100.

27. Woollcott, *New York Times Theatre Reviews*, 1922.

28. Banner, *American Beauty*, 133.
29. Ibid.
30. Roach, *The Player's Passion*, 52.
31. Latham, *Posing a Threat*, 103.
32. As Rebecca Schneider has observed, "The explicit body in performance is foremost a site of social markings [. . .] all of which bear ghosts of historical meaning" (2).
33. Zeidman, *The American Burlesque Show*, 171.
34. Banner, *American Beauty*, 11.
35. Ibid., 206.
36. 1927 Ziegfeld *Follies* program, Ziegfeld Collection, Box 1.21, Harry Ransom Center.
37. Allen, *Horrible Prettiness*, 84.
38. Quoted in Minsky, *Minsky's Burlesque*, 274.
39. Banner, *American Beauty*, 208.
40. "A Night of Triumph for Mineralava," *Madison Square Garden Beauty Bulletin*, November 28, 1923, Billy Rose Theatre Collection, New York Public Library at Lincoln Center.
41. *Austin Statesman*, January 18, 1928, Ziegfeld Collection, Box 4.21, Harry Ransom Center.
42. Nathan, *The Popular Theatre*, 87.
43. Banner, *American Beauty*, 208.
44. Allen, *Horrible Prettiness*, 84.
45. Kingsley, "About Beauties," *Daily Mirror*, July 3, 1920.
46. Rogers St. John, "The Girls Who Glorified Ziegfeld" (a series of four articles), July 14, 1946, Florenz Ziegfeld—Billie Burke Papers, Series III, Box 14, Folder 37, Billy Rose Theatre Collection, New York Public Library at Lincoln Center.
47. Cantor, "Ziegfeld and His Follies," February 10, 1934, 40.
48. Quoted in Etcoff, *Survival of the Prettiest*, 40.
49. "Beauty contestants don Gadhafi tees." <www.CNN.com>, November 2, 2002.
50. *Austin Statesman,* January 18, 1928, Ziegfeld Collection, Box 4.21, Harry Ransom Center.
51. Kingston, "What I have learned from Florenz Ziegfeld," November 2, 1924, Ziegfeld Collection, Box 4.21, Harry Ransom Center.
52. *New York Evening Journal,* July 23, 1932: 4, Ziegfeld Collection, Box 4.21, Harry Ransom Center.
53. Quoted in McArthur, *Actors and American Culture, 1880–1920*, 188.
54. Zeidman, *The American Burlesque Show*, 142.
55. Ibid., 233.
56. Cantor and Freedman, "Ziegfeld and His Follies," January 13, 1934.
57. As noted by a *New York Times* reviewer in 1920, "It is, of course, pre-eminently as a show place for feminine pulchritude that the Ziegfeld roof has made its name." Woolcott, *New York Times Theatre Reviews 1920–1926, Volume 1.*

58. Gross, "It's the same show—but 'Miss A' is a big winner." September 13, 1965. Billy Rose Theatre Collection, New York Public Library at Lincoln Center.

59. *New York Herald Tribune*, September 9, 1963, file under "Miss America, 1960s," Billy Rose Theatre Collection, New York Public Library at Lincoln Center.

60. Lee, "Miss America, Inc.: Beauty Show that Started as a Boardwalk Carnival is Now a Refined Business," September 3, 1961.

61. Ibid.

62. Riverol, *Live from Atlantic City*, 27.

63. *Variety*, September 16, 1964, Miss America Folder 1960s, Billy Rose Theatre Collection, New York Public Library at Lincoln Center.

64. Carroll *Vanities* program, 8th Edition, 1930, emphasis mine.

65. *Time*, March 11, 1957, Ziegfeld Collection, Box 1.23, Harry Ransom Center.

66. Langer, *Feeling and Form: A Theory of Art*, 93.

67. Banet-Weiser, *The Most Beautiful Girl in the World*, 33.

68. Zeidman, *The American Burlesque Show*, 11.

69. Banet-Weiser, *The Most Beautiful Girl in the World*, 38.

70. Gypsy Rose Lee Papers, publicity papers, Box 79, Folder 1, Billy Rose Theatre Collection, New York Public Library at Lincoln Center.

71. Bambi Vawn Papers, transcript of a 1989 Sally Jesse Raphael Program, Series I, Box 1, Folder 1, Billy Rose Theatre Collection, New York Public Library at Lincoln Center.

72. Banet-Weiser, *The Most Beautiful Girl in the World*, 38.

73. Perlmutter, "Miss America: Whose Ideal?" *Beauty Matters*, 156.

74. Osborne, *Miss America: The Dream Lives On*, 86.

75. Quoted in Minsky, *The American Burlesque Show*, 255.

76. Stanley, *The Crowning Touch*, 78.

77. Ibid., 89.

78. Goffman, *The Presentation of Self in Everyday Life*, 13.

79. Bell, "City Beat Column," *New York Daily News*, August 14, 1989. Bambi Vawn Papers, Series I, Box 1, Folder 3, Billy Rose Theatre Collection, New York Public Library at Lincoln Center.

80. "A Night of Triumph for Mineralava," *Madison Square Garden Beauty Bulletin*, November 28, 1923, Billy Rose Theatre Collection, New York Public Library at Lincoln Center.

81. E.D. Price, editorial, 1931 Ziegfeld *Follies* program, Ziegfeld Collection, Box 1.22, Harry Ransom Center.

82. Minsky, *Minsky's Burlesque*, 267.

83. Friedman, *Prurient Interests*, 92.

84. Ibid.

85. Quoted in Dworkin, *Miss America, 1945: Bess Myerson's Own Story*, 105.

86. Minsky, *Minsky's Burlesque*, 268.

87. Ibid., 245.

88. 1928 Ziegfeld Theatre *Rosalie* program, 19.

89. *Star and Garter* Souvenir Book, 1943.
90. Ibid.
91. Zeidman, *The American Burlesque Show*, 94.
92. Ibid., 121.
93. 1931 Ziegfeld *Follies* program, Ziegfeld Collection, Box 1.22, Harry Ransom Center.
94. Carlton, *Looking for Little Egypt*, 80.
95. Interview, Amy Slattum, Miss New Hampshire contestant, NHPR, Spring 1999.
96. Zeidman, *The American Burlesque Show*, 38.
97. Ibid., 144.
98. McCullough, *Living Pictures*, 80.
99. *Cavalcade of Burlesque*, Vol. 1, No. 1, Fall 1951, 46. Bambi Vawn Papers, Series I, Box 1, Folder 6, Billy Rose Theatre Collection, New York Public Library at Lincoln Center.
100. Kruh, <www.bambinomusical.com/Scollay/Howard.html.>.
101. Bodian, "Burlesque at the Empire theatre," <www.virtualnewarknj.comememories/burlesqu/bodianempire.htm.>.
102. Starker, <www.columbusalive.com/2001>.
103. Folly Theater History, <www.follytheater.com/history_burlesque.html.>.
104. Victoria Theatre, <www. victoriatheatre.org/about.htm.>.
105. Amorosi, "Nightlife's Nine Lives," September 17–24, 1998.
106. Levine, *Highbrow/Lowbrow*, 7.
107. Program for the 28th Annual Wheatheart of the Nation Contest, August 24, 1974.
108. Bambi Vawn papers, Sally Jessy Raphael transcript, 1989, Series I, Box 1, Folder 1, Billy Rose Theatre Collection, New York Public Library at Lincoln Center.
109. Mortimer, *Woman Confidential*, 109.
110. Personal Interview, "Silver," May 30, 2002. All subsequent references to remarks made by "Silver" are excerpted from this same interview.
111. Bambi Vawn papers, Sally Jessy Raphael transcript, 1989, Series I, Box 1, Folder 1, Billy Rose Theatre Collection, New York Public Library at Lincoln Center.
112. Carlton, *Looking for Little Egypt*, 46.
113. Personal Interview, Grace Swank Davis, April 2000. All subsequent references to remarks made by Ms. Davis are excerpted from this same interview.
114. Stanley, *The Crowning Touch*, 1.
115. Personal Interview, former Miss Rhode Island contestant, Spring 1999. All subsequent references to remarks made by this contestant are excerpted from the same interview.
116. Personal Interview, Laura Lawless, Miss Arizona 2002, September 19, 2002. All subsequent references to remarks made by Ms. Lawless are excerpted from this same interview.
117. Lawless's question is a telling echo of the early rhetoric against beauty pageants. In 1968, when the Miss America Pageant was disrupted both from within and

without by a contestant who unraveled a banner of protest on the stage and the vociferous debate raging outside on the Boardwalk, pageant denunciators focused public scrutiny on the objectification of women's bodies, insisting that women be recognized as more than "lips and hips." Yet, in spite of its historical remembrance as a kind of watershed moment in the feminist movement of the 1960s, and the very real changes made in the public's awareness of its own constructions and impositions of gender, the protest was ultimately ineffective with respect to squelching the kinds of displays that initiated the infamous demonstration. There are more beauty pageants today than ever before, and sexualized female display as entertainment is endemic in American popular entertainment.

118. (MAO) Unofficial Miss Oklahoma Message Board, <www.voy.com/79996>, accessed September 19, 2004.

119. *Boston Herald American,* September 6, 1976. Paul Jordan Collection, Box 5, Folder M, Harvard Theatre Collection, Houghton Library, Cambridge, MA.

120. Wohlfert-Wihlborg, "Here She Comes," *People Magazine,* September 19, 1983.

121. *Newsday,* July 26, 1984.

122. DePaulo, "Behind Those Smiles: Inside the Mind of Miss America," *TV Guide* September 10, 1988: 7.

123. Wohlfert-Wihlborg, "Here She Comes," *People Magazine,* September 19, 1983: 95.

124. Gross, "It's the same show—but 'Miss A' is a big winner," *New York Daily News* September 13, 1965. Billy Rose Theatre Collection, New York Public Library at Lincoln Center.

125. Lee, "Miss America, Inc.: Beauty Show that Started as a Boardwalk Carnival is Now a Refined Business," *New York Sunday News,* September 3, 1961.

126. *Variety* (review), 1959, Miss America folder 1950–59, Billy Rose Theatre Collection, New York Public Library at Lincoln Center.

127. Simon, "For God, for love—and for West Allis, Wisconsin," September 11, 1976, Miss America folder 1970s, Billy Rose Theatre Collection, New York Public Library at Lincoln Center.

128. Gill, "The Miss America Uproar: What it says about us all," September 15, 1984.

129. Ibid.

130. *New York Press,* September 11, 1978: 11, Miss America folder 1970s, Billy Rose Theatre Collection, New York Public Library at Lincoln Center.

131. O'Reilly, *TV Guide* September 17, 1983, Miss America folder 1970s, Billy Rose Theatre Collection, New York Public Library at Lincoln Center.

132. *Newsday,* July 26, 1984, Miss America folder 1980s, Billy Rose Theatre Collection, New York Public Library at Lincoln Center.

133. Spivak, "Poststructuralism, Marginality, Postcoloniality and Value," 204.

134. Hornick, *Cavalcade of Burlesque,* 5.

135. Grosz, *Space, Time, and Perversion,* 26.

136. Ibid., 37.

137. debord, *The Society of the Spectacle,* 13.

138. Hornick, *Cavalcade of Burlesque,* Vol. 2, No. 1, December 1952: 32.

3 ARTIFICE AND AUTHENTICITY: PARALLELS IN PERFORMANCE APPROACH

1. "Some Girls," May 2, 1980, Billy Rose Theatre Collection, New York Public Library at Lincoln Center.
2. Hornick, *Cavalcade of Burlesque*, Vol. 2, No. 2, 11.
3. Carpozi, "America's Dream Girls," September 11, 1982.
4. Burana, *Strip City*, 260.
5. Wolfflin, *Renaissance and Baroque*, 77.
6. Liepe-Levinson, *Strip Show*, 122.
7. Quoted in Carlton, *Looking for Little Egypt*, 29.
8. Burana, *Strip City*, 258.
9. Roger Simon, "For God, for Love—and for West Allis, Wisconsin," September 11, 1976: 29.
10. Quoted in Stanley, *The Crowning Touch*, 51.
11. Etcoff, *Survival of the Prettiest*, 115.
12. Personal Interview, Susan Scotto, November, 3, 2000. All subsequent references to remarks made by Ms. Scotto are excerpted from this same interview.
13. *New York Press* September 11, 1978: 11, Miss America folder 1970s, Billy Rose Theatre Collection, New York Public Library at Lincoln Center.
14. Ibid.
15. States, *Reckonings in Little Rooms*, 25.
16. Zeidman, *The American Burlesque Show*, 126.
17. *Stripper of the Year*, Westwood Productions, 1990.
18. Mankowitz, *Mazeppa*, 119.
19. Alexander, *Strip Tease*, 35.
20. Roger Simon, "For God, for Love and for West Allis, Wisconsin," 1976: 28.
21. Henley, *Body Politics*, 90.
22. Stanley, *The Crowning Touch*, 63.
23. Axum, *The Outer You . . .* , 21.
24. Quoted in Stanley, *The Crowning Touch*, 6.
25. *American Weekly*, June 16, 1946, Florenz Ziegfeld—Billie Burke papers, Series III, Box 14, Folder 37, Billy Rose Theatre Collection, New York Public Library at Lincoln Center.
26. "Ziegfeld and his *Follies*" [retrospective] January 9, 1957. Billy Rose Theatre Collection, New York Public Library at Lincoln Center.
27. Hornick, *Cavalcade of Burlesque*, Vol. 2, No. 2, March 1953: 9.
28. Personal Interview, Miss South Dakota 2002, September 20, 2002. All subsequent references are excerpted from this same interview.
29. *Variety* clipping review, Miss America folder 1950–59, Billy Rose Theatre Collection, New York Public Library at Lincoln Center.
30. Zeidman, *The American Burlesque Show*, 140.
31. Personal Interview, Amateur runway model, Providence, Rhode Island, Spring 2000.

32. Zeidman, *The American Burlesque Show*, 140.
33. George Carpozi, "America's Dream Girls," September 11, 1982.
34. Burana, *Strip City*, 258.
35. "Some Girls," May 2, 1980, Billy Rose Theatre Collection, New York Public Library at Lincoln Center.
36. Stanley, *The Crowning Touch*, 56.
37. Peiss, *On Beauty . . . and the History of Business*, 18.
38. Bentley, *Sisters of Salome*, 5.
39. Personal Interview, Erika Harold, Miss Illinois 2002, September 19, 2002. Ms. Harold was later crowned Miss America 2003. All subsequent references are excerpted from this same interview.
40. Barthes, *Mythologies*, 86.
41. Axum, *The Outer You . . .* , 43.
42. Hornick, *Cavalcade of Burlesque*, Vol. 2, No. 1, December 1952.
43. Hornick, *Cavalcade of Burlesque*, Vol. 1, No. 1, 1951.
44. Arnheim, *The Split and the Structure*, 42.
45. Davis, *SMUT: Erotic Reality/Obscene Ideology*, 23.
46. Burana, *Strip City*, 257.
47. Personal Interview, "Nightshade," Florida strip club DJ, conducted by email, 1999.
48. Quoted in Futterman, *Dancing Naked in the Material World*, 120.
49. Quoted in Scott, *Behind the G-String*, 66.
50. Davis, *SMUT: Erotic Reality/Obscene Ideology*, 20.
51. Zeidman, *The American Burlesque Show*, 110.
52. Scott, *Behind the G-String*, 221.
53. Bentley, *Sisters of Salome*, 14.
54. Scott, *Behind the G-String*, 221.
55. Davis, *SMUT: Erotic Reality/Obscene Ideology*, 150.
56. *New York World Telegram*, June 11, 1934, Gypsy Rose Lee Collection, Box 79, Folder 2, Billy Rose Theatre Collection, New York Public Library at Lincoln Center.
57. Arnheim, *The Split and the Structure*, 44.
58. Paul Jordan Collection, unidentified loose papers, Box 5, Harvard Theatre Collection.
59. Hornick, *Cavalcade of Burlesque*, Vol. 2, No. 2, March 1953.
60. Gypsy Rose Lee Collection, unidentified promotional materials, Box 79, Folder 2, Billy Rose Theatre Collection, New York Public Library at Lincoln Center.
61. Personal Interview, "Nicki," Charlie's Bikini Club, June 2, 2002. All subsequent references to remarks made by "Nicki" are excerpted from this same interview.
62. Hanna, "Undressing the First Amendment and Corsetting the Striptease Dancer," TDR.
63. Scott, *Behind the G-String*, 231.
64. Bentley, *Sisters of Salome*, 31.
65. Paul Jordan Collection, uncatalogued papers, unnamed Buffalo New York newspaper, 1967, Harvard Theatre Collection.

66. Thanks to David Richman for pointing out this connection.

67. Hornick, *Cavalcade of Burlesque*, Vol. 2, No. 2, March 1953, 22.

68. States, *Great Reckonings in Little Rooms*, 151.

69. Nathan, *Theatre, Drama, Girls*, 43.

70. Grosz, *Volatile Bodies*, x.

71. Quoted in Schneider, *The Explicit Body in Performance*, 22.

72. Grosz, *Space Time Perversion*, 32.

73. Logan, *Before the Footlights and Behind the Scenes*, 584.

74. *Webster's New World College Dictionary*, Fourth Edition.

75. Logan, *Apropos of Women and Theatre*, 135.

76. Quoted in Logan, *Before the Footlights and Behind the Scenes*, 590.

77. Ibid., 589.

78. Kubiak, "Splitting the Difference," 1998.

79. Quoted in Logan, *The Mimic World*, 589.

80. Quoted in Dudden, *Women in American Theatre*, 185.

81. This analysis is borrowed from Bert States, who has characterized theater as "a re-presentation, a re-presence (if that), perfected in the rehearsal process and locked into the fraud of self-repetition" (*Great Reckonings in Little Rooms*, 108).

82. Quoted in Meiselas, *Carnival Strippers*, 122, emphasis mine.

83. Quoted in Dworkin, *Miss America 1945*, 94.

84. " 'It' Depends," *Night and Day*, March 1950: 46–47.

85. Scott, *Behind the G-String*, 73.

86. Parsons, "Gypsy Rose Lee Jests About Her Art And Ranks Success as Mere Luck," (n.d.) Gypsy Rose Lee Collection, Box 79, Folder 3, Billy Rose Theatre Collection, New York Public Library at Lincoln Center.

87. *Sunday Mirror,* September 27, 1936, Gypsy Rose Lee, Box 79, Folder 2, Billy Rose Theatre Collection, New York Public Library at Lincoln Center.

88. Goffman, *The Presentation of the Self*, 8.

89. Futterman, *Dancing Naked in the Material World*, 116.

90. Goffman, *The Presentation of the Self*, 9.

91. Wigley, "Untitled: The Housing of Gender," 386.

92. Quoted in Fuchs, *The Death of Character*, 3.

93. Burana, *Strip City*, 68.

94. Quoted in Scott, *Behind the G-String*, 68.

95. <www.stripperpower.com>, accessed on January 6, 2002.

96. Quoted in Scott, *Behind the G-String*, 68.

97. Burana, *Strip City*, 83.

98. Goffman, *The Presentation of the Self*, 67.

99. Ibid., 66.

100. Quoted in Scott, *Behind the G-String*, 80.

101. Quoted in Scott, *Behind the G-String*, 72.

102. <www.stripperpower.com>, accessed on January 6, 2002.

103. Quoted in Scott, *Behind the G-String*, 46.

104. Liepe-Levinson, *Strip Show*, 116.
105. Personal Interview, former Miss Rhode Island contestant, Providence Rhode Island, Spring 1999.
106. Stanley, *The Crowning Touch*, 1.
107. Goffman, *The Presentation of the Self*, 252, emphasis his.
108. Personal Interview, former Miss Rhode Island contestant, Providence Rhode Island, Spring 1999.
109. Since fulfilling her duties as Miss Arizona, Lawless, in addition to attending law school, has continued her work toward raising public awareness of Mental Health issues. As part of that work she coached Miss New York 2003 in the presentation of her platform topic.
110. The "reality show" concept was taken a step further by producers of the 2003 pageant, who hired the winning couple (Trista Rehn and Ryan Sutter) from ABC's *The Bachelorette* to provide running commentary during the course of the competition, *American Idol* runner-up Clay Aiken to sing the opening number, and Tom Bergeron, game show host of *Hollywood Squares* and *America's Funniest Home Videos*, to serve as emcee.
111. Scott A. Zamost, "Strippers want to Dress up their Image," *Las Vegas Sun* (n.d.) Paul Jordan Collection, Box 4, Harvard Theatre Collection.
112. <www.stripperpower.com>, accessed on January 6, 2002.
113. Stanley, *The Crowning Touch*, 25.
114. Quoted in Meiselas, *Carnival Strippers*, 65.
115. Quoted in Scott, *Behind the G-String*, 65.
116. Miss America 2003 Scholarship Competition, Atlantic City, NJ, September 20, 2003, ABC televised event.
117. Personal Interview, Rachel Wadsworth, Miss Maine 2002, September 17, 2002. All subsequent references are excerpted from this same interview.
118. *Miss Exotic World Contest*, June 1, 2002, Helendale, California.
119. *St. Louis Daily Globe-Democrat* March 3, 1918, Ziegfeld Collection, Box 1.12, Harry Ransom Center.
120. Yang, "A Question of Accent: Ethnicity and Transference," 142.
121. Nathan, *The World in Falseface*, 244.
122. Quoted in Etcoff, *Survival of the Prettiest*, 102.
123. Beauvoir, *The Second Sex*, 533.
124. Mortimer, *Women Confidential*, 111.
125. Francis, *That Certain Something*, 13.
126. Prus and Styllianoss, *Hookers, Rounders and Desk Clerks*, 98.
127. "In Texas, Two Kings of the Beauty Queen Business," February 28, 1988, Billy Rose Theatre Collection, New York Public Library at Lincoln Center.

4   PERFORMING NORMALCY

1. Quoted in Scott, *Behind the G-String*, 35.

2. Deford, "Confessions of a Miss America Judge," *TV Guide,* September 2, 1978, quoting Don Galloway, Billy Rose Theatre Collection, New York Public Library at Lincoln Center.

3. Quoted in Minsky, *Minsky's Burlesque*, 249.

4. Terry and Urla, *Deviant Bodies*, 2.

5. Ibid.

6. "As Jean Genet repeatedly illustrated," points out Rebecca Schneider, "the illicit enactment of taboo is the ideological twin to licit or normative social orders of appropriate behavior," *The Explicit Body in Performance*, 79.

7. Terry and Urla, *Deviant Bodies*, 4.

8. Barthes, *Mythologies*, 98.

9. Scott, *Behind the G-String*, 78.

10. Allen, *Horrible Prettiness*, 235.

11. Liepe-Levinson, *Strip Show*, 25.

12. Carlton, *Looking for Little Egypt*, 33.

13. 1909 Ziegfeld *Follies* program, Ziegfeld Collection, Harry Ransom Center, Austin, TX.

14. Allen, *Horrible Prettiness*, 246.

15. McCullough, *Living Pictures*, 41.

16. Ibid., 121.

17. Zeidman, *The American Burlesque Show*, 84.

18. *Vanities*, 8th Edition, 1930 program.

19. "Arlington Mother Named Ms. International Nude," September 6, 1976, Paul Jordan Collection, Box 5, Folder M, Harvard Theatre Collection.

20. *Boston Evening Globe*, September 8, 1976.

21. "Arlington Mother Named Ms. International Nude," September 6, 1976, Paul Jordan Collection, Box 5, Folder M, Harvard Theatre Collection.

22. Allen, *Horrible Prettiness*, 245.

23. Ibid., 246.

24. Stanley, *The Crowning Touch*, 81.

25. 1928 Ziegfeld Theater program advertisement, 12, Billy Rose Theatre Collection, New York Public Library at Lincoln Center. Ned Wayburn was an early-twentieth-century American choreographer of stage and films, well known for a military-like synchronization of the women in his routines.

26. Stanley, *The Crowning Touch*, 5.

27. Amy Slattum, NHPR interview, Spring 1999.

28. Etcoff, *Survival of the Prettiest*, 68.

29. Stanley, *The Crowning Touch*, 1.

30. Ibid., 27.

31. Axum, *The Outer You . . . The Inner You*, 19.

32. Stanley, *The Crowning Touch*, 2.

33. Chapkis, *Beauty Secrets*, 5.

34. Kingsley, "About Beauties," July 3, 1920.

35. Lois Banner has remarked that, specifically, "since the 1920s, to be beautiful has involved the adoption of artificial means" (*American Beauty*, 274).

36. Quoted in Latham, *Posing a Threat*, 20.

37. Axum, *The Outer You . . . The Inner You*, 28.

38. Bordo, "The Body and the Reproduction of Femininity," 91.

39. Goffman, *The Presentation of the Self*, 47.

40. Axum, *The Outer You . . . The Inner You*, 23.

41. Stanley, *The Crowning Touch*, 4.

42. Ibid., 9.

43. Guy Livingston publicity agency promotional flyer, folder M., Paul Jordan Collection, Harvard Theatre Collection.

44. Stanley, *The Crowning Touch*, 73.

45. Ibid., 28.

46. Quoted in Trilling, *Sincerity and Authenticity*, 70.

47. Quoted in Etcoff, *Survival of the Prettiest*, 102.

48. Frank, *G-Strings and Sympathy*, 33.

49. Nathan, *The Theatre, The Drama, The Girls*, 308.

50. Osborne, *The Dream Lives On*, 69.

51. Banet-Weiser, *The Most Beautiful Girl in the World*, 32.

52. Segal, "There She Goes" <www.washingtonpost.com>, <http://www.washingtonpost.com/wp-dyn/articles/A30500-2004Sep17.html>, September 18, 2004, accessed September 25, 2004.

53. Garfinkel, *Studies in Ethnomethodology*, 125.

54. Urla and Swedlund, "The Anthropometry of Barbie," 277.

55. Stanley, *The Crowning Touch*, 43.

56. Quoted in Urla and Swedlund, "The Anthropometry of Barbie," 300.

57. CBS television feature transcript, August 28, 1958: "The Perfect Miss America," Billy Rose Theatre Collection, New York Public Library at Lincoln Center.

58. According to Lois Banner, "There was a political as well as a scientific dimension to the notion that all women could be beautiful. Just as Progressive reformers viewed their reform work as advancing democracy, so did beauty specialists see their goal as a democratic demand. As one author stated the oft-expressed sentiment, beauty was a 'natural right' of American women" (*American Beauty*, 205).

59. *New York Times*, Friday June 12, 1970, "Miss America: Dreams and Boosters," Billy Rose Theatre Collection, New York Public Library at Lincoln Center.

60. Stanley, *The Crowning Touch*, 3.

61. Wolf, *The Beauty Myth*, 14.

62. Etcoff, *Survival of the Prettiest*, 108.

63. Burana, *Strip City*, 10.

64. Ibid., 149.

65. Terry and Urla, *Deviant Bodies*, 6.

66. <http://strippers.cc/index.html>, link from <www.stripperpower.com>

67. "Know No's: Stripper Kung Fu," <http://www.stripperpower.com/articles/kungfu.shtml>, accessed January 6, 2002.

68. "Unnatural Beauty: Miss Brazil Boasts 19 Procedures" ABCnews.com. <http://abcnews.go.com/sections/primetime/2020/PRIMETIME_010503_miss brazil_feature>, May 3, 2002, accessed January 4, 2003.

69. Ibid.

70. "Pageant Hopes Soap—Opera Spoof Enlivens Show," September 15, 1984 Billy Rose Theatre Collection, New York Public Library at Lincoln Center.

71. Bordo, "The Body and the Reproduction of Femininity," 91.

72. MAO Message Board, <http://www.missamerica.org>, Official MAO webpage.

73. Quoted in Schur, *Labeling Women Deviant*, 112.

74. Wohlfert-Wihlborg, "Here She Comes," September 19, 1983: 97. Billy Rose Theatre Collection, New York Public Library at Lincoln Center.

75. Grosz, *Volatile Bodies*, 14.

76. "Beauty Pageant Contestants Remain Underfed," <www.womens-enews.com>, December 4, 2002.

77. Wohlfert-Wihlborg, "Here She Comes," September 19, 1983: 97. Billy Rose Theatre Collection, New York Public Library at Lincoln Center.

78. Bivens, *Miss America: In Pursuit of the Crown*, 69.

79. Ibid., 70.

80. Unidentified news materials, Miss America 1970s folder, Billy Rose Theatre Collection, New York Public Library at Lincoln Center.

81. Garfinkel, *Studies in Ethnomethodology*, 118–121.

82. Ibid., 119.

83. Kemp and Squire, *Feminisms*, 386.

84. Quinlan, "How NOW, Miss America," *New York Post,* September 6, 1974.

85. Garfinkel, *Studies in Ethnomethodology*, 131.

86. Ibid., 172.

87. Kemp and Squire, *Feminisms*, 387.

88. Garfinkel, *Studies in Ethnomethodology*, 134.

89. Quoted in States, *Great Reckonings in Little Rooms*, 25.

90. Senelick, *Gender in Performance*, ix.

91. Senelick, *Gender in Performance*, xi.

92. <www.missgayamerica.com>. Rules and Regulations page.

93. "Not Your Father's Miss America" (AP) December 13, 1999. <http://www.CBSnews.com/stories/199/09/20/entertainment/,ain62943.shtml>, accessed January 4, 2003.

94. Ibid.

95. Barillas, C., Ed. "Miss'd America Captures Sought After Crown," *The Data Lounge*. <http://www.datalounge.com/datalounge/news/record.html?record = 4670>, accessed September 20, 1999.

96. "Beauty Pageant Contestants Remain Underfed," <www.womens-enews.com>, December 4, 2002.

97. Lemons, "Selene Luna: Bad-ass Goddess of the Night," Gettingit.com Webzine, <http://www.Gettingit.com>, December 17, 1999, accessed December 30, 2002.
98. Rothfels, "Aztecs, Aborigines, and Ape-People," 159.
99. Quoted in Meiselas, *Carnival Strippers*, 41.
100. Ibid.
101. Simon, "For God, for Love—and for West Allis, Wisconsin," September 11, 1976: 34.
102. Rose, "Sexuality in the Field of Vision," 390.
103. Liepe-Levinson, *Strip Show*, 133.
104. Burana, *Strip City*, 57.
105. Liepe-Levinson, *Strip Show*, 83.
106. Personal Interview, "Jezebel," Charlie's Bikini Club, June 2, 2002.
107. Alexander, *Strip Tease*, 32.
108. Ibid.
109. *That Girl*, produced by Bernie Orenstein and Saul Turteltaub, distributed by Anchor Bay, Inc., 1999.
110. Terry and Urla, *Deviant Bodies*, 13.
111. Barthes, *S/Z*, 8.
112. Unidentified publicity materials, Paul Jordan Collection, Box 5, Harvard Theatre Collection.
113. Zolot, *Reporter* (Jaycee newsletter, n.d.) Paul Jordan Collection, Box 5, Folder C, Harvard Theatre Collection.
114. Rose, "Sexuality in the Field of Vision," 389.
115. Burana, *Strip City*, 46.
116. Message Board, <www.missamerica.org>.
117. DePaulo, "Behind Those Smiles: Inside the Mind of Miss America," September 10, 1988: 8.
118. Banet-Weiser, *The Most Beautiful Girl in the World*, 80.
119. Frank, *G-Strings and Sympathy*, 142.
120. Bordo, "The Body and the Reproduction of Femininity," 91.
121. O'Reilly, *TV Guide*, September 17, 1983, emphasis mine.
122. Etcoff, *Survival of the Prettiest*, 6.

5   ECONOMICS AND ADVANCEMENT: OR, FLESH-FOR-CASH TRANSACTIONS AND THE CINDERELLA MYTH

1. Etcoff, *Survival of the Prettiest*, 84.
2. Quoted in Banet-Weiser, *The Most Beautiful Girl in the World*, 193. Originally from Laura Mulvey's "The Spectacle is Vulnerable," 5.
3. Baxandall, *America's Working Women*, 208.
4. Dudden, *Women in the American Theatre*, 180.

5. Latham, *Posing a Threat*, 113.

6. Baxandall, *America's Working Women*, 329.

7. Bentley, *Sisters of Salome*, 12.

8. Robert C. Allen has stated that in the early twentieth century "the concept of show invaded the domain of culture"; that Flo Ziegfeld's *Follies* of 1907 "represented the acceptable face of feminine sexual spectacle" in its "expressive but controlled sexuality" (*Horrible Prettiness*, 245). Although I have argued that such a concept was put in play decades earlier, and, certainly, as Kathy Peiss has noted, "the 'fashion system' predated the emergence of a widespread commercial beauty culture," unquestionably, for women, the *business* of show gained remarkable momentum in the first quarter of the twentieth century ("On Beauty and the History of Business," 10).

9. Kennedy, *If All We Did Was to Weep at Home*, 108.

10. Ibid.

11. McEvoy, "He Knew What They Wanted," September 10, 1932: 11. Ziegfeld Collection, Box OB 5.5. Harry Ransom Center.

12. Peiss, "On Beauty and the History of Business," 15.

13. Carter, *The Sadeian Woman*, 57.

14. Quoted in Thomas, Robert McG., Jr. "Lili St. Cyr, 80, Burlesque Star Famous for Her Bubble Baths," *New York Times* on the Web (Obit.). February 6, 1999. <http://www.nytimes.com>.

15. McCullough, *Living Pictures on the New York Stage*, 45.

16. McEvoy, "He Knew What They Wanted," September 10, 1932: 11. Ziegfeld Collection, Box OB 5.5. Harry Ransom Center.

17. Banner, *American Beauty*, 180.

18. Zeidman, *The American Burlesque Show*, 66.

19. Banner, *American Beauty*, 200.

20. Kennedy, *If All We Did Was to Weep at Home*, 112.

21. Hornick, *Cavalcade of Burlesque*, Vol. 1, No. 2, Winter 1951.

22. Alexander, *Strip Tease*, 46.

23. Ziegfeld, "What Becomes of the Ziegfeld Girls?" May 1925.

24. Personal Interview, "Lolita" *Miss Exotic World* Contest, June 1, 2002.

25. McEvoy, "He Knew," 11. Ziegfeld Collection, Box OB 5.5. Harry Ransom Center.

26. McEvoy, "He Knew What They Wanted," September 1932, 8.

27. Minsky, *Minsky's Burlesque*, 197.

28. Baxandall, *America's Working Women*, 218.

29. Ibid., 204.

30. Zeidman, *The American Burlesque Show*, 217.

31. Baxandall, *America's Working Women*, 222.

32. Rogers St. Johns, "The Girls Who Glorified Ziegfeld," July 7, 1946. Florenz Ziegfeld—Billie Burke papers, Series III, Box 14, Folder 37. Billy Rose Theatre Collection, New York Public Library at Lincoln Center,

33. Banner, *American Beauty*, 181.

34. Ibid., 182.
35. McEvoy, "He Knew What They Wanted," September 10, 1932, 4. Ziegfeld Collection, Box OB 5.5. Harry Ransom Center.
36. Farnsworth, *The Ziegfeld Follies*, 129.
37. Quoted in Banner, *American Beauty*, 264.
38. Hornick, *Cavalcade of Burlesque*, Vol. 1, No. 2, Winter 1951.
39. Ibid., 18.
40. Banner, *American Beauty*, 183.
41. Zeidman, *The American Burlesque Show*, 142.
42. Ibid., 144.
43. Alexander, *Strip Tease*, 46.
44. Hornick, *Cavalcade of Burlesque*, Vol. 2, No. 2, March 1953, 9.
45. Zeidman, *The American Burlesque Show*, 83.
46. Peiss, "On Beauty and the History of Business," 15.
47. Unidentified promotional materials, Paul Jordan Collection, Box 5, Harvard Theatre Collection.
48. Alexander, *Strip Tease*, 26.
49. Hornick, *Cavalcade of Burlesque*, Vol. 2, No. 3, June 1953.
50. Banner, *American Beauty*, 182.
51. Quoted in Banner, *American Beauty*, 217, from the early twentieth-century journal *Woman Beautiful*.
52. Bivens, *101 Secrets to Winning Beauty Pageants*, 31.
53. Boynoff, *Daily News,* June 8, 1939. Earl Carroll Collection, March 1939–October, 1939. Billy Rose Theatre Collection, New York Public Library at Lincoln Center.
54. Lauterbach, "Close-Up," news clipping, Gypsy Rose Lee Collection, Box 79, Folder 3. Billy Rose Theatre Collection, New York Public Library at Lincoln Center.
55. Unidentified promotional material, Paul Jordan Collection, Box 5, folder J. Harvard Theatre Collection,
56. Mortimer, *Women Confidential*, 103–104.
57. Ibid.
58. Ibid., 104.
59. Burns, *Modern Man*, December 1955, Vol. V, No. 6–54.
60. Ibid.
61. Ibid., 36.
62. Ibid., 46.
63. "*Look* looks at Dorian Dennis," *New York Mirror* 1958, Paul Jordan Collection, Box 5, Folder E. Harvard Theatre Collection.
64. Kilgallen, "The Voice of Broadway," (unidentified news column), March 29, 1958. Paul Jordan Collection, Box 5, Folder E. Harvard Theatre Collection.
65. *Peep Show Magazine* (n.d.) Paul Jordan Collection, Box 7, Folder O. Harvard Theatre Collection.

66. Zamost, "Strippers want to dress up their image; converge in LV," *Las Vegas Sun* (n.d.). Paul Jordan Collection, Box 4. Harvard Theatre Collection.

67. Mortimer, *Women Confidential*, 101.

68. Ibid.

69. Burns, *Modern Man*, December 1955, Vol. V, No. 6–54.

70. Banner, *American Beauty*, 182.

71. Glenn, *Female Spectacle*, 196.

72. Bettelheim, *The Uses of Enchantment*, 236–237.

73. Halprin, *Look at My Ugly Face*, 189–190.

74. Bettelheim, *The Uses of Enchantment*, 251.

75. Simon, "For God, for Love—and for West Allis, Wisconsin," September 11, 1976: 30.

76. Craig, *Ain't I a Beauty Queen?*, 66.

77. Knight, "Miss USA," 6.

78. Personal Interview, anonymous bystander, Miss America 2002 Boardwalk Parade Atlantic City, September 20, 2002.

79. Bivens, *Miss America*, 2.

80. *Pageantry Magazine*. Edited by Lisa Nees. 1996, 146.

81. Cinderella Scholarship Pageants, <www.netstat.com/pageants/cinderella/history.html>.

82. Ibid.

83. Ibid.

84. Simon, "For God, for Love—and for West Allis, Wisconsin," September 11, 1976, 30.

85. Knight, "Miss USA," 6.

86. Banner, *American Beauty*, 249.

87. Knight, "Miss USA," 4.

88. Frank Bruni, "A Search for Girls, Girls, Girls Around Italy's Dial," September 3, 2002.

89. Banet-Weiser, *The Most Beautiful Gird in the World*, 81.

90. Unidentified promotional collage, Paul Jordan Collection, Box 5, Harvard Theatre Collection.

91. Hal Rosen, "Tips for Tables," unidentified clipping, Paul Jordan Collection, Box 5, Folder H, Harvard Theatre Collection.

92. Rause, "Gibby's Number One Girl: What Makes a Stripper Strip?" July 17, 1977: 2, Paul Jordan Collection, Box 5, Folder D, Harvard Theatre Collection.

93. Slocum, unidentified news column, Paul Jordan Collection, Box 5, Folder E, Harvard Theatre Collection.

94. Banet-Weiser, *The Most Beautiful Girl in the World*, 31.

95. Miss America Scholarship Competition 2002, Atlantic City, NJ, September 2002.

96. *The Secret World of Beauty Pageants*, Film Garden Entertainments, produced for the Learning Channel, 1998.

97. Amy Slattum, NHPR interview, Spring 1999.
98. Perlmutter, "Miss America," 163.
99. Miss Mountain State Pageant in West Virginia, Link found on <www. qualitypageants.com/wv.pageants>.
100. <http://forestrypageant.tripod.com>.
101. <www.bbtel.com/~majestic/>.
102. <www.missmarylandteen.com>.
103. <www.herheighness.com>.
104. Craig, *Ain't I a Beauty Queen?*, 53.
105. Ibid.
106. Burana, *Strip City*, 236.
107. Ibid.
108. Personal Interview, Miss New Hampshire 2002, Manchester, New Hampshire, September 5, 2002.
109. DePaulo, "Behind Those Smiles: Inside the Mind of Miss America," *TV Guide* September 10, 1988.
110. <www.voy.com/41982>.
111. Burana, *Strip City*, 298.
112. Transcript of a 1989 Sally Jessy Raphael program on striptease artists, Bambi Vawn papers, Series I, Box 1, folder 1, Billy Rose Theatre Collection, New York Public Library at Lincoln Center.
113. Unidentified promotional materials, Paul Jordan Collection, Box 5, Harvard Theatre Collection.
114. Scott, *Behind the G-String*, 70.
115. Minsky, *Minsky's Burlesque*, 232.
116. Beyond, Chris, The No-Fi "Magazine," <www.nofimagazine.com/dixieint1. htm>, accessed March 8, 2004.
117. Rause, "Gibby's Number One Girl: What Makes a Stripper Strip?" July 17, 1977: 2, Paul Jordan Collection, Box 5, Folder D, Harvard Theatre Collection.
118. Hornick, *Cavalcade of Burlesque*, Vol. 2, No. 1, December 1952.
119. A personal letter to Paul Jordan dated March 23, 1962, Paul Jordan Collection, Box 5, Harvard Theatre Collection.
120. <www.abbierabine.com>.
121. Belkin, "In Texas, Two Kings of the Beauty Queen Business," February 28, 1988.
122. Knight, "Miss USA," 4.
123. Ibid.
124. DePaulo, "Behind Those Smiles: Inside the Mind of Miss America," September 10, 1988: 6–7.
125. Di Maggio, "All that glitters . . . is only rhinestone," <www.geocities.com/ TelevisionCity/9699/reluctant.html>.
126. Ibid.
127. Simon, "For God, for Love—and for West Allis, Wisconsin," September 11, 1976: 30.

128. Ibid., 34.
129. Bookkeeping records from Paul Jordan Collection, Box 3, folder titled "Burlesque circuit 1969," Harvard Theatre Collection.
130. Unidentified accounting papers, Paul Jordan Collection, Box 3, Harvard Theatre Collection.
131. Bambi Vawn papers, Series I, Box 1, Folder 1, Billy Rose Theatre Collection, New York Public Library at Lincoln Center.
132. Burana, *Strip City*, 38.
133. Letter to Paul Jordan, Paul Jordan Collection, Box 4, Harvard Theatre Collection.
134. Rause, "Gibby's Number One Girl: what Makes a Stripper Strip?" July 17, 1977: 2, Paul Jordan Collection, Box 5, Folder D, Harvard Theatre Collection.
135. Zamost, "Strippers want to dress up their image; converge in LV," *Las Vegas Sun* (n.d.). Paul Jordan Collection, Box 4. Harvard Theatre Collection.
136. Rause, "Gibby's Number One Girl: What Makes a Stripper Strip?" July 17, 1977: 2, Paul Jordan Collection, Box 5, Folder D, Harvard Theatre Collection.
137. Burana, *Strip City*, 260.
138. Ibid., 268.
139. Quoted in Burana, *Strip City*, 274.
140. Burana, *Strip City*, 38.
141. Rattray, "Texas Playmate," Paul Jordan Collection, loose promotional materials, Box 5, Harvard Theatre Collection.
142. *The Secret World of Beauty Pageants*, Film Garden Entertainments, produced for the Learning Channel, 1998.
143. Belkin, "In Texas, Two Kings of the Beauty Queen Business," February 28, 1988.
144. Banet-Weiser, *The Most Beautiful Girl in the World*, 47.
145. Gross, "It's the same show—but 'Miss A' is a big winner," September 13, 1965.
146. Banet-Weiser, *The Most Beautiful Girl in the World*, 44.
147. <www.mrsamerica.com/sponsors>.
148. Banet-Weiser, *The Most Beautiful Girl in the World*, 52.
149. "Miss America: Dreams and Boosters," June 12, 1970.
150. Ibid.
151. <www.netstat.com/pageants/cinderella/history.html>.
152. Ibid.
153. *The Secret World of Beauty Pageants*, Film Garden Entertainments, produced for the Learning Channel, 1998.
154. Gross, "It's the same show—but 'Miss A' is a big winner," September 13, 1965.
155. Pennington, "Bare Necessity? The Miss America Pageant is all About Scholarship—and Swimsuits," September 11, 1997, <www.highbeam.com/library/doc3.asp?DOCID>, accessed June 16, 2004.
156. Kindel, "Beauty You Can Take to the Bank," June 18, 1984, accessed June 16, 2004, <www.highbeam.com/library/doc3.asp?DOCID>.
157. Atlantic City, September 2002.

158. Kravitz, "Miss Americ-Lite?," Atlantic City Weekly, week of January 9–February 4, 2004, accessed June 16, 2004, <www.atlanticcitycasinos. net/archives/ 01.29.04/pinky.html>.
159. Banet-Weiser, *The Most Beautiful Girl in the World*, 193.
160. Personal Interview, Jerry Seelig, Harrah's Casino, Atlantic City, September 21, 2002.
161. Quoted in Schroeder and Janet L. Borgerson, "Marketing Images of Gender: A Visual Analysis," 180.
162. Personal Interview, Heather French, former Miss America, Harrah's Casino, Atlantic City, September 21, 2002.
163. Ibid.
164. Scott, *Behind the G-String*, 5.
165. Schneider, *The Explicit Body in Performance*, 5.
166. Etcoff, *Survival of the Prettiest*, 3–4.
167. Personal Interview, Miss America Boardwalk Parade bystander, Atlantic City, September 20, 2002.
168. Banner, *American Beauty*, 199.
169. Wohlfert-Wihlborg, "Here She Comes," September 19, 1983: 94.
170. Quoted in Murray, *The Body Merchant*, Prologue.

6   NAKED POLITICS: REGULATING AND LEGISLATING FEMALE DISPLAY

1. Quoted in Johnson, *The Feminist Difference*, 187.
2. McCullough, *Living Pictures*, 45.
3. Carlton, *Looking for Little Egypt*, 46.
4. Logan, *Before the Footlights and Behind the Scenes*, 583.
5. Davis, Kathy, *Embodied Practices*, 14.
6. Levine, *Highbrow/Lowbrow*, 253.
7. Lacey, *Unspeakable Subjects*, emphasis mine.
8. Ibid., emphasis hers.
9. Quoted in Friedman, *Prurient Interests*, 93.
10. "The Church Wars on Burlesque," May 31, 1937: 20.
11. Friedman, *Prurient Interests*, 75.
12. Strossen, *Defending Pornography Rights*, 44.
13. Ibid., 55.
14. Zeidman, *The American Burlesque Show*, 63–64.
15. Strossen, *Defending Pornography*, 54.
16. Zeidman, *The American Burlesque Show*, 143.
17. McCullough, *Living Pictures*, 91.
18. Alexander, *Strip Tease*, 51.
19. Murray, *The Body Merchant*, 45.
20. Hornick, *Cavalcade of Burlesque*, Vol. 1, No. 1, 1951.

21. Quoted in Burana, *Strip City*, 145.

22. Burana, *Strip City*, 65.

23. Johnson, *The Feminist Difference*, 177.

24. Zeidman, *The American Burlesque Show*, 139.

25. Burana, *Strip City*, 81.

26. Banner, *American Beauty*, 266.

27. Ibid., 267.

28. Strossen, *Defending Pornography*, 55.

29. "*Look* looks at Dorian Dennis," *New York Mirror,* 1958, Paul Jordan Collection, Harvard Theatre Collection.

30. Farnsworth, *The Ziegfeld Follies*, 11.

31. Cantor and Freedman, "Ziegfeld and His Follies," January 27, 1934: 24.

32. Farnsworth, *The Ziegfeld Follies*, 84.

33. Ibid.

34. Murray, *The Body Merchant*, 199.

35. Ibid.

36. Murray, *The Body Merchant*, 186.

37. Riverol, *Live from Atlantic City*, 10.

38. Osborne, *The Dream Lives On*, 160.

39. Latham, *Posing a Threat*, 103.

40. Banner, *American Beauty*, 264.

41. "Women's lives," states Judith Baer, "do not fit into American constitutional law. Gender is a deviant case, a doctrinal outlier, in the law of equality. Early in this century, *Muller v. Oregon* put sex discrimination outside the scope of equal protection law, placing 'woman . . . in a class by herself.' As the century ends, woman is still in a special class." *Our Lives Before the Law*, 97.

42. Alexander, *Strip Tease*, 113.

43. Freidman, *Prurient Interest*, 67.

44. Grosz, *Volatile Bodies*, 203.

45. Alexander, *Strip Tease*, 291.

46. Zeidman, *The American Burlesque Show*, 219.

47. Ibid.

48. Quoted in Zeidman, *The American Burlesque Show*, 223.

49. Friedman, *Prurient Interest*, 80.

50. Ibid.

51. Quoted in Friedman, *Prurient Interest*, 93

52. Minsky and Machlin, *Minsky's Burlesque*, 274.

53. Friedman, *Prurient Interest*, 63.

54. Alexander, *The American Burlesque Show*, 113.

55. Minsky, *Minsky's Burlesque*, 271.

56. Alexander, *Strip Tease*, 290.

57. Zeidman, *The American Burlesque Show*, 63–64.

58. Minsky, *Minsky's Burlesque*, 266.

59. Quoted in Minsky, *Minsky's Burlesque*, 266.

60. Friedman, *Prurient Interest*, 80.

61. Alexander, *Strip Tease*, 114.

62. Ibid., 220.

63. Quoted in Friedman, *Prurient Interest*, 73.

64. Ibid.

65. "The Church Wars on Burlesque," *Life Magazine,* Vol. 2, No. 22, May 31, 1937: 20.

66. Zeidman, *The American Burlesque Show*, 235.

67. Heckman, "Weekend Hours for Exotic Dancers Mulled," August 20, 2002.

68. Ibid., B5.

69. Ibid.

70. Quoted in Friedman, *Prurient Interest*, 82.

71. Banet-Weiser, *The Most Beautiful Girl in the World*, 38.

72. Bentley, *Sisters of Salome*, 9.

73. Burana, *Strip City*, 67.

74. Ibid., 78.

75. Ibid.

76. Quoted in Alexander, *Strip Tease*, 112.

77. Gill, "The Miss America Uproar: What it says about us all," September 15, 1984. Billy Rose Theatre Collection, New York Public Library at Lincoln Center.

78. *The Secret World of Beauty Pageants*, Film Garden Entertainments, produced for the Learning Channel, 1998.

79. Geoffrey Stokes, "The Last Miss America Story," *Village Voice,* August 7, 1984.

80. Goffman, *The Presentation of Self in Everyday Life*, 64–65.

81. "Jill Nicolini, Relinquished Pageant Crown," *On the Record*. Host: Greta Van Susteren. September 4, 2002, Partial Transcript. <http://www.foxnews.com/story/0,2933,62191,00.html>, accessed January 6, 2003.

82. Playboy webpage, <www.playboy.com/nss/features/nicolini>, accessed January 6, 2003.

83. Ibid.

84. "Pageant queen resigned over topless photos," (AP) <http://www.CNN.com/2002/SHOWBIZ/News/07/29/missnc.resigns.ap/index.html>, accessed July 29, 2002.

85. Strossen, *Defending Pornography*, 53.

86. Ibid.

87. Ibid.

88. "Miss North Carolina case reveals little-known clauses in contract." News-Journal Wire Services. <www.news-journalonline.com/2002/Nov/3/NOTE2.htm>, accessed November 3, 2002.

89. "Pageant queen resigned over topless photos," CNN.com July 29, 2002.

90. Chapkis, *Beauty Secrets*, 173.

91. "Miss North Carolina case reveals little-known clauses in contract." News-Journal Wire Services. <www.news-journalonline.com/2002/Nov/3/NOTE2.htm>, accessed November 3, 2002.

92. Findlaw.com byline, <http://news.findlaw.com/ap_stories/e/1404/5-21-2003/20030521204500_4.html>.

93. Civil Action, United States District Court for the District of New Jersey, MAO, Inc., *Plaintiff v. Infinite Broadcasting Corporation.* <http://news.corporate.findlaw.com/hdocs/docs/missamerica/missamerica.pdf>.

94. "Miss America told to zip it on chastity talk," <www.washtimes.com/national/>.

95. Ibid.

96. Ibid.

97. <www.news-journalonline.com/2002/Nov/3/NOTE2.htm>.

98. Ibid.

99. Burana, *Strip City*, 78.

100. <www.news-journalonline.com/2002/Nov/3/NOTE2.htm>.

101. Heckman, "Weekend Hours for Exotic Dancers Mulled," August 2002: 20.

102. "Bare Intentions," <www.wcug.www.edu/~klipsun/april98/strippers.html>.

103. Strossen, *Defending Pornography*, 38.

104. "Student Chooses Stripping Over Sports," Excite News March 29, 2001, <http://news.excite.com/news/r/010329/11/odd-stripper-dc>.

105. Keichline, "Stripped of Athletic Status," March 16, 2001 n.p.

106. Ibid., emphasis mine.

107. Justice O'Connor announced the judgment of the Court and delivered the opinion with respect to Parts I and II, in which Rehnquist, C.J., and Kennedy, Souter, and Breyer, JJ., joined, and an opinion with respect to Parts III and IV, in which Rehnquist, C.J., and Kennedy, and Breyer, J.J., joined. Scalia, J., filed an opinion concurring in the judgment, in which Thomas, J., joined. Souter, J., filed an opinion concurring in part and dissenting in part. Stevens, J., filed a dissenting opinion, in which Ginsburg, J., joined. All citations in this article are excerpted from these case opinions, unless otherwise noted. *City of Erie v. PAP'S A. M.*, 529 US 277, 120 S.Ct. 1522 (2000) at 6.

108. PAP's AM at 1–3.

109. Williams, *The Alchemy of Race and Rights*, 139.

110. Turner, *Dramas, Fields, and Metaphors*, 14.

111. PAP's AM at 16.

112. PAP's AM at 10; see *Barnes v. Glen Theatre, Inc.*, supra, at 568, 111 S.Ct. 2456.

113. Dudden, *Women in the American Theatre*, 143.

114. Allen, *Horrible Prettiness*, 109.

115. Qtd in Allen, *Horrible Prettiness*, 111–112.

116. Qtd in Bank, *Theatre Culture in America, 1825–1860*, 167.

117. PAP's AM at 5.

118. PAP's AM at 10, Italics mine; see *US v. O'Brien*, 391 U.S., 367, 88 S.Ct. 1673 (1967).

119. PAP's AM at 6.
120. PAP's AM at 27.
121. PAP's AM at 17.
122. PAP's AM at 5.
123. PAP's AM at 23.
124. PAP's AM at 5.
125. Ibid.
126. *Renton v. Playtime Theatres, Inc.*, 475 U.S. 41, 106 S.Ct. 925 (1986).
127. *PAP's AM at 3.*
128. PAP's AM at 19.
129. PAP's AM at 21.
130. Grosz, "Bodies -Cities," 242.
131. Wigley, "Untitled: The Housing of Gender," 358.
132. Qtd in Wigley "Untitled: The Housing of Gender," 355.
133. PAP's AM at 10.
134. PAP's AM at 27.
135. PAP's AM at 21.
136. PAP's AM at 6.
137. PAP's AM at 5.
138. Strossen, *Defending Pornography*, 50.
139. Butler, *Excitable Speech*, 132.
140. Quoted in Krips, *Fetish: An Erotics of Culture*, 180.
141. Butler, *Excitable Speech*, 130, Italics hers.
142. Hall, "Cultural Identity and Diaspora," 112.

AFTERWORD

1. "Siss! Boom! Ah!," *Boston Herald*, 1919.
2. Comstock, quoted in Dudden, *Women in the American Theatre*, 176.
3. Green, "Is Less More? Broadway's Naked Truths," *New York Times* online, <www.nytimes.com>, July 6, 2003.
4. *All-American Girl* 2003 Pageant, ABC, March 12, 2003, produced by Simon Fuller.
5. Rose, "Sexuality in the Field of Vision," 388.
6. Dudden, *Women in the American Theatre*, 2.
7. Banner, *American Beauty*, 24.
8. "Miss World Leaves Nigeria," <www.CNN.com.2002WORLD/africa/11/22/nigeria.missworld/index.html>.
9. Ibid.
10. CNN.com, "Miss Turkey named Miss World," December 7, 2002.
11. Ibid.
12. "Miss World Leaves Nigeria," <www.CNN.com.2002WORLD/africa/11/22/nigeria.missworld/index.html>.

13. CNN.com, "Miss Turkey named Miss World, December 7, 2002.
14. Ibid.
15. *Mrs. America Pageant 2002*. PAX television. October 12, 2002.
16. Mike Brunker, "Hunts for nude women draw fire," <www.msnbcnews.com>, July 16, 2003. According to recent investigations, "Hunting for Bambi" is, rather than an actual event for public participation, purported to be a video depicting naked actresses getting shot for entertainment purposes.
17. Geraldine Maschio, "A Prescription for Femininity," 42–49.
18. Barthes, *Mythologies*, 84.
19. Quoted in Allen, *Horrible Prettiness*, 36.
20. Baer, *Our Lives Before the Law*, 200.
21. Rose, *Feminism and Geography*, 88.

Bibliography ❧

SPECIFIC COLLECTIONS

Bambi Vawn Papers (1967–91). Billy Rose Theatre Collection, New York Public Library at Lincoln Center.

Black Crook Collection. Harry Ransom Humanities Research Center, Austin, TX.

Earl Carroll Collection. Billy Rose Theatre Collection, New York Public Library at Lincoln Center.

Exotic World Burlesque Museum. Helendale, CA.

Florenz Ziegfeld Collection. Harry Ransom Humanities Research Center, Austin, TX.

Florenz Ziegfeld—Billie Burke Papers (1907–84). Billy Rose Theatre Collection, New York Public Library at Lincoln Center.

Gypsy Rose Lee Collection. Billy Rose Theatre Collection, New York Public Library at Lincoln Center.

Paul Jordan Collection (uncatalogued). Harvard Theatre Collection, Houghton Library, Cambridge, MA.

Tony Pastor Collection. Harry Ransom Humanities Research Center, Austin, TX.

BOOKS AND ESSAYS IN BOOKS

Alexander, H.M. *Strip Tease: The Vanished Art of Burlesque*. New York: Knight Publishers, 1938.

Allen, Robert C. *Horrible Prettiness: Burlesque and American Culture*. Chapel Hill, NC: University of North Carolina Press, 1991.

Anderson, Benedict. *Imagined Communities*. London: Verso, 1983.

Arnheim, Rudolf. *The Split and the Structure*. Berkeley, CA: University of California Press, 1996.

Axum, Donna. *The Outer You . . . The Inner You*. Waco, TX: Word Books, 1978.

Baer, Judith A. *Our Lives Before the Law: Constructing a Feminist Jurisprudence*. Princeton, NJ: Princeton University Press, 1999.

Banet-Weiser, Sarah. *The Most Beautiful Girl in the World: Beauty Pageants and National Identity*. Los Angeles, CA: University of California Press, 1999.

Bank, Rosemarie. *Theatre Culture in America, 1825–1860*. New York and Cambridge: Cambridge University Press, 1997.

Banner, Lois. *American Beauty*. New York: Alfred A. Knopf, 1983.

Barthes, Roland. *Mythologies*. Trans. Annette Lavers. New York: Hill and Wang, 1957.

———. *S/Z*. Translated by Richard Miller. New York: Hill and Wang, 1974.

Baxandall, Rosalyn Fraad and Linda Gordon, eds. *America's Working Women: A Documentary History 1600 to the Present*. New York: W.W. Norton & Company, 1995.

Bentley, Toni. *Sisters of Salome*. New Haven, CT: Yale University Press, 2002.

Bhabha, Homi K., ed. *Nation and Narration*. New York: Routledge, 1990.

Bivens, Ann-Marie. *Miss America: In Pursuit of the Crown*. New York: MasterMedia Limited, 1991.

Bland, Lucy. "Trial by Sexology?" *Sexology in Culture: Labeling Bodies and Desire*. Edited by Lucy Bland and Laura Doan. London: Polity Press, 1998.

Blau, Herbert. *To All Appearances: Ideology and Performance*. London and New York: Routledge, 1992.

Bordo, Susan. "The Body and the Reproduction of Femininity," *Writing on the Body: Female Embodiment and Feminist Theory*. Edited by Katie Conboy, Nadia Medina, and Sarah Stanbury. New York: Columbia University Press, 1997.

Buckley, Peter. "The Culture of 'Leg-Work': The Transformation of Burlesque after the Civil War." *The Mythmaking Frame of Mind: Social Imagination and American Culture*. Belmont, CA: Wadsworth Publishing Company, 1993.

Burana, Lily. *Strip City: A Stripper's Farewell Journey Across America*. New York: Hyperion, 2001.

Butler, Judith. "Bodies that Matter." *Feminist Theory and the Body*. Edited by Janet Price and Magrit Shildrick. London and New York: Routledge, 1999.

——— *Excitable Speech: A Politics of the Performative*. New York: Routledge, 1997.

Carlton, Donna. *Looking for Little Egypt*. Bloomington, IN: IDD Books, 1994.

Carter, Angela. *The Sadeian Woman: And the Ideology of Pornography*. New York: Penguin Books, 1979.

Chapkis, Wendy. *Beauty Secrets: Women and the Politics of Appearance*. Boston, MA: South End Press, 1986.

———. *Live Sex Acts: Women Performing Erotic Labor*. New York: Routledge, 1997.

Chow, Rey. "Where Have all the Natives Gone?" *Contemporary Postcolonial Theory*. Edited by Padmini Mongia. New York: St. Martin's Press, 1996.

Craig, Maxine Leeds. *Ain't I a Beauty Queen?: Black Women, Beauty, and the Politics of Race*. London: Oxford University. Press, 2002.

Crary, John. "Modernizing Vision." *Vision and Visuality*. Edited by Hal Foster. Seattle, WA: Bay Press, 1988.

Davis, Kathy, ed. *Embodied Practices: Feminist Perspectives on the Body*. London: SAGE Publications, 1997.

Davis, Murray S. *SMUT: Erotic Reality/Obscene Ideology*. Chicago, IL: The University of Chicago Press, 1983.

Davis, Tracy C. *Actresses as Working Women: Their Social Identity in Victorian Culture*. New York: Routledge, 1991.

De Beauvoir, Simone. *The Second Sex.* Translated by H.M. Parshley. New York: Knopf, 1953.

Debord, Guy. *The Society of the Spectacle.* Translated by Donald Nicholson-Smith. New York: Zone Books, 1995.

Douglas, Mary. *Purity and Danger: An Analysis of Concepts of Pollution and Taboo.* New York: Routledge, 1966.

Dudden, Faye E. *Women in the American Theatre: Actresses and Audiences 1790–1870.* New Haven, CT: Yale University Press, 1994.

Dworkin, Susan. *Miss America, 1945: Bess Myerson's Own Story.* New York: Newmarket Press, 1987.

Eaves, Elisabeth. *Bare: On Women, Dancing, Sex, and Power.* New York: Alfred A. Knopf, 2002.

Etcoff, Nancy. *Survival of the Prettiest: The Science of Beauty.* New York: Anchor Books, 2000.

Ewen, Stuart. *All Consuming Images: The Politics of Style in Contemporary Culture.* New York: Basic Books, 1988.

Farmer, Norman K., Jr. *Poets and the Visual Arts in Renaissance England.* Austin, TX: University of Texas Press, 1984.

Farnsworth, Marjorie. *The Ziegfeld Follies: A History in Text and Pictures.* New York: Bonanza Books, 1956.

Felski, Rita. "The Dialectic of 'Feminism' and 'Aesthetics.' " *Feminisms.* Edited by Sandra Kemp and Judith Squires. New York: Oxford University Press, 1997.

Fish, Charles. *Blue Ribbons and Burlesque: A Book of Country Fairs.* Woodstock, VT: Countryman Press, 1998.

Francis, Arlene. *That Certain Something: The Magic of Charm.* New York: Julian Messner, Inc., 1960.

Frank, Katherine. *G-Strings and Sympathy: Strip Club Regulars and Male Desire.* Durham, NC: Duke University Press, 2002.

Fraser, Antonia. *The Weaker Vessel.* New York: Vintage books, 1994.

Friedman, Andrea. *Prurient Interests: Gender, Democracy, and Obscenity in New York City, 1909–1945.* New York: Columbia University Press, 2000.

Fuchs, Eleanor. *The Death of Character: Perspectives on Theater after Modernism.* Bloomington, IN: Indiana University Press, 1996.

Futterman, Marilyn Suriani. *Dancing Naked in the Material World.* New York: Prometheus Books, 1992.

Gänzl, Kurt. *Lydia Thompson: Queen of Burlesque.* New York: Routledge, 2002.

Garfinkel, Harold. *Studies in Ethnomethodology.* Los Angeles, CA: Polity Press, 1967.

Gilbert, Douglas. *American Vaudeville: Its Life and Times.* New York: Dover Publications, 1940.

Goffman, Erving. *The Presentation of the Self in Everyday Life.* New York: Doubleday Anchor Books, 1959.

Grosz, Elizabeth. *Space, Time, and Perversion.* New York: Routledge, 1995.

———. *Volatile Bodies: Toward a Corporeal Feminism.* Bloomington, IN: Indiana University Press, 1994.

Hall, Stuart. "Cultural Identity and Diaspora." *Contemporary Postcolonial Theory.* Edited by Padmini Mongia. New York: St. Martin's Press, 1996.

Halprin, Sara. *Look at My Ugly Face: Myths and Musings on Beauty and Other perilous Obsessions with Women's Appearance.* New York: Viking Press, 1995.

Haraway, Donna. "The Persistence of Vision." *Writing on the Body: Female Embodiment and Feminist Theory.* Edited by Katie Conboy, Nadia Medina, and Sarah Stanbury. New York: Columbia University Press, 1997.

Henley, Nancy. *Body Politics: Power, Sex and Nonverbal Communication.* Englewoods Cliffs, NJ: Prentice-Hall, 1977.

Jarrett, Lucinda. *Stripping in Time.* London: Rivers Oram Press, 1997.

Johnson, Barbara. *The Feminist Difference: Literature, Psychoanalysis, Race, and Gender.* Cambridge, MA: Harvard University Press, 1998.

Johnson, Herrick. *Plain Talks about the Theater.* Chicago, IL: F. H. Revell, 1882.

Kemp, Sandra and Judith Squire, eds. *Feminisms.* New York: Oxford University Press, 1997.

Kennedy, Susan E. *If All We Did Was to Weep at Home: A History of White Working-Class Women in America.* Bloomington, IN: Indiana University Press, 1981.

Kibler, M. Alison. *Rank Ladies: Gender and Cultural Hierarchy in American Vaudeville.* Chapel Hill, NC: University of North Carolina Press, 1999.

Knight, Emma. "Miss USA." *American Dreams: Lost and Found.* Edited by Studs Terkel. New York: New York Press, 1999.

Kott, Jan. *The Memory of the Body: Essays on Theater and Death.* Translated by Mark Rosenzweig. Evanston, IL: Northwestern University Press, 1992.

Lacey, Nicola. *Unspeakable Subjects: Feminist Essays in Legal and Social Theory.* Oxford: Hart Publishing, 1998.

Langer, Susanne K. *Feeling and Form: A Theory of Art.* New York: Charles Scribner's Sons, 1953.

Latham, Angela J. *Posing a Threat: Flappers, Chorus Girls, and Other Brazen Performers of the American 1920s.* Hanover, NH: University Press of New England, 2000.

Levine, Lawrence W. *Highbrow/Lowbrow: The Emergence of Cultural Hierarchy in America.* Cambridge, MA: Harvard University Press, 1988.

Liepe-Levinson, Katherine. *Strip Show: Performances of Gender and Desire.* New York: Routledge, 2002.

Logan, Olive. *Before the Footlights and Behind the Scenes.* Philadelphia, PA: Pharmalee and Company, 1870.

———. *The Mimic World.* Philadelphia, PA: n.p., 1871.

———. *Apropos of Women and Theatres.* New York: Carleton, 1869.

MacKinnon, Catherine A. *Only Words.* Cambridge, MA: Harvard University Press, 1993.

Maginnis, Tara. *Fashion Shows, Strip Shows, Beauty Pageants: Theatre of the Feminine Ideal.* Unpublished PhD dissertation, University of Georgia, 1991.

Mankowitz, Wolf. *Mazeppa.* London: Blond & Briggs, 1982.

McArthur, Benjamin. *Actors and American Culture, 1880–1920.* Philadelphia, PA: Temple University Press, 1984.

McConachie, Bruce. *Melodramatic Formations: American Theatre and Society, 1820–1870.* Iowa City, IA: University of Iowa Press, 1992.

McCullough, Jack W . *Living Pictures on the New York Stage.* Ann Arbor, MI: UMI Research Press, 1981.

Meiselas, Susan. *Carnival Strippers.* New York: Farrar, Straus and Giroux, 1976.

Minsky, Morton and Milt Machlin. *Minsky's Burlesque: A Fast and Funny Look at America's Bawdiest Era.* New York: Arbor House, 1986.

Mizejewski, Linda. *Ziegfeld Girl: Image and Icon in Culture and Cinema.* Durham, NC: Duke University Press, 1999.

Modleski, Tania. "Feminism and the Power of Interpretation: Some Critical Readings." *Feminist Studies, Critical Studies.* Edited by Teresa de Lauretis. Bloomington, IN: Indiana University Press, 1986.

Moi, Toril. "Feminist, Female, Feminine." *Feminisms.* Edited by Sandra Kemp and Judith Squires. New York: Oxford University Press, 1997.

Mortimer, Lee. *Women Confidential.* New York: Paperback Library, 1960.

Murray, Ken. *The Body Merchant: The Story of Earl Carroll.* Pasadena, CA: Ward Ritchie Press, 1976.

Nathan, George Jean. *The Theatre, The Drama, The Girls.* New York: Alfred A. Knopf, Inc., 1921.

———. *The Popular Theatre.* New York: Alfred A. Knopf, Inc., 1918.

———. *The World in Falseface.* New York: Alfred A. Knopf, Inc., 1923.

Osborne, Angela Saulino. *Miss America: The Dream Lives On.* Dallas, TX: Taylor Publishing Company, 1995.

Peiss, Kathy. "On Beauty . . . and the History of Business." *Beauty and Business: Commerce, Gender, and Culture in Modern America.* Edited by Philip Scranton. London and New York: Routledge, 2001.

———. *Cheap Amusements: Working Women and Leisure in turn-of-the-Century New York.* Philadelphia, PA: Temple University Press, 1986

Perlmutter, Dawn. "Miss America: Whose Ideal?" *Beauty Matters.* Edited by Peg Zeglin Brand. Bloomington: Indiana University Press, 2000.

Phelan, Peggy. *Unmarked: The Politics of Performance.* New York: Routledge, 1993.

Price, Janet and Margrit Shildrick, editors. *Feminist Theory and the Body.* New York: Routledge, 1999.

Prus, Robert and Irini Styllianoss. *Hookers, Rounders and Desk Clerks.* Toronto: Gage Publishing Ltd., 1980.

Read, Alan. *Theatre and Everyday Life: An Ethics of Performance.* New York: Routledge, 1993.

Riverol, A.R. *Live from Atlantic City: The History of the Miss America Pageant Before, After, and in Spite of Television.* Bowling Green, OH: Bowling Green State University Popular Press, 1992.

Roach, Joseph. *The Player's Passion: Studies in the Science of Acting*. Ann Arbor, MI: University of Michigan Press, 1993.

Rose, Gillian. *Feminism and Geography: The Limits of Geographical Knowledge*. Minneapolis, MN: University of Minnesota Press, 1993.

Rose, Jacqueline. "Sexuality in the Field of Vision," *Feminisms*. Edited by Sandra Kemp and Judith Squires. New York: Oxford University Press, 1997.

Rosen, Marjorie. *Popcorn Venus: Women, Movies, and the American Dream*. New York: Coward, McCann and Geoghegan, 1973.

Rothfels, Nigel. "Aztecs, Aborigines, and Ape-People: Science and Freaks in Germany, 1850–1900." *Freakery: Cultural Spectacles of the Extraordinary Body*. Edited by Rosemarie Garland Thomson. New York: New York University Press, 1996.

Russo, Mary. "Female Grotesques: Carnival and Theory." *Feminist Studies/Critical Studies*. Edited by Teresa de Lauretis. Bloomington, IN: Indiana University Press, 1986.

Schneider, Rebecca. *The Explicit Body in Performance*. New York: Routledge, 1997.

Schur, Edwin M. *Labeling Women Deviant: Gender, Stigma, and Social Control*. Philadelphia, PA: Temple University Press, 1983.

Scott, David A. *Behind the G-String: An Exploration of the Stripper's Image, Her Person and Her Meaning*. Jefferson, NC: McFarland & Co., 1996.

Senelick, Laurence, ed. *Gender in Performance: The Presentation of Difference in the Performing Arts*. Hanover, NH: University Press of New England, 1992.

Shattuck, Roger. *Forbidden Knowledge: From Prometheus to Pornography*. New York: Harcourt Brace & Company, 1996.

Snyder, Robert W. *The Voice of the City: Vaudeville and Popular Culture in New York*. New York: Oxford University Press, 1989.

Spivak, Gayatri Chakravorty. "Poststructuralism, Marginality, Postcoloniuality and Value." *Contemporary Postcolonial Theory*. Edited by Padmini Mongia. New York: St. Martin's Press, 1996.

Stanley, Anna. *The Crowning Touch: Preparing for Beauty Pageant Competition*. San Diego, CA: Box of Ideas Publishing, 1989.

States, Bert O. *Great Reckonings in Little Rooms: On the Phenomenology of Theater*. Los Angeles, CA: University of California Press, 1985.

Stencell, A. W. *Girl Show: Into the Canvas World of Bump and Grind*. Toronto: ECW Press, 1999.

Stratton, Jon. *The Desirable Body: Cultural Fetishism and the Erotics of Consumption*. Chicago, IL: University of Illinois Press, 2001.

Strossen, Nadine. *Defending Pornography: Free Speech, Sex, and the Fight for Women's Rights*. New York: New York University Press, 1995.

Terry, Jennifer and Jacqueline Urla, Eds. *Deviant Bodies*. Bloomington, IN: Indiana University Press, 1995.

Trilling, Lionel. *Sincerity and Authenticity*. Cambridge, MA: Harvard University Press, 1971.

Turner, Victor. *Dramas, Fields, and Metaphors: Symbolic Action in Human Society.* Ithaca, NY: Cornell University Press, 1974.

Urla, Jacqueline and Alan C. Swedlund. "The Anthropometry of Barbie: Unsettling Ideals of the Feminine Body in Popular Culture." Edited by Jennifer Terry and Jacqueline Urla. *Deviant Bodies.* Bloomington, IN: Indiana University Press, 1995.

Webster's New World College Dictionary, Fourth Edition. Editor in Chief, Michael Agnes. New York: Macmillan, 1997.

Whitton, Joseph. *The Naked Truth! An Inside History of The Black Crook.* Philadelphia, PA: H.W. Shaw Co., 1897.

Wigley, Mark. "Untitled: The Housing of Gender." *Sexuality and Space.* Edited by Beatriz Colomina. Princeton, NJ: Princeton Architectural Press, 1992.

Williams, Patricia J. *The Alchemy of Race and Rights.* Cambridge, MA: Harvard University Press, 1991.

Wilmeth, Don B. with Tice L. Miller. *Cambridge Guide to American Theatre.* New York and London: Cambridge University Press, 1996.

Wolf, Naomi. *Beauty Myth: How Images of Beauty Are Used Against Women.* New York: Doubleday, 1991.

Wolfflin, Heinrich. *Renaissance and Baroque.* Translated by Kathrin Simon. Ithaca, NY: Cornell University Press, 1966.

Woolcott, Alexander. *New York Times Theatre Reviews 1920–1926, Volume 1.* New York: Arno Press, 1971.

Wortley, Richard. *A Pictorial History of Striptease: 100 Years of Undressing to Music.* Seacaucus, NJ: Chartwell Books, distributed by Book Sales, 1976.

Yang, Suzanne. "A Question of Accent: Ethnicity and Transference." *The Psychoanalysis of Race.* Edited by Christopher Lane. New York: Columbia University Press, 1998.

Zeidman, Irving. *The American Burlesque Show.* New York: Hawthorn Books, 1967.

NEWSPAPER ARTICLES

"Arlington Mother Named Ms. International Nude." *Boston Herald American* September 6, 1976: 3. Paul Jordan Collection, Harvard Theatre Collection.

Austin Statesman (TX), January 18, 1928. Ziegfeld Collection, Harry Ransom Center.

Belkin, Lisa. "In Texas, Two Kings of the Beauty Queen Business." *The New York Times* February 28, 1988. Billy Rose Theatre Collection, New York Public Library at Lincoln Center.

Bell, Bill. "City Beat Column." *New York Daily News* August 14, 1989. Bambi Vawn Papers. Billy Rose Theatre Collection, New York Public Library at Lincoln Center. *Boston Evening Globe* September 8, 1976.

Boynoff, Sara. *Daily News* June 8, 1939. Earl Carroll Collection, March 1939 to October 1939. Billy Rose Theatre Collection, New York Public Library at Lincoln Center.

Bruni, Frank. "A Search for Girls, Girls, Girls Around Italy's Dial." *New York Times International* September 3, 2002: A4.

Cantor, Eddie and David Freedman. "Ziegfeld and His Follies." *Collier's National Weekly* January 13, 1934.

———. January 27, 1934.

———. February 10, 1934.

Carpozi, George. "America's Dream Girls." *New York Post* September 11, 1982. Billy Rose Theatre Collection, New York Public Library at Lincoln Center.

Carter, Alan. "Hey Big Spender!: Spend a Little Time Getting to Know Janette Boyd." *New York Daily News* January 30, 1986: C23. Paul Jordan Collection. Harvard Theatre Collection.

Corbin, John. "Puritan Attacks on the Stage and its Clothes." *New York Times Magazine* June 1, 1919. Black Crook Collection, Harry Ransom Center.

"Days When the Black Crook was Daring." *The New York Times* March 10, 1929.

Gross, Ben. "It's the same show—but 'Miss A' is a big winner." *New York Daily News* September 13, 1965. Billy Rose Theatre Collection, New York Public Library at Lincoln Center.

Hammond, Percy. *Dallas News* November 4, 1923. Ziegfeld Collection, Harry Ransom Center.

Hearn, Don. "Tips on Tables." Unidentified promotional material. Paul Jordan Collection. Harvard Theatre Collection.

Heckman, Meg. "Weekend Hours for Exotic Dancers Mulled." *Concord Monitor* (NH) August 20, 2002: 20.

Keichline, Seth. "Stripped of Athletic Status." *Daily Titan* (Fullerton, CA) March 16, 2001 n.p.

Kerr, Walter. *Herald Tribune* March 17, 1957: n.p. Ziegfeld Collection. Harry Ransom Center.

Kilgallen, Dorothy. "The Voice of Broadway" (Unidentified news column). March 29, 1958: n.p. Paul Jordan Collection. Harvard Theatre Collection.

Kingsley, Walter. "About Beauties." *Daily Mirror* July 3, 1920: n.p.

Kingston, Samuel F. "What I have learned from Florenz Ziegfeld." *Dallas News* November 2, 1924: n.p.

Kravitz, Pinky. "Miss Americ-Lite?," Atlantic City Weekly, week of January 9—February 4, 2004, accessed June 16, 2004, <www.atlanticcitycasinos.net/archives/01.29.04/pinky.html>.

Lauterbach, Richard E. "Close-Up." Unidentified news clipping (n.d. n.p.) Gypsy Rose Lee Collection. Billy Rose Theatre Collection, New York Public Library at Lincoln Center.

Lee, Henry. "Miss America, Inc.: Beauty Show that Started as a Boardwalk Carnival is Now a Refined Business." *New York Sunday News* September 3, 1961.

"*Look* looks at Dorian Dennis." *New York Mirror* 1958: n.d, n.p. Paul Jordan Collection. Harvard Theatre Collection.

Melcher, E.S. *New York Journal* (clipping, n.d.)1932. Florenz Ziegfeld—Billie Burke Papers (1907–1984), Billy Rose Theatre Collection, New York Public Library at Lincoln Center.

"Miss America: Dreams and Boosters," *New York Times* June 12, 1970. Billy Rose Theatre Collection, New York Public Library at Lincoln Center.

Mortimer, Lee. *Daily Mirror* (clipping). Unidentified promotional material. Paul Jordan Collection. Harvard Theatre Collection.

New York Evening Journal, July 23, 1932: n.p. Ziegfeld Collection, Harry Ransom Center.

New York Herald Tribune September 9, 1963. Billy Rose Theatre Collection, New York Public Library at Lincoln Center.

New York Press September 11, 1978. Billy Rose Theatre Collection, New York Public Library at Lincoln Center.

New York Sunday Mirror September 27, 1936. Gypsy Rose Lee Collection. Billy Rose Theatre Collection, New York Public Library at Lincoln Center.

New York Woman (clipping) September 1936. Gypsy Rose Lee Collection, Billy Rose Theatre Collection, New York Public Library at Lincoln Center.

New York World Telegram (clipping) June 11, 1934. Gypsy Rose Lee Collection, Billy Rose Theatre Collection, New York Public Library at Lincoln Center.

Newsday July 26, 1984. Billy Rose Theatre Collection, New York Public Library at Lincoln Center.

"Pageant Hopes Soap—Opera Spoof Enlivens Show," *New York Times* September 15, 1984. Billy Rose Theatre Collection, New York Public Library at Lincoln Center.

Parsons, Louella. "Gypsy Rose Lee Jests About Her Art And Ranks Success as Mere Luck." Unidentified news materials, Gypsy Rose Lee Collection, Billy Rose Theatre Collection, New York Public Library at Lincoln Center.

Pennington, Gail. "Bare Necessity? The Miss America Pageant is all About Scholarship—and Swimsuits," *St. Louis Post Dispatch*, September 11, 1997, <www.highbeam.com/library/doc3.asp?DOCID>, accessed June 16, 2004.

Quinlan, Anna. "How NOW, Miss America," *New York Post* September 6, 1974. Billy Rose Theatre Collection, New York Public Library at Lincoln Center.

Rattray, Jim. "Texas Playmate." *Playpen* (n.d.) Promotional clipping for Dior Angel. Paul Jordan Collection. Harvard Theatre Collection

Reid, Louis. "Vaudeville in Many Cities." *New York Dramatic Mirror: The Screen and Stage Weekly* July 3, 1920: n.p.

Rosen, Hal. "Tips for Tables." Unidentified promotional clipping. Paul Jordan Collection. Harvard Theatre Collection.

"Siss! Boom! Ah!." *Boston Sunday Herald* May 25, 1919: n.p.

"Some Girls." *Soho Weekly News* May 2, 1980.

St. Johns, Adela Rogers. "The Girls Who Glorified Ziegfeld" (a series of four articles). *American Weekly* June 23, 1946: n.p. Florenz Ziegfeld—Billie Burke Papers (1907–1984), Billy Rose Theatre Collection, New York Public Library at Lincoln Center.

St. Johns, Adela Rogers. July 7, 1946.

———. July 14, 1946.

St. Louis Daily Globe-Democrat March 3, 1918. Ziegfeld Collection, Harry Ransom Center.

Stokes, Geoffrey. "The Last Miss America Story." *Village Voice* August 7, 1984.

Variety. September 16, 1964, Billy Rose Theatre Collection, New York Public Library at Lincoln Center.

———. 1959.

World Telegraph. (n.d.) Unidentified Dorian Dennis promotional clipping, Paul Jordan Collection, Harvard Theatre Collection.

Zamost, Scott A. "Strippers want to Dress up their Image." *Las Vegas Sun* (n.d., n.p.) Paul Jordan Collection, Harvard Theatre Collection.

"Ziegfeld and his *Follies."* *Variety* [retrospective] January 9, 1957. Billy Rose Theatre Collection, New York Public Library at Lincoln Center.

Zolot, Cary. *Reporter* (Jaycee newsletter, n.d., n.p.) Paul Jordan Collection, Harvard Theatre Collection.

MAGAZINE AND JOURNAL ARTICLES

Cavalcade of Burlesque Fall 1951. Philadelphia, PA: Burlesque Historical Company.

———. December 1952.

———. March 1953.

———. June 1953.

Christopher, Dan. "Burlesque Intellectual." *Modern Man: The Man's Picture Magazine.* December 1955: 35+.

Deford, Frank. "Confessions of a Miss America Judge." *TV Guide* September 2, 1978. Billy Rose Theatre Collection, New York Public Library at Lincoln Center.

DePaulo, Lisa. "Behind Those Smiles: Inside the mind of Miss America." *TV Guide* September 10, 1988. Billy Rose Theatre Collection, New York Public Library at Lincoln Center.

Gill, Brendan. "The Miss America Uproar: What it says about us all." *TV Guide* September 15, 1984. Billy Rose Theatre Collection, New York Public Library at Lincoln Center.

Hanna, Judith Lynne. "Undressing the First Amendment and Corsetting the Striptease Dancer." *The Drama Review* 42, Summer 1998: 9–37.

Hornick, Jay. *Cavalcade of Burlesque* Fall 1951. Philadelphia, PA: Burlesque Historical Company.

" 'It' Depends." *Night and Day: America's Picture Magazine of Entertainment.* March 1950: 46–47.

Kindel, Stephen. "Beauty You Can Take to the Bank," *Forbes Magazine,* June 18, 1984, <www.highbeam.com/library/doc3.asp? DOCID>, accessed June 16, 2004.

Kubiak, Anthony. "Splitting the Difference: Performance and Its Double in American Culture." *The Drama Review* 42, Winter 1998.

Maschio, Geraldine. "A Prescription for Femininity: Male Interpretation of the Feminine ideal at the Turn of the Century." *Women and Performance: A Journal of Feminist Theory*. Vol. 4, 1988/89: 42–49.

McEvoy, J.P. "He Knew What They Wanted." *Saturday Evening Post* September 10, 1932: n.p. Ziegfeld Collection. Harry Ransom Center.

Montrelay, M. "Inquiry into Femininity." *M/F*. Volume 1: 83–102.

O'Reilly, Jane. *TV Guide*. September 17, 1983. Billy Rose Theatre Collection, New York Public Library at Lincoln Center.

Pageantry Magazine: The Magazine for the Pageant, Fashion, Talent and Modeling Industries. Edited by Lisa Nees. 1996 Issue. Published quarterly by Pageantry, Talent and Entertainment Services, Inc. Altamonte Springs, FL.

Peep Show Magazine (n.d.). Paul Jordan Collection. Harvard Theatre Collection.

Rause, Vince. "Gibby's Number One Girl: What Makes a Stripper Strip?" *Focus Magazine* July 17, 1977: n.p. Paul Jordan Collection. Harvard Theatre Collection.

Schroeder, Jonathan E. and Janet L. Borgerson. "Marketing Images of Gender: A Visual Analysis." *Consumption, Markets and Culture* Vol. 2(2) 1998: 161–201.

Simon, Roger. "For God, for Love—and for West Allis, Wisconsin." *TV Guide* September 11, 1976.

"The Church Wars on Burlesque."*Life Magazine* May 31, 1937 Vol. 2, No. 22: 20.

Time March 11, 1957: n.p. Ziegfeld Collection, Harry Ransom Center, Austin, TX.

Wohlfert-Wihlborg, Lee. "Here She Comes." *People Magazine* September 19, 1983. Billy Rose Theatre Collection, New York Public Library at Lincoln Center.

Ziegfeld, Flo. "What becomes of the Ziegfeld Girls?" *Pictorial Review* May 1925: n.p. Ziegfeld Collection. Harry Ransom Center.

THEATRE AND BEAUTY CONTEST PROGRAMS

"A Night of Triumph for Mineralava." *Madison Square Garden Beauty Bulletin* November 28, 1923, Billy Rose Theatre Collection, New York Public Library at Lincoln Center.

Earl Carroll *Vanities* program, 8th Edition. 1930. Author's personal collection.

1922 Ziegfeld *Follies* program. Ziegfeld Collection. Harry Ransom Center.

1924 Ziegfeld *Follies* New Amsterdam Theatre program. Ziegfeld Collection. Harry Ransom Center.

1927 Ziegfeld *Follies* New Amsterdam Theatre program. Ziegfeld Collection. Harry Ransom Center.

1928 Ziegfeld Theatre *Rosalie* program. Ziegfeld Collection. Harry Ransom Center.

1931 Ziegfeld *Follies* program. Ziegfeld Collection. Harry Ransom Center.

Price, E.D., editorial, 1931 Ziegfeld *Follies* program. Ziegfeld Collection. Harry Ransom Center.

Star and Garter Souvenir program. Produced by Michael Todd. Staged by Hassard Short. Handwritten date April 13, 1943. Author's personal collection.

"The Economic Interpretation of Beauty: Why Pulchritude Conquers Where Brains Fail!" *Madison Square Garden Beauty Bulletin* November 28, 1923.

"28th Annual Wheatheart of the Nation Contest" program. August 24, 1974. Author's personal collection.

INTERVIEWS (ALL INTERVIEWS WERE CONDUCTED IN PERSON UNLESS OTHERWISE NOTED)

Amateur runway model (Interviewee wishes to remain anonymous). Brown University, Providence, RI. Spring 2000.
Anonymous bystander, Miss America Boardwalk Parade. Atlantic City, NJ. September 20, 2002.
French, Heather. Harrah's Casino, Atlantic City, NJ. September 21, 2002.
Harold, Erika, Miss Illinois 2002, Atlantic City, NJ. September 19, 2002.
"Jezebel." Charlie's Bikini Club. Adelanto, CA. June 2, 2002.
Lawless, Laura, Miss Arizona 2002, Atlantic City, NJ. September 19, 2002.
"Lolita." *Miss Exotic World 2002* contestant. Helendale, CA. June 1, 2002.
Luna, Selene. *Miss Exotic World 2002* contestant (performed under the pseudonym "Starlet O'Hara"). Helendale, CA. May 30, 2002.
Mills, Susan. Providence, RI. May 1, 2001.
Miss Rhode Island Contestant (former). (Interviewee wishes to remain anonymous) Brown University, Providence, RI. Spring 1999.
Morin, Mary, Miss New Hampshire 2002, Atlantic City, NJ. September 17, 2002.
————. Manchester, NH. September 5, 2002.
"Nicki." Charlie's Bikini Club. Adelanto, CA. June 2, 2002.
"Nightshade." Florida strip club DJ. Interview conducted by email. Spring 1999.
Scotto, Susan. Mt. Holyoke, MA. November 3, 2000.
Seelig, Jerry. Harrah's Casino, Atlantic City, NJ. September 21, 2002.
Shortbull, Vanessa, Miss South Dakota, Atlantic City, NJ. September 20, 2002.
"Silver." *Miss Exotic World Contest*, Helendale, CA. May 30, 2002.
Slattum, Amy. Former Miss New Hampshire Contestant. New Hampshire Public Radio. Spring 1999.
Swank Davis, Grace. 15th Annual Theatre History Seminar, Mt. Pleasant, Iowa. April 2000.
Wadsworth, Rachel, Miss Maine 2002, Atlantic City, NJ. September 17, 2002.

TELEVISED BEAUTY PAGEANTS AND VIDEOS

Miss America. Writ. Michelle Ferrari. Dir. Lisa Ades and Leslie Klainberg. Narr. Cherry Jones. American Experience, PBS, WGBH Boston. 2002.
"Call of the Wild." *That Girl*. Writ. Milton Pascal. Dir. Hall Cooper. Prod. Bernie Orenstein and Saul Turteltaub. Anchor Bay Entertainment, Inc., 1999.
Mrs. America Pageant 2002. PAX television Channel. October 12, 2002.

Sally Jessy Raphael. Syndicated Talk Show 1989 episode on striptease artists. Bambi Vawn papers. Billy Rose Theatre Collection, New York Public Library at Lincoln Center. Transcript.

Striporama. Dir. Jerald Intrator. Something Weird Video, Venus Productions, 1952.

Stripper of the Year. Produced by Bert Rhine, Westwood Productions. 1990.

The Perfect Miss America. CBS, New York. August 28, 1958. Billy Rose Theatre Collection, New York Public Library at Lincoln Center. Transcript.

The Secret World of Beauty Pageants. Film Garden Entertainments. Produced for The Learning Channel. 1998.

WEBPAGES

Abbie Rabine's webpage. Miss Massachusetts 2001. <www.abbierabine.com>. Accessed May 2003.

Amorosi, A.D. "Nightlife's Nine Lives," Philadelphia City Paper.net, September 17–24, 1998. <http://citypaper.net/articles/091798/ear.clubs.shtml>. Accessed March 10, 2003.

Archibald, George. "Miss America told to zip it on chastity talk." Washington Times Online. <www.washtimes.com/national/>. Written October 9, 2002. Accessed March 10, 2003.

"Bare Intentions." <www.wcug.www.edu/~klipsun/april98/strippers.html>. Accessed March 12, 2003.

Barillas, C., Ed. "Miss'd America Captures Sought After Crown." *The Data Lounge.* <http://www.datalounge.com/datalounge/news/record.html?record = 4670>. Accessed September 20, 1999.

"Beauty contestants don Gadhafi tees." <CNN.com> November 2, 2002. <http://www.CNN.com/2002/WORLD/africa/11/02/libya.beauty.ap/index. html>.

Beyond, Chris. The No-Fi "Magazine," <www.nofimagazine.com/dixieint1.htm>. Accessed March 8, 2004.

Bodian, Nat. "Burlesque at the Empire theatre," <www.virtualnewarknj.com/memories/burlesque/bodianempire.html>. Accessed March 8, 2004.

Brunker, Mike. "Hunts for nude women draw fire." <www.msnbcnews.com>. July 16, 2003.

Cinderella Scholarship Pageants Webpage. <http://www.netstat.com/pageants/cinderella/history.html>. Accessed May 2003.

Civil Action, United States District Court for the district of New Jersey, MAO, Inc., Plaintiff v. Infinite Broadcasting Corporation. <http://news. corporate.findlaw.com/ hdocs/docs/missamerica/missamerica.pdf>.

Di Maggio, Phil. "All that glitters . . . is only rhinestone." Amateur Pageant website. <http://www.geocities.com/TelevisionCity/9699/reluctant.html> a web link from the homepage <http://www.geocities.com/TelevisionCity/9699/ menu.htm>. Accessed May 30, 2003.

Findlaw.com   byline.   <http://news.findlaw.com/ap_stories/e/1404/5–21–2003/ 20030521204500_4.html. MAO lawsuit>. Accessed May 21, 2003.

Folly Theater History. Starker, <www.columbusalive.com/2001>. Accessed March 8, 2004.

Her Heighness Pageant Coaching. <www.herheighness.com>. Accessed May 2003.

Huey, Stephen. Commentary. "Beauty Pageant Contestants Remain Underfed." <www.womens-enews.com>. December 4, 2002.

"Jill Nicolini, Relinquished Pageant Crown." *On the Record.* Host: Greta Van Susteren. September 4, 2002. Partial Transcript. <http://www.foxnews.com/story/ 0,2933,62191,00.html>. Accessed January 6, 2003.

"Know No's: Stripper Kung Fu." <http://www.stripperpower.com/articles/kungfu. shtml> (site no longer functional) accessed on January 6, 2002.

Kruh, David. <www.bambinomusical.com/Scollay/Howard.html>. Accessed March 8, 2004.

Lemons, Stephen. "Selene Luna: Bad-ass Goddess of the Night." Gettingit.com Webzine. <http://www.Gettingit.com>. December 17, 1999. Accessed December 30, 2002.

Majestic Beauty Pageants website. <www.bbtel.com/~majestic/>. Accessed May 2003.

MAO Message Board. <http://www.missamerica.org>. Official MAO webpage. Accessed May 1999.

"Miss America Pageant Cans Talent Spots," July 30, 2004, CNN, <http://www. cnn.com/2004/US/Northeast/07/29/pageant.talent.ap/>.

Miss Baltimore Teen All-American Pageant. <www.missmarylandteen.com>. Accessed May 2003.

Miss Gay America webpage. <http://www.missgayamerica.com>. Copyright © 1973 Norma Kristie, Inc.

Miss Georgia Forestry Pageant website <http://forestrypageant.tripod.com>. Accessed May 2003.

Miss Mountain State Pageant in West Virginia <http://www.qualitypageants.com/ wv.pageants>. Accessed May 2003.

"Miss North Carolina case reveals little-known clauses in contract." News-Journal Wire   Services.   <www.news-journalonline.com/2002/Nov/3/NOTE2.htm>. Accessed November 3, 2002.

Mrs. America Pageant webpage. <www.mrsamerica.com/sponsors>. Accessed October 15, 2002.

"Not Your Father's Miss America." (AP) December 13, 1999. <http://www. CBSnews.com/stories/199/09/20/entertainment/,ain62943.shtml>.   Accessed January 4, 2003.

"Pageant queen resigned over topless photos," (AP) <http://www.CNN.com/2002/ SHOWBIZ/News/07/29/missnc.resigns.ap/index.html>. Accessed July 29, 2002.

Playboy webpage. <http://www.playboy.com/nss/features/nicolini>. Playboy link to Jill Nicoloni story. Accessed January 6, 2003.

Segal, David. "There She Goes," <www.washingtonpost.com>, <http://www. washingtonpost.com/wp-dyn/articles/A30500–2004Sep17. html>, September 18, 2004. Accessed September 25, 2004.

Starker, Melissa <www.columbusalive.com/2001/20010524/052401/05240101.html>. Accessed March 8, 2004.

Strippers Directory. <http://strippers.cc/index.html> Website link from <http://www.stripperpower.com> Accessed on January 6, 2002.

"Student Chooses Stripping Over Sports," Excite News March 29, 2001. <http://news.excite.com/news/r/010329/11/odd-stripper-dc>.

Thistle, Franklin L. "The Off-Stage Shenanigans of Strippers." Java's Bachelor Pad reprinted essay from *Adam*, Vol. 3 No. February 8, 1959. <http://www.javabach-elor.100megs4.com>.

Thomas, Robert McG., Jr. "Lili St. Cyr, 80, Burlesque Star Famous for Her Bubble Baths." *New York Times* on the Web (Obit.). February 6, 1999.<http://www. nytimes.com>.

"Unnatural Beauty: Miss Brazil boasts 19 Procedures." ABCnews.com. <http://abcnews.go.com/sections/primetime/2020/PRIMETIME_010503_mis sbrazil_feature>. May 3, 2003. Accessed January 4, 2003.

"Unofficial Miss America Message Board." <www.voy.com/41982>. Accessed May 2003.

Victoria Theatre, <www.victoriatheatre.org/about.html>. Accessed March 8, 2004.

"Warren G. Harding calls for a "Return to Normalcy," Boston, MA, May 14, 1920." <http://www.pbs.org/greatspeeches/timeline/w_harding_s.html>. Accessed June 15, 2003.

Index ❧

Page numbers in italics indicate figures.